# GPU Programming Fundamentals with CUDA

Jamie Flux

https://www.linkedin.com/company/golden-dawn-engineering/

# Contents

1

11

# Chapter 1

# Introduction to GPU Architecture

## Overview of GPU Architecture

The Graphics Processing Unit (GPU) is a dedicated processor designed to execute the parallel processing of multiple threads, making it an ideal architecture for tasks spanning high-throughput graphics rendering and general-purpose scientific computations. A GPU is distinguished by its massive number of cores, where each core is a simple processing element, contributing to its parallel capabilities.

## 1  GPU Cores

GPU cores are designed to handle simple computations concurrently. Let $C$ denote the number of cores in a GPU, then the processing power $P$ can be expressed as:

$$P = C \cdot F \cdot IPC$$

where $F$ is the clock frequency, and $IPC$ is the instructions per cycle. The design favors high throughput over low latency, contrasting typical CPU designs.

## 2  Memory Hierarchy

The memory architecture of a GPU is structured hierarchically to accommodate a wide range of access latencies and bandwidth requirements. The key components include global memory, shared memory, and cache levels. The memory transfer time $T_m$ can generally be modeled as:

$$T_m = T_{access} + \frac{D}{B}$$

where $T_{access}$ is the fixed access time, $D$ is the data size, and $B$ is the bandwidth. Higher levels of caching (e.g., L1 and L2) aim to minimize $T_m$.

## 3  Comparison with CPU Processing

The architectural divergence between CPUs and GPUs can be primarily understood through their design philosophies. CPUs are optimized for sequential task execution with sophisticated control and data flow mechanisms. In comparison, GPUs prioritize data parallelism for throughput.

Considering the task execution time $T$ on a CPU and GPU can be differentiated as:

$$T_{CPU} = \frac{N}{S \cdot F_{cpu}}$$

$$T_{GPU} = \frac{N}{(P) \cdot F_{gpu}}$$

where $N$ is the operation count, $S$ is the number of cores in a CPU, $F_{cpu}$ and $F_{gpu}$ are the respective frequencies. GPUs achieve a reduction in $T$ for certain tasks by leveraging their higher core count.

These comparative advantages result in GPUs being particularly suited for workloads with higher parallelism.

# Conclusion

This architecture provides a compelling solution to parallel computational problems by efficiently utilizing its multiple cores and optimized memory hierarchy. Continued exploration of these units facilitates advancements across multiple domains requiring intensive computational capabilities.

# Python Code Snippet

Below is a Python code snippet for leveraging GPU architecture concepts with PyCUDA, demonstrating the core computational elements, including core utilization, memory management, and task execution parallelism.

```python
import pycuda.autoinit
import pycuda.driver as drv
import numpy as np
from pycuda.compiler import SourceModule

# GPU kernel for simple parallel computation
mod = SourceModule("""
__global__ void process_data(float *data, int size) {
    int idx = blockIdx.x * blockDim.x + threadIdx.x;
    if (idx < size) {
        data[idx] = data[idx] * data[idx];
    }
}
""")


def gpu_square_array(data):
    """
    Function to compute the square of each element in the array
    ↪ using GPU.
    :param data: numpy array of float32
    :return: squared numpy array
    """
    # Allocate memory on the GPU
    data_gpu = drv.mem_alloc(data.nbytes)
    drv.memcpy_htod(data_gpu, data)

    # Calculate block and grid size
    block_size = 256
    grid_size = (data.size + block_size - 1) // block_size

    # Get the kernel function
    func = mod.get_function("process_data")

    # Execute the kernel
    func(data_gpu, np.int32(data.size), block=(block_size, 1, 1),
    ↪ grid=(grid_size, 1))

    # Copy the result back to host
    data_out = np.empty_like(data)
    drv.memcpy_dtoh(data_out, data_gpu)

    return data_out

# Example usage
```

```
size = 1000
data = np.random.randn(size).astype(np.float32)
squared_data = gpu_square_array(data)

print("Original Data: ", data[:10])
print("Squared Data: ", squared_data[:10])
```

This code defines several key functions necessary for basic understanding and implementation of GPU architecture concepts:

- The `process_data` kernel performs parallel square computations on a GPU's cores, showcasing parallel processing capabilities.

- The `gpu_square_array` function handles memory operations and kernel invocation, demonstrating memory management within PyCUDA.

- Block and grid size calculations ensure optimal GPU resource utilization, reflecting core design considerations related to `GPU Cores`.

The final block of code executes the provided kernel on a sample data array, illustrating how to offload computation to a GPU using PyCUDA.

# Chapter 2

# Setting Up CUDA Development Environment

## Introduction to CUDA Toolkit

The CUDA toolkit serves as the foundation for developing applications that harness GPU acceleration. It provides essential tools such as compilers, libraries, and debugging utilities, enabling developers to efficiently interface with NVIDIA GPUs. The installation of this toolkit is pivotal for setting up a CUDA development environment.

## 1   CUDA Toolkit Installation

For installing the CUDA toolkit, a sequence of actions must be performed, which includes verifying compatibility, selecting the proper version, and executing the installation. Let the set $V$ represent all CUDA versions, with $v_c \in V$ denoting the chosen compatible version. Formally, we have:

$$\text{Select } v_c \text{ such that } \begin{cases} \text{OS version compatibility with } v_c, \\ \text{GPU architecture compatibility with } v_c \end{cases}$$

The selection can be expressed through a decision function $D_{\text{compat}}$:

$$D_{\text{compat}}(v, av) = \begin{cases} 1 & \text{if } v \text{ is applicable for } av \\ 0 & \text{otherwise} \end{cases}$$

where $av$ represents the active environment variables. The appropriate $v_c$ maximizes $D_{\text{compat}}$.

# Configuring the Development Environment

Post-installation, environment configuration is requisite for ensuring proper toolkit integration with the system's path variables. The configuration process involves setting environment paths which can be represented by a set union operation:

$$E = E_{\text{system}} \cup E_{\text{cuda}}$$

where $E_{\text{system}}$ denotes existing system paths and $E_{\text{cuda}}$ includes paths specific to CUDA binaries and libraries.

## 1 Path Specification

Let `PATH` indicate the path environment variable. The configuration requires appending CUDA directories:

`PATH` $= $ `PATH` $\cup$ $\{$`/usr/local/cuda/bin`, `/usr/local/cuda/lib64`$\}$

This modifies the operation space for locating CUDA executables and libraries as a set transformation `PATH`$' = f($`PATH`$)$.

# Verifying Installation

To ensure a successful setup, a verification process must be employed. This can be outlined as an algorithm.

**Data:** CUDA toolkit path and sample codes
**Result:** Verification of CUDA installation
```
// Compile sample CUDA program
```
Load sample;
Compile using NVCC;
```
// Execute compiled program
```
**if** *execution result shows CUDA version* **then**
  └ return success
**else**
  └ return failure

The algorithm relies on function calls to `nvcc` for compilation verification, thus ensuring proper configuration through an expected output.

# Preparing the Development Machine

A development machine's readiness for GPU programming necessitates requisite system specifications and driver availability. The underlying architecture, denoted by $\mathcal{A}$, must align with technological prerequisites for optimal execution:

$$\text{Required Specs} \subseteq \mathcal{A}$$

Moreover, CUDA requires compatible drivers expressed as $D_{\min} \leq D_{\text{actual}}$, where $D_{\min}$ is the minimal driver version and $D_{\text{actual}}$ is the installed driver version.

# Python Code Snippet

Below is a Python code snippet that includes setting up the CUDA environment, verifying installation, and establishing paths using PyCUDA. These functions ensure your system is properly configured for GPU programming with CUDA.

```python
import pycuda.driver as cuda
import pycuda.autoinit
from pycuda.compiler import SourceModule
import numpy as np
import os

# Function to check CUDA enabled GPUs
def check_cuda_devices():
```

```python
cuda.init()
print(f"Detected {cuda.Device.count()} CUDA Capable device(s).")
for i in range(cuda.Device.count()):
    dev = cuda.Device(i)
    print(f"[Device {i}] {dev.name()}, compute capability:
    ↪  {dev.compute_capability()}, Total Memory:
    ↪  {dev.total_memory() // (1024 ** 2)} MB")

# CUDA kernel to verify installation
kernel_code = """
__global__ void verify_installation(float *a, float *b, float *c,
↪  int N) {
    int idx = blockIdx.x * blockDim.x + threadIdx.x;
    if (idx < N) {
        c[idx] = a[idx] + b[idx];
    }
}
"""

def verify_cuda_installation():
    # Create a simple array addition task
    N = 1024
    a = np.random.randn(N).astype(np.float32)
    b = np.random.randn(N).astype(np.float32)
    c = np.empty_like(a)

    # Allocate memory on the device
    a_gpu = cuda.mem_alloc(a.nbytes)
    b_gpu = cuda.mem_alloc(b.nbytes)
    c_gpu = cuda.mem_alloc(c.nbytes)

    # Copy the arrays to the GPU
    cuda.memcpy_htod(a_gpu, a)
    cuda.memcpy_htod(b_gpu, b)

    # Compile and get the kernel function
    mod = SourceModule(kernel_code)
    func = mod.get_function("verify_installation")

    # Launch the kernel
    block_size = 256
    grid_size = int(np.ceil(N / block_size))
    func(a_gpu, b_gpu, c_gpu, np.int32(N), block=(block_size, 1, 1),
    ↪  grid=(grid_size, 1))

    # Copy the result back to the host
    cuda.memcpy_dtoh(c, c_gpu)

    # Check the result
    if np.allclose(c, a + b):
        print("CUDA installation verified: Array addition
        ↪  successful.")
    else:
```

```
    print("Error: CUDA result does not match expected output.")

def configure_environment_paths():
    # Assuming environment setup function
    cuda_path = "/usr/local/cuda"
    os.environ["PATH"] = os.environ["PATH"] + os.pathsep +
    ↪    os.path.join(cuda_path, "bin")
    os.environ["LD_LIBRARY_PATH"] = os.environ["LD_LIBRARY_PATH"] +
    ↪    os.pathsep + os.path.join(cuda_path, "lib64")
    print("Environment paths configured for CUDA binaries and
    ↪    libraries.")

# Running the setup checks and configurations
check_cuda_devices()
configure_environment_paths()
verify_cuda_installation()
```

This code defines several key functions necessary for the implementation and verification of your CUDA development environment:

- `check_cuda_devices` uses PyCUDA to detect and list all CUDA-enabled devices available on your machine, providing basic details.

- `verify_cuda_installation` performs a simple array addition to ensure CUDA is correctly installed and functional. It compiles a basic CUDA kernel to sum arrays on the GPU.

- `configure_environment_paths` appends necessary CUDA directories to system environment variables to facilitate finding binaries and libraries.

The final block of code executes these functions, providing verification and configuration for your CUDA setup.

# Chapter 3

# Understanding CUDA Programming Model

## CUDA Threads

In the CUDA programming model, threads serve as the fundamental unit of execution. Each thread is assigned a unique identifier, allowing it to execute instructions independently. The thread index `threadIdx` is represented by a three-dimensional vector, expressed mathematically as:

$$\texttt{threadIdx} = (\texttt{threadIdx}.x, \texttt{threadIdx}.y, \texttt{threadIdx}.z)$$

This multi-dimensional indexing enables the efficient division and execution of tasks within the CUDA kernels, with each thread performing computations on distinct data elements.

The role of these threads can be likened to SIMD (Single Instruction, Multiple Data) execution, where each executes a kernel procedure concurrently. The total number of threads launched is described by the relationship:

$$T = B_x \times B_y \times B_z \times \texttt{blockDim}.x \times \texttt{blockDim}.y \times \texttt{blockDim}.z$$

where $B_x$, $B_y$, and $B_z$ denote the dimensions of the grid of thread blocks.

# Thread Blocks

A thread block, denoted by `blockIdx`, acts as a collection of threads that can cooperate through shared memory and synchronization operations. Each block is identified by a block index, a three-dimensional vector:

$$\texttt{blockIdx} = (\texttt{blockIdx}.x, \texttt{blockIdx}.y, \texttt{blockIdx}.z)$$

Thread blocks execute independently of each other; therefore, they can be scheduled on any available processor core with their shared data. The number of threads per block, given by `blockDim`, must obey the constraint:

$$\texttt{blockDim}.x \times \texttt{blockDim}.y \times \texttt{blockDim}.z \leq T_{\max}$$

where $T_{\max}$ is the maximum allowable number of threads per block, typically constrained by the architecture specifications of the NVIDIA GPU.

## 1    Shared Memory and Synchronization

Threads within a single block can communicate efficiently by using the block's shared memory. This shared memory is represented as a limited resource:

$$S = \sum_{i=1}^{N} s_i$$

where $S$ is the total shared memory size and $s_i$ denotes the memory allocation per thread. Synchronization points, such as `__syncthreads()`, ensure that computation across threads within a block remains coherent and access sequences do not lead to race conditions.

# Grids of Blocks

The grid configuration in CUDA, indicated by a multidimensional index `gridDim`, organizes the collection of blocks. The grid encompasses the execution space across the GPU as given by:

$$\texttt{gridDim} = (\texttt{gridDim}.x, \texttt{gridDim}.y, \texttt{gridDim}.z)$$

Blocks within a grid are independent units of execution, and the total structure of execution is defined by:

$$N_{\text{blocks}} = \texttt{gridDim}.x \times \texttt{gridDim}.y \times \texttt{gridDim}.z$$

The execution model allows complex algorithms to be expressed concisely by mapping computational tasks to a grid of blocks, maximizing data parallelism.

# Kernel Launch and Execution Declaration

The launch configuration of CUDA kernels dictates the number of threads and blocks through the execution configuration syntax: `«<grid, block, shared_memory, stream»>`. Each execution aspect influences performance characteristics, optimized by selecting suitable grid and block sizes.

In this operational context, the grid and block dimensions $(G, B)$ are parameterized choices formulated by:

$$\texttt{kernel} <<< (G_x, G_y, G_z), (B_x, B_y, B_z) >>> (\texttt{args})$$

The appropriate allocation for these parameters is often empirically determined, balancing between latency, memory access patterns, and computational throughput.

---

**Data:** Configuration of kernel execution
**Result:** Optimized parallel computation
Determine best grid $(G_x, G_y, G_z)$ and block sizes $(B_x, B_y, B_z)$;
**foreach** *task chunk* **do**
    Assign to thread block;
    **while** *block not complete* **do**
        Compute and synchronize;

---

# Python Code Snippet

Below is a Python code snippet that encompasses the core elements of the CUDA programming model, including setting up a CUDA environment, managing threads and blocks, and launching a kernel using PyCUDA.

```python
import pycuda.driver as cuda
import pycuda.autoinit
from pycuda.compiler import SourceModule
import numpy as np

# Kernel code string, implementing a simple addition for
↪    demonstration
kernel_code = """
__global__ void addVectors(float *a, float *b, float *c, int n) {
    int tid = blockIdx.x * blockDim.x + threadIdx.x;
    if (tid < n) {
        c[tid] = a[tid] + b[tid];
    }
}
"""

# Initialize host input vectors
n = 256
a = np.random.rand(n).astype(np.float32)
b = np.random.rand(n).astype(np.float32)

# Allocate memory on the device
a_gpu = cuda.mem_alloc(a.nbytes)
b_gpu = cuda.mem_alloc(b.nbytes)
c_gpu = cuda.mem_alloc(a.nbytes)

# Transfer the arrays to the GPU
cuda.memcpy_htod(a_gpu, a)
cuda.memcpy_htod(b_gpu, b)

# Compile the kernel code
mod = SourceModule(kernel_code)

# Get the kernel function from the compiled module
add_vectors = mod.get_function("addVectors")

# Determine block and grid sizes
block_size = 128  # Threads per block
grid_size = (n + block_size - 1) // block_size

# Launch the kernel
add_vectors(a_gpu, b_gpu, c_gpu, np.int32(n), block=(block_size, 1,
↪    1), grid=(grid_size, 1))

# Create an empty array to receive the result
c = np.empty_like(a)

# Copy the result from the GPU back to the host
cuda.memcpy_dtoh(c, c_gpu)
```

```
# Verify the result
if np.allclose(c, a + b):
    print("The result is correct!")
else:
    print("There is an error in the computation.")
```

This code consists of key components necessary for setting up a simple CUDA program using PyCUDA:

- `addVectors` is the CUDA kernel function, which adds two vectors element-wise.

- Initialization of vectors a and b for computation and memory allocation on the GPU.

- The kernel is compiled and executed via PyCUDA's `SourceModule` and `get_function`.

- Grid and block sizes are calculated to determine the proper configuration for the kernel execution.

- After kernel execution, results are copied back to verify correctness.

This concise example demonstrates the steps involved in setting up and running CUDA kernels for basic computations in Python using PyCUDA.

# Chapter 4

# Basics of CUDA Memory Management

## Memory Allocation

In the CUDA framework, memory allocation on the GPU device is fundamental to facilitate parallel computations. GPU memory is allocated using the `cudaMalloc` API, which reserves a specified amount of bytes on the device memory. This function returns a pointer to the allocated memory location. Mathematically, the process is denoted as:

$$P_{\text{device}} = \texttt{cudaMalloc}(\texttt{\&d\_ptr}, \text{size})$$

where $P_{\text{device}}$ represents the device pointer and size is the length of bytes for allocation. The memory allocation must adhere to the constraints posed by the GPU's architecture limit, denoted by:

$$\text{size} \leq M_{\text{total}}$$

where $M_{\text{total}}$ is the total available memory on the device.

## Memory Transfer

Efficient data transfer between host (CPU) and device (GPU) is executed using the `cudaMemcpy` function. The copy direction plays a crucial role in data management and is categorized as either host to device (H2D), device to host (D2H), or device to device (D2D).

The transfer operation can be encapsulated in the following function signature:

$$\texttt{cudaMemcpy}(\texttt{dest}, \texttt{src}, \text{count}, \texttt{cudaMemcpyKind})$$

where `cudaMemcpyKind` specifies the direction, and the effectiveness of this transfer is significantly influenced by user-controlled parameters like buffer size count.

---

**Data:** Host and device pointers `h_ptr` and `d_ptr`
**Result:** Data correctly transferred between host and
device
Call `cudaMemcpy` operation;
Determine optimal `cudaMemcpyKind`;
Adjust buffer size according to requirements;

---

With regards to mathematical notation, the relationship of effective bandwidth $B$ during memory transfer is represented as:

$$B = \frac{n \cdot \text{element size}}{\text{time}}$$

where $n$ is the number of elements being transferred, serving as a pivotal factor in optimizing performance.

# Memory Deallocation

Post computation, it is crucial to deallocate the memory previously reserved on the device to prevent memory leakage, employing the `cudaFree` function:

$$\texttt{cudaFree}(P_{\text{device}})$$

where $P_{\text{device}}$ is the pointer to the memory space allocated to be freed. This function ensures that resource consumption is minimized, maintaining system integrity and performance efficiency.

Sleeving an additional operation, device memory can be reset by:

$$\texttt{cudaDeviceReset}()$$

which reclaims all currently allocated memory and resets all device states, safeguarding against erroneous memory states in subsequent operations.

# Unified Memory Access

Unified memory in CUDA enables seamless data sharing between host and device, effectively abstracting memory management for ease of use. Memory is allocated using:

$$\text{cudaMallocManaged}(\&\text{ptr}, \text{size})$$

which provides cross-platform transparent access, summarizing the beneficial paradigm where the physical separation of memory is logically unified, thereby expressed in rigid formalism as:

$$M_{\text{unified}} \equiv M_{\text{host}} \cup M_{\text{device}}$$

This feature automates data migration between the host and device, advancing the development of sophisticated parallel programs.

# Python Code Snippet

Below is a Python code snippet that encompasses memory allocation, transfer, and deallocation operations in CUDA using the PyCUDA library. This snippet includes handling of device pointers, memory operations, and performance measurement.

```python
import pycuda.driver as cuda
import pycuda.autoinit
import numpy as np
from time import time

# Initialize variables
size = 1024 * 1024   # 1MB of data
host_data = np.random.randn(size).astype(np.float32)
device_data = cuda.mem_alloc(host_data.nbytes)

# Memory Allocation and Transfer
def allocate_and_transfer_memory(host_array):
    """
    Allocate memory on the GPU and transfer data from host to
    ↪  device.
    :param host_array: Array of data on the host.
    :return: Device pointer to allocated memory.
    """
    # Allocate memory on the device
    device_pointer = cuda.mem_alloc(host_array.nbytes)
```

```python
    # Transfer data to device
    cuda.memcpy_htod(device_pointer, host_array)

    return device_pointer

# Calculate Effective Bandwidth
def calculate_bandwidth(num_bytes, transfer_time):
    """
    Calculate effective memory bandwidth.
    :param num_bytes: Total number of bytes transferred.
    :param transfer_time: Time taken for the transfer.
    :return: Effective bandwidth.
    """
    return num_bytes / (transfer_time * 1e9)  # GB/s

# Memory Deallocation
def deallocate_memory(device_pointer):
    """
    Free allocated memory on the device.
    :param device_pointer: Pointer to the device memory to free.
    """
    device_pointer.free()

# Unified Memory Access
def unified_memory_access(array_size):
    """
    Using unified memory to manage host and device memory
    ↪ seamlessly.
    :param array_size: Number of elements in the unified array.
    :return: CUDA managed array.
    """
    managed_array = cuda.pagelocked_zeros(array_size,
    ↪ dtype=np.float32, mem_flags=cuda.host_alloc_flags.DEVICEMAP)
    return managed_array

# Main code execution
try:
    # Allocate and transfer memory
    start_time = time()
    d_ptr = allocate_and_transfer_memory(host_data)
    transfer_time = time() - start_time

    # Calculate and print bandwidth
    bandwidth = calculate_bandwidth(host_data.nbytes, transfer_time)
    print(f"Effective Bandwidth: {bandwidth:.2f} GB/s")

    # Allocate unified memory
    unified_array = unified_memory_access(size)

finally:
    # Clean up memory
    deallocate_memory(d_ptr)
```

This code defines several core functions necessary for CUDA memory management using PyCUDA, including:

- `allocate_and_transfer_memory` function allocates memory on the GPU and transfers data from host to device.

- `calculate_bandwidth` computes effective memory bandwidth during data transfer.

- `deallocate_memory` is responsible for freeing GPU memory, ensuring efficient resource management.

- `unified_memory_access` demonstrates how to use CUDA's unified memory for simplified management across host and device.

This code brings together the essential elements for managing and utilizing GPU memory in parallel computations using CUDA and PyCUDA.

# Chapter 5

# Writing Your First CUDA Program

## Preparing the Development Environment

To initiate the CUDA programming journey, the development environment must be configured. This involves setting up the appropriate software, which is pivotal to executing CUDA code efficiently. The CUDA toolkit must be installed on a system meeting specific hardware and software requirements. Variables are set as:

$$env\_variables = \{CUDA\_PATH, PATH, LD\_LIBRARY\_PATH\}$$

## Understanding CUDA Kernels

Within the realm of GPU programming, kernels are the functions written to execute on the GPU. These functions embody parallel computation tasks distributed across multiple threads. The architecture of the kernel is defined by:

$$kernel\_launch(\ll<grid\_dim, block\_dim\gg>)$$

where grid_dim and block_dim denote the dimensions of the grid and the blocks respectively. These dimensions assign the workload across the GPU's parallel processors.

# Creating a Simple CUDA Program

A simple CUDA program consists of four central components: data initialization, memory allocation, kernel execution, and result retrieval.

## 1   Data Initialization

Data that will be processed on the GPU must be initialized within the host environment. Example of initializing a data pointer:

$$h\_array[i] = f(i) \quad \forall i \in [0, N) \tag{5.1}$$

where $h\_array$ is the host array intended to be transferred to the GPU.

## 2   Kernel Execution and Launch Configuration

Kernel execution is initiated by configuring the launch parameters. Optimal grid and block configurations are crucial for performance:

```
kernel <<< grid_dim, block_dim >>> (d_array)
```

Grid and block dimensions are chosen in accordance with:

$$\texttt{grid\_dim} = \lceil \frac{N}{\texttt{block\_dim}} \rceil \tag{5.2}$$

---

**Data:** Integer array size $N$ and appropriate device
 pointers
**Result:** Array processed and data retrieved to host
Initialize data on host;
Allocate memory on device using `cudaMalloc`;
Transfer data to device using `cudaMemcpy`;
Configure execution with calculated grid and block
 dimensions;
Execute kernel on device;
Retrieve data back to host using `cudaMemcpy`;
Free device memory using `cudaFree`;

---

# Compiling and Running a CUDA Program

Compilation of a CUDA program is executed using the NVIDIA compiler, nvcc. The typical compilation command is:

$$nvcc - o\, output\_exe\, source.cu$$

The executable, output_exe, is subsequently run to observe the results on the GPU device.

# Python Code Snippet

Below is a Python code snippet that encompasses the core computational elements of writing a simple CUDA program, including data initialization, memory management, kernel execution, and result retrieval, using PyCUDA.

```python
import numpy as np
import pycuda.driver as cuda
import pycuda.autoinit
from pycuda.compiler import SourceModule

# Kernel code as a string
kernel_code = """
__global__ void add(int *d_array, int N) {
    int idx = blockIdx.x * blockDim.x + threadIdx.x;
    if (idx < N) {
        d_array[idx] += 1;
    }
}
"""

# Compile the kernel code
mod = SourceModule(kernel_code)
add = mod.get_function("add")

def initialize_data(N):
    '''
    Initialize data on the host.
    :param N: Size of the array.
    :return: Initialized host array.
    '''
    h_array = np.arange(N).astype(np.int32)
    return h_array

def allocate_and_transfer(h_array):
```

```
    '''
    Allocate device memory and transfer data from host to device.
    :param h_array: Host array.
    :return: Device array pointer.
    '''
    d_array = cuda.mem_alloc(h_array.nbytes)
    cuda.memcpy_htod(d_array, h_array)
    return d_array

def execute_kernel(d_array, N):
    '''
    Execute the kernel on the GPU.
    :param d_array: Device array pointer.
    :param N: Size of the array.
    '''
    block_dim = 256
    grid_dim = (N + block_dim - 1) // block_dim
    add(d_array, np.int32(N), block=(block_dim, 1, 1),
    ↪   grid=(grid_dim, 1))

def retrieve_and_cleanup(d_array, N):
    '''
    Retrieve data back to host and clean up device memory.
    :param d_array: Device array pointer.
    :param N: Size of the array.
    :return: Retrieved host array.
    '''
    h_result = np.empty(N, dtype=np.int32)
    cuda.memcpy_dtoh(h_result, d_array)
    d_array.free()
    return h_result

# Example usage
N = 1024
h_array = initialize_data(N)
d_array = allocate_and_transfer(h_array)
execute_kernel(d_array, N)
h_result = retrieve_and_cleanup(d_array, N)

print("Original Array:", h_array)
print("Result Array:", h_result)
```

This code defines several key functions necessary for the setup and execution of a simple CUDA-accelerated addition operation:

- initialize_data function initializes a numpy array on the host, simulating data preparation.

- allocate_and_transfer allocates memory on the GPU and transfers data from host to device.

- `execute_kernel` sets up the execution configuration and launches the CUDA kernel on the GPU.

- `retrieve_and_cleanup` retrieves the modified data back to host memory and frees device memory.

The final block of code provides an example of initializing data, performing a simple addition operation via CUDA, and retrieving the results back on the host.

# Chapter 6

# CUDA Threads and Synchronization

## Overview of CUDA Thread Model

The CUDA thread model is fundamental in harnessing the parallelism offered by Graphics Processing Units (GPUs). Within this architecture, a kernel function is executed by a multitude of threads, which are organized into blocks and grids. The execution hierarchy is structured such that each block constitutes a sequential group of threads, while a grid comprises numerous blocks. Mathematically, this structure can be expressed as:

$$\text{Threads per block} = T_b, \quad \text{Blocks per grid} = B_g$$

The total number of threads, $T_{\text{total}}$, is given by:

$$T_{\text{total}} = T_b \times B_g$$

Each thread is identified by a unique index calculated as:

$$\text{threadIdx} = \text{blockIdx} \times T_b + \text{threadIdx}$$

This index captures the thread's position within the entire grid, facilitating data parallel operations across large datasets.

# Synchronization Techniques

Ensuring correct execution order and preventing data hazards in a parallel environment is paramount. CUDA offers synchronization primitives to achieve these objectives within a single block. The primary device-level synchronization technique is `__syncthreads()`, which acts as a barrier ensuring that all threads within a block have reached the barrier before any thread can proceed. Formally, for any operation $O$ to be dependent on another operation $P$:

$$O \mid P \Rightarrow \texttt{\_\_syncthreads()}$$

This guarantees the ordering of operations, i.e., all instances of operation $P$ must be completed before any instance of $O$ is commenced.

# Avoiding Race Conditions

Race conditions occur when multiple threads simultaneously access shared data, leading to inconsistent results. The synchronization primitives play a crucial role in circumventing these issues by protecting the critical sections of code that access shared variables.

Consider a shared variable $x$ updated inside a parallel block:

$$\text{Naive Addition:} \quad x = x + 1$$

This increment operation must be atomic to prevent race conditions. Series of operations, represented as:

$$x = x + v$$

are to be enclosed within atomic operations provided by CUDA, such as `atomicAdd()`:

$$\text{Atomic Addition:} \quad \texttt{atomicAdd(} \quad x, v\texttt{)}$$

This ensures that during the execution of the atomic operation, no other thread can modify the value of $x$.

---

**Data:** Initial shared variable $x$ and increment value $v$
**Result:** Atomic increment of the shared variable
**while** *there exists a thread operating on $x$* **do**
  atomicAdd(&x, v);
  __syncthreads();

---

The correct execution relies on atomic primitives for sequential consistency and `__syncthreads()` for barrier synchronization. These mechanisms combine to form the basis of ensuring cooperative execution while avoiding race conditions across multiple threads in a block.

# Optimal Thread Synchronization to Prevent Deadlocks

Thread synchronization when overused or improperly configured can lead to deadlocks. A deadlock scenario occurs when two or more threads wait forever for a condition that never occurs. The prevention of such conditions necessitates a careful design where synchronization is minimized and assured not to form cyclic dependencies.

The criteria for deadlock prevention in CUDA can be mathematically modeled as:

$$R_i \leq M - H,$$

where $R_i$ is resources requested by thread $i$, $M$ is the total available resources, and $H$ is the hold condition met by $i$.

In CUDA programming, ensuring all resources are correctly defined and that threads do not indefinitely wait for others to release resources is crucial. Using atomic operations effectively and ensuring proper barrier placements eliminates potential deadlocks.

# Case Study: Synchronization in Parallel Reduction Algorithm

A typical application of thread synchronization in CUDA is seen in the parallel reduction algorithm, which systematically reduces an array to a single value, such as the sum or maximum. This process involves successive halving of array segments and requires synchronization to ensure partial results are correctly computed:

$$x[i] = x[2i] + x[2i + 1]$$

Following calculations, `__syncthreads()` is crucial:

---

**Data:** Input array $x$ of size $N$
**Result:** Reduced sum stored in $x[0]$
**while** $N > 1$ **do**
  **for** $i = 0$ to $N/2$ - $1$ **do**
    Perform partial sum;
    `__syncthreads()` to ensure completion;
  Update $N$ to $\lceil N/2 \rceil$;

---

This structured use of barrier synchronization ensures that intermediate calculations are completed before threads continue, culminating in a consistent final result.

# Python Code Snippet

Below is a Python code snippet that encompasses the key elements of CUDA thread synchronization, avoidance of race conditions, and a demonstration of a parallel reduction algorithm using PyCUDA.

```python
import pycuda.autoinit
import pycuda.driver as drv
import numpy as np
from pycuda.compiler import SourceModule

# CUDA Kernel code
kernel_code = """
__global__ void incrementArray(float *arr, int N, float v) {
    int idx = blockIdx.x * blockDim.x + threadIdx.x;
    if(idx < N) {
        atomicAdd(&arr[idx], v);
    }
}

__global__ void parallelReduction(float *g_idata, float *g_odata,
 unsigned int n) {
    extern __shared__ float sdata[];

    unsigned int tid = threadIdx.x;
    unsigned int i = blockIdx.x*(blockDim.x*2) + threadIdx.x;
    sdata[tid] = (i < n) ? g_idata[i] + g_idata[i+blockDim.x] : 0;
```

```
    __syncthreads();

    for(unsigned int s=blockDim.x/2; s>0; s>>=1) {
        if (tid < s) {
            sdata[tid] += sdata[tid + s];
        }
        __syncthreads();
    }

    if (tid == 0) g_odata[blockIdx.x] = sdata[0];
}
"""

# Compile the kernel code
mod = SourceModule(kernel_code)
increment = mod.get_function("incrementArray")
parallel_reduction = mod.get_function("parallelReduction")

# Initialize data
N = 1024
x = np.random.rand(N).astype(np.float32)
v = 1.0
x_gpu = drv.mem_alloc(x.nbytes)
drv.memcpy_htod(x_gpu, x)

# Define grid and block size
block_size = 256
grid_size = (N + block_size - 1) // block_size

# Call the increment kernel, providing a demonstration of atomic
↪   operations
increment(x_gpu, np.int32(N), np.float32(v), block=(block_size, 1,
↪   1), grid=(grid_size, 1))

# Set up for reduction
sdata = np.zeros(grid_size).astype(np.float32)
sdata_gpu = drv.mem_alloc(sdata.nbytes)

# Perform parallel reduction, demonstrating the use of shared memory
↪   and __syncthreads()
parallel_reduction(x_gpu, sdata_gpu, np.uint32(N),
↪   block=(block_size, 1, 1), grid=(grid_size, 1), shared=block_size
↪   * np.float32().nbytes)

# Retrieve results
drv.memcpy_dtoh(sdata, sdata_gpu)
result = np.sum(sdata)  # final reduction on CPU

# Outputs
print("Atomic Increment Operation Results: ", x[:10])  # Print first
↪   10 elements after increment
```

```
print("Result of Parallel Reduction: ", result)
```

This code defines several key functions necessary for executing critical CUDA operations and provides working examples implemented with PyCUDA:

- The CUDA kernel `incrementArray` showcases the use of `atomicAdd` for avoiding race conditions while incrementing array values.

- The `parallelReduction` kernel performs reduction across an array through shared memory and `__syncthreads()` to synchronize thread blocks.

- Python code initializes data, sets up memory handling, and manages the GPU interaction required for executing the provided CUDA kernels.

- The final block retrieves and prints outcomes from both the atomic increment operations and the parallel reduction process.

# Chapter 7

# Optimizing Memory Bandwidth

## Memory Bandwidth Considerations

Optimizing memory bandwidth is a fundamental aspect of enhancing performance in CUDA-accelerated applications. The transfer rate, $BW$, between host and device memory, can be mathematically expressed as follows:

$$BW = \frac{\text{Data Size}}{\text{Transfer Time}}$$

where the data size is often measured in bytes, and the transfer time in seconds. The relation implies maximizing $BW$ requires minimizing transfer time while efficiently managing data size.

## Coalesced Memory Access Patterns

Coalesced memory access is crucial in optimizing device memory bandwidth. When memory transactions are coalesced, a single transaction serves multiple access requests from different threads. For threads in a warp that are accessing contiguous memory locations, coalesced access can be mathematically modeled as minimizing the non-coalesced memory footprint $F_{\text{non-coalesced}}$:

$$F_{\text{non-coalesced}} = (N \times T) - \text{Coalesced Memory Size}$$

where $N$ is the number of threads, and $T$ is the transaction size. By designing access patterns that minimize $F_{\text{non-coalesced}}$, bandwidth usage is effectively optimized.

# Asynchronous Memory Transfers and Overlapping

Asynchronous memory transfers become paramount when attempting to overlap data copy and execution tasks, thus reducing the effective transfer time. The formal representation of achievable throughput, $\eta$, with overlap operations incorporated is:

$$\eta = \frac{BW_{\text{mem}} \times BW_{\text{comp}}}{\max(BW_{\text{mem}}, BW_{\text{comp}})}$$

Asynchronous operations utilize streams, where `cudaMemcpyAsync` allows data transfer to occur concurrently with kernel execution, thereby modifying throughput $\eta$ positively.

# Pinned Memory Utilization

Allocating pinned memory buffers on the host side facilitates higher throughput compared to pageable memory. If $P$ denotes the overhead of pageable memory and PMC is the pinned memory contribution to performance:

$$\text{PMC} = \eta_{\text{cached}} - \eta_{\text{pinned}}$$

Here, $\eta_{\text{cached}}$ is the effective bandwidth when using pageable (potentially cached) memory, while $\eta_{\text{pinned}}$ represents the bandwidth from pinned memory execution, usually ensuring $\eta_{\text{pinned}} > \eta_{\text{cached}}$.

---

**Data:** Datasets for transfer from host to device
**Result:** Enhanced transfer efficiency through pinned memory
        Allocate pinned memory on host
`cudaHostAlloc` for dataset
Initiate async transfer with `cudaMemcpyAsync`
Declare non-blocking streams

---

Integration of pinned memory allocation is explicitly depicted, generating a notable bandwidth improvement versus conventional pageable memory allocations.

# Near-Peak Throughput with Unified Memory

Unified Memory simplifies memory management by providing a single memory space accessible from both the host and the device. However, accurately accounting for throughput and latency changes reveals peak throughput $\eta_{\text{unified}}$ approaching:

$$\eta_{\text{unified}} = f(\text{data locality, operational loads})$$

Data locality dictates performance; the memory access pattern impacts how often data is migrated between host and device, which can either be an advantage or impediment.

# Efficient Memory Latency Hiding

Latency hiding strategies aim to mitigate delays intrinsic in memory transactions. Using a latency masking factor $\lambda$, the effective execution time $T_{\text{exec}}$ of operations is reduced:

$$T_{\text{exec}} = T_{\text{theoretical}} \times (1 - \lambda)$$

Key techniques include kernel overlap with prefetching and double-buffering, both enhancing throughput by concealing load times within execution cycles.

---

**Data:** Memory-intensive workloads
**Result:** Reduction in latency; Enhanced execution throughput
Prepare consecutive kernel launches
Activate prefetching strategies
Deploy double buffering to layer execution pipelines

---

This approach exploits the pipeline nature of modern CUDA architectures, providing methodological pathways to optimize data transfer rates and merging computational loads for enhanced efficiency.

# Python Code Snippet

Below is a Python code snippet that encompasses the core computational aspects discussed in the chapter, including optimizing memory bandwidth, coalesced memory access patterns, asynchronous memory transfers, pinned memory utilization, and efficient memory latency hiding using PyCUDA.

```python
import pycuda.driver as cuda
import pycuda.autoinit
import numpy as np
from pycuda.compiler import SourceModule

# Example kernel that simulates a simple operation using threads
mod = SourceModule("""
__global__ void simple_kernel(float *a, float *b, float *c)
{
    int idx = threadIdx.x + blockIdx.x * blockDim.x;
    if (idx < N) {
        c[idx] = a[idx] + b[idx];
    }
}
""")

# Allocate host data
N = 1024
a_host = np.random.randn(N).astype(np.float32)
b_host = np.random.randn(N).astype(np.float32)

# Allocate device memory
a_device = cuda.mem_alloc(a_host.nbytes)
b_device = cuda.mem_alloc(b_host.nbytes)
c_device = cuda.mem_alloc(a_host.nbytes)

# Pinned memory allocation for improved data transfer performance
a_pinned, event_a = cuda.register_host_memory(a_host)
b_pinned, event_b = cuda.register_host_memory(b_host)

# Copy data to device using asynchronous transfer
cuda.memcpy_htod_async(a_device, a_pinned)
cuda.memcpy_htod_async(b_device, b_pinned)

# Launch kernel
function = mod.get_function("simple_kernel")
function(a_device, b_device, c_device, block=(256,1,1),
    grid=(int(N/256) + 1,1))

# Copy result back to host
c_host = np.empty_like(a_host)
cuda.memcpy_dtoh(c_host, c_device)
```

```
# Utilize streams for asynchronous operations (Data transfer and
↪   kernel execution)
stream = cuda.Stream()
cuda.memcpy_htod_async(a_device, a_pinned, stream)
cuda.memcpy_htod_async(b_device, b_pinned, stream)

function(a_device, b_device, c_device, block=(256,1,1),
↪   grid=(int(N/256) + 1,1), stream=stream)

# Prefetching and double-buffer technique
for _ in range(10):
    cuda.memcpy_dtod_async(a_device, b_device, a_host.nbytes,
    ↪   stream)

# Close stream
stream.synchronize()
stream = None

# Free resources
a_device.free()
b_device.free()
c_device.free()
event_a.unregister()
event_b.unregister()
```

This code snippet implements several key concepts using Py-CUDA:

- Launching a CUDA kernel with `simple_kernel` to perform computations in parallel on the GPU.

- Pinned memory allocation with `cuda.register_host_memory` provides higher data transfer throughput compared to pageable memory.

- Asynchronous memory transfer is enabled by `cuda.memcpy_htod_async`, overlapping data copy and kernel execution to maximize bandwidth.

- CUDA streams are employed to manage asynchronous kernels and data transfers effectively, improving overall computation and data handling efficiency.

- Techniques such as prefetching and double-buffering are highlighted to demonstrate memory latency hiding strategies in action.

These implementations demonstrate how to optimize memory bandwidth and handle data efficiently using CUDA and PyCUDA, which are critical for developing high-performance GPU-accelerated applications.

# Chapter 8

# Streamlining Data Transfers with Streams

## Conceptual Overview of Streams

CUDA streams are pivotal in optimizing GPU performance by enabling concurrent execution of data transfers and kernel operations. The concept of streams can be formally depicted as a sequence of operations that execute in the order they are issued, providing an organized framework for overlapping memory transfers and computational kernels. Let $S_i$ represent a stream; operations within $S_i$ execute sequentially, while operations in distinct streams $S_i$ and $S_j$ $(i \neq j)$ can execute concurrently.

## Mathematical Modeling of Stream Operations

The execution timeline $T_{\text{stream}}$ of CUDA kernels and memory transfers using streams can be formulated mathematically. Suppose $K$ is a CUDA kernel, and $M$ represents memory operations; the time taken for sequential execution $T_{\text{seq}}$ without streams is:

$$T_{\text{seq}} = T(K) + \sum_{i=1}^{N} T(M_i)$$

where $N$ is the number of memory operations. Leveraging

streams, the effective execution time $T_{\text{stream}}$, with overlapping, is given by:

$$T_{\text{stream}} = \max \left( T(K), \max_i T(M_i) \right)$$

This relationship illustrates how streams can reduce the execution time significantly by enabling simultaneous execution of memory and compute tasks.

## Implementation of Streams in CUDA

CUDA streams are implemented using the `cudaStream_t` object. Consider the following pseudo-code for using streams to perform matrix addition operations while overlapping data transfers with kernel execution.

---

**Input:** Two matrices A, B
**Output:** Resultant matrix C
Create `cudaStream_t stream1, stream2`;
`cudaStreamCreate(&stream1)`;
`cudaStreamCreate(&stream2)`;
Copy A to GPU via `cudaMemcpyAsync` in `stream1`;
Copy B to GPU via `cudaMemcpyAsync` in `stream2`;
Launch kernel `matAddKernel` in `stream1`;
Copy C from GPU via `cudaMemcpyAsync` in `stream2`;
Synchronize `stream1, stream2`;
Destroy streams `cudaStreamDestroy(stream1, stream2)`;

---

The above algorithm demonstrates the conceptualization and utilization of CUDA streams, showcasing overlap between memory operations and kernel execution.

## Analyzing Throughput and Latency with Streams

Consider the throughput $\eta_{\text{stream}}$ of a system using streams. It can be described as a function of both compute and memory bandwidths:

$$\eta_{\text{stream}} = \frac{BW_{\text{comp}} \times BW_{\text{mem}}}{\max(BW_{\text{comp}}, BW_{\text{mem}})}$$

where $BW_{\mathrm{comp}}$ and $BW_{\mathrm{mem}}$ are the compute and memory bandwidths, respectively. The expression encapsulates how the combined performance comes close to the ideal concurrency performance bounds.

Latency $L_{\mathrm{stream}}$ can be mathematically analyzed as:

$$L_{\mathrm{stream}} = L_{\mathrm{comp}} + L_{\mathrm{mem}} - \delta$$

where $\delta$ is the latency reduction achieved due to concurrent operations enabled by streams. Streams effectively preside in achieving reduced latency values by permitting task overlap.

# Measuring the Impact of CUDA Streams

Empirical metrics for assessing stream performance include effective throughput and the occupation ratio of concurrent tasks. If $\Gamma$ represents the workload, its partitioning into streams is achieved as $\Gamma = \{\Gamma_1, \Gamma_2, \ldots, \Gamma_n\}$. The throughput difference factor $\Delta\eta$:

$$\Delta\eta = \eta_{\mathrm{stream}} - \eta_{\mathrm{no\text{-}stream}}$$

is used to quantify the gain from streamlining operations.

# Applications and Examples

CUDA streams find applications across various domains, particularly in scenarios requiring high throughput and low latency, thanks to their concurrent execution capabilities. They are extensively used in real-time video processing, deep learning batch execution, and high-performance scientific computations. By formulating compute-bound kernels and memory transfers in structured streams, applications benefit from reduced stalls and maximal throughput.

# Algorithm Synchronization in Streams

Synchronization is critical in stream-based programming. Consider an application employing multiple streams; synchronization constructs such as events are deployed, aligning streams to prevent data races:

$$E_{\text{sync}} = \begin{cases} 1 & \text{if synchronized,} \\ 0 & \text{otherwise.} \end{cases}$$

Employing `cudaEventRecord` and `cudaEventSynchronize` ensures that tasks in different streams are correctly ordered when dependencies exist, maintaining data coherency and execution fidelity.

# Python Code Snippet

Below is a Python code snippet that illustrates the use of CUDA streams to perform concurrent memory transfers and computations. The example shows how matrix addition can be conducted using PyCUDA with CUDA streams for efficient execution.

```python
import pycuda.driver as cuda
import pycuda.autoinit
import numpy as np
from pycuda.compiler import SourceModule

# CUDA Kernel for matrix addition
mod = SourceModule("""
__global__ void matAddKernel(float *A, float *B, float *C, int
↪   width) {
    int idx = threadIdx.x + blockIdx.x * blockDim.x;
    if (idx < width) {
        C[idx] = A[idx] + B[idx];
    }
}
""")


def execute_cuda_streams(A, B, width):
    """
    Executes matrix addition using CUDA streams for overlapping
    ↪   computational and memory operations.

    :param A: 1D numpy array representing matrix A.
    :param B: 1D numpy array representing matrix B.
    :param width: The width of the matrices.
    :return: Resultant matrix after addition.
    """
    # Convert input matrices to float32
    A = A.astype(np.float32)
    B = B.astype(np.float32)

    # Allocate memory on the device
    A_gpu = cuda.mem_alloc(A.nbytes)
```

```
    B_gpu = cuda.mem_alloc(B.nbytes)
    C_gpu = cuda.mem_alloc(A.nbytes)

    # Create CUDA streams
    stream1 = cuda.Stream()
    stream2 = cuda.Stream()

    # Asynchronous memory copies
    cuda.memcpy_htod_async(A_gpu, A, stream=stream1)
    cuda.memcpy_htod_async(B_gpu, B, stream=stream2)

    # Kernel function
    mat_add = mod.get_function("matAddKernel")

    # Launching the kernel on stream1
    mat_add(A_gpu, B_gpu, C_gpu, np.int32(width), block=(256, 1, 1),
    ↪  grid=(int((width + 255)/256), 1), stream=stream1)

    # Prepare output array for the result
    C = np.empty_like(A)

    # Asynchronous memory copy for the output
    cuda.memcpy_dtoh_async(C, C_gpu, stream=stream2)

    # Synchronize streams
    stream1.synchronize()
    stream2.synchronize()

    # Cleanup
    A_gpu.free()
    B_gpu.free()
    C_gpu.free()
    stream1.synchronize()
    stream2.synchronize()

    return C

# Example usage
if __name__ == "__main__":
    width = 1024
    A = np.random.rand(width).astype(np.float32)
    B = np.random.rand(width).astype(np.float32)

    # Run matrix addition
    C = execute_cuda_streams(A, B, width)

    # Display the resultant matrix
    print("Resultant matrix C:")
    print(C)
```

This code encompasses several key functionalities:

- A simple CUDA kernel, 'matAddKernel', is defined to perform element-wise addition of two matrices.

- The 'execute_cuda_streams' function employs PyCUDA to allocate device memory and perform asynchronous data transfers and kernel execution using CUDA streams (`cudaStream_t`).

- Two streams are created to perform memory transfers and computation concurrently, leveraging the CUDA runtime.

- The resultant matrix is transferred back to the host memory asynchronously, showcasing the overlap between computation and data transfer.

- The use of `stream.synchronize()` methods ensures proper synchronization and correctness of operations.

This example highlights the use of CUDA streams to effectively streamline data transfers and computation, reducing execution time and achieving improved hardware utilization.

# Chapter 9

# Understanding and Handling Errors

## Error Classification in CUDA Programming

Error handling in CUDA programming is paramount for ensuring robust and efficient GPU applications. Errors can be broadly classified into two categories: compile-time and runtime errors. Compile-time errors $E_c$ are detected during the compilation phase and are often syntax-related. Runtime errors $E_r$ occur during program execution and are primarily due to incorrect API usage or resource exhaustion.

$$E_{\text{total}} = E_c + E_r \tag{9.1}$$

In practice, effective handling seeks to minimize both $E_c$ and $E_r$.

## General Error Handling Strategies

CUDA provides several mechanisms to address errors that arise during execution, often requiring checks after specific operations. A standard practice involves utilizing error codes returned by CUDA API functions. Each function call returns a `cudaError_t` type, indicating the status of the operation:

```
cudaError_t status = cudaFunction(...);
```
The error check should follow the function call:

$$E_r = \begin{cases} 0, & \text{if status} = \texttt{cudaSuccess} \\ 1, & \text{otherwise.} \end{cases} \qquad (9.2)$$

# Systematic Error Identification Techniques

Validation of successful execution is achieved by employing
`cudaGetErrorString` to convert the error code into a human-readable
format. The pseudocode example below demonstrates this practice.

---

**Input:** CUDA function call status status
**if** $status \neq cudaSuccess$ **then**
   | Print `cudaGetErrorString(status)`;
   | Terminate program;

---

# Propagating Errors

When CUDA functions are encapsulated within modular components, error propagation becomes essential. This process can be
defined mathematically by considering the composite error status
$E_{\text{comp}}$:

$$E_{\text{comp}} = \bigvee_{i=1}^{n} E_{r_i} \qquad (9.3)$$

where $E_{r_i}$ denotes individual errors arising from each component.

# Asynchronous Errors Detection

CUDA operations often execute asynchronously, complicating error detection. Errors may not immediately manifest but arise when
launching subsequent operations or synchronizing streams. The
CUDA function `cudaPeekAtLastError` provides an immediate in-
dicative error status for asynchronous calls, whereas
`cudaDeviceSynchronize` confirms error presence post-execution.

# Corrective Measures and Resource Recovery

Once an error is identified, corrective measures are crucial to mitigate any adverse effects. Common strategies involve deallocation of memory and resetting the device to a clean state:

$$\text{cudaFree(resource)} \rightarrow \text{cudaDeviceReset()}$$

These functions ensure that all resources are relinquished, and the device returns to initial conditions suitable for subsequent operations.

# Optimizing Error Resilience

To optimize the resilience of CUDA programs against errors, a combination of redundancy strategies and rigorous input validation is recommended. Implementing checksum architectures and parity checks enhances resilience:

$$R = \text{validate}(I) + \text{checksum}(I)$$

where $I$ is the input data set.

Implementing this systematic approach ensures a comprehensive framework for error detection and management, thereby enhancing the robustness of CUDA-accelerated applications.

# Python Code Snippet

Below is a Python code snippet that demonstrates the implementation of crucial error handling strategies in CUDA programming using PyCUDA. It includes error checking for memory allocation, kernel execution, and device synchronization.

```
import pycuda.driver as cuda
import pycuda.autoinit
import numpy as np
from pycuda.compiler import SourceModule

# Kernel code in C for CUDA
cuda_source = """
__global__ void add(int *a, int *b, int *c, int N) {
```

```python
        int index = blockIdx.x * blockDim.x + threadIdx.x;
        if (index < N) {
            c[index] = a[index] + b[index];
        }
}
"""

# Compile the kernel
mod = SourceModule(cuda_source)
add_kernel = mod.get_function("add")

def check_cuda_errors():
    """
    Checks for errors in CUDA functions and displays them.
    """
    err = cuda.Context.get_current().get_last_error()
    if err != cuda.cudaError_t['cudaSuccess']:
        raise RuntimeError("CUDA Error: " +
        ↪    cuda.get_error_string(err))

def example_cuda_operation():
    """
    Example CUDA operation to illustrate error handling with PyCUDA.
    """
    N = 512   # Number of elements
    a = np.random.randint(0, 10, size=N).astype(np.int32)
    b = np.random.randint(0, 10, size=N).astype(np.int32)
    c = np.zeros_like(a)

    # Allocate device memory
    a_gpu = cuda.mem_alloc(a.nbytes)
    b_gpu = cuda.mem_alloc(b.nbytes)
    c_gpu = cuda.mem_alloc(c.nbytes)

    # Copy data to device
    cuda.memcpy_htod(a_gpu, a)
    cuda.memcpy_htod(b_gpu, b)

    # Launch the kernel
    block_size = 256
    grid_size = (N + block_size - 1) // block_size
    add_kernel(a_gpu, b_gpu, c_gpu, np.int32(N), block=(block_size,
    ↪    1, 1), grid=(grid_size, 1))

    # Check for errors in the kernel launch
    check_cuda_errors()

    # Copy the result back to the host
    cuda.memcpy_dtoh(c, c_gpu)

    # Check for errors when copying the results back
    check_cuda_errors()
```

```
    return a, b, c

# Execute the example and print results
a, b, c = example_cuda_operation()
print("Array A:", a)
print("Array B:", b)
print("Array C (Result):", c)
```

This code implements key error handling strategies:

- `check_cuda_errors` checks for errors after CUDA operations to ensure smooth execution.

- `example_cuda_operation` performs a vector addition on the GPU, demonstrating the allocation, execution, and error detection process.

- The kernel `add` performs element-wise addition of two vectors, showcasing a basic CUDA operation and handling potential errors.

This approach ensures structured error management when programming with CUDA, helping developers identify and fix issues efficiently to maintain application robustness.

# Chapter 10

# CUDA Shared Memory and Tiling

## Fundamentals of CUDA Shared Memory

In CUDA programming, shared memory is a programmable cache that resides on-chip, offering significantly lower latency than global memory. Each multiprocessor features distinct shared memory space, accessible by all threads within a block.

Let $SM$ denote the shared memory space and $TM$ for thread-local memory. For a given multiprocessor, the shared memory can be represented as:

$$SM = \{s_i \mid s_i \in \text{shared memory region}, \forall i \equiv 0, \ldots, N-1\}$$

where $N$ denotes the number of elements in shared memory. Each thread $t_j$ in a block can access $SM$ through explicit load and store instructions.

## Advantages of Data Locality

The efficiency of CUDA applications can be significantly enhanced by maximizing data locality. Shared memory access latency is orders of magnitude lower compared to accesses to global memory. Therefore, arranging data to be reused within shared memory enhances performance.

Memory access time is denoted by $\tau$, such that:

$$\tau_{\text{shared}} \ll \tau_{\text{global}}$$

where $\tau_{\text{shared}}$ and $\tau_{\text{global}}$ represent the access times for shared and global memory respectively. Thus, optimizing $SM$ usage minimizes $\tau_{\text{total}}$.

# Tiling Techniques for Efficient Memory Access

Tiling is a method employed to partition data into smaller chunks or tiles, allowing threads to load necessary portions into shared memory, operate on them, and store results back. Given a data matrix $M_{m \times n}$, it is partitioned into tiles $T$ of size $b \times b$.

$$T = \{T_{i,j} \mid T_{i,j} \subseteq M \, \forall \, i = \left\lceil \frac{m}{b} \right\rceil, j = \left\lceil \frac{n}{b} \right\rceil\}$$

Thus, the efficiency of tiled operations using shared memory is described by:

$$E_T \sim O\left(\frac{m \cdot n}{b}\right)$$

where $E_T$ represents computational efficiency.

# Algorithmic Implementation of Tiling

Algorithmic realization of tiling can be demonstrated via matrix multiplication. The following pseudocode illustrates these principles:

---

**Input:** Matrices $A$ and $B$ of dimension $m \times k$ and $k \times n$
**Output:** Matrix product $C = A \times B$
**foreach** *Tile T in A and B* **do**
    Load $T(A)$ and $T(B)$ into shared memory;
    Compute partial products in shared memory;
    Store results into matrix $C$;

---

The pseudocode ensures matrix operations are confined to $SM$ as much as possible, thereby reducing $\tau_{\text{total}}$.

# Synchronization in Shared Memory Usage

Synchronization between threads is crucial during shared memory operations to prevent race conditions. The synchronization barrier `__syncthreads()` is employed such that:

$$t_{i,\, j} = \texttt{\_\_syncthreads()} \ \forall \ t_{i,j} \in \text{block}$$

Ensuring consistent state of $SM$.

# Latency Reduction through Tiling

Utilizing tiling not only improves memory access patterns but also reduces the latency associated with global memory transactions. Given the operations $R_i$ running with shared memory, the effective latency $\lambda$ can be described by:

$$\lambda_{\text{effective}} = \frac{\lambda_{\text{global}}}{b}$$

when the overhead $O$ introduced by tiling is less than the gain:

$$O < \lambda_{\text{global}} - \lambda_{\text{effective}}$$

Optimization is achievable when data locality is maximized and latency reduced accordingly.

# Mathematical Formalism of Shared Memory Utilization

The optimization problem revolves around maximizing operations within shared memory and minimizing global memory exchanges. Let $\mathcal{O}$ denote the operations count, we aim to reach:

$$\max_{OP} \mathcal{O}_{\text{shared}}, \quad \min_{DM} \mathcal{O}_{\text{global}}$$

subject to capacity constraints given by $\dim(SM)$.

This theoretical appraisal showcases shared memory and tiling as potent strategies for enhancing CUDA application performance by focusing on memory hierarchy and data locality.

# Python Code Snippet

Below is a Python code snippet that implements the core computational techniques of using CUDA shared memory and tiling in matrix multiplication. This code leverages PyCUDA to perform actual GPU computation.

```python
import pycuda.autoinit
import pycuda.driver as cuda
import numpy as np
from pycuda.compiler import SourceModule

# Kernel code for matrix multiplication with shared memory tiling
kernel_code = """
__global__ void matrixMulShared(float *A, float *B, float *C, int N)
↪ {
    __shared__ float tile_A[BLOCK_SIZE][BLOCK_SIZE];
    __shared__ float tile_B[BLOCK_SIZE][BLOCK_SIZE];

    int row = blockIdx.y * BLOCK_SIZE + threadIdx.y;
    int col = blockIdx.x * BLOCK_SIZE + threadIdx.x;
    float value = 0;

    for (int k = 0; k < gridDim.x; ++k) {
        tile_A[threadIdx.y][threadIdx.x] = A[row * N + k *
        ↪ BLOCK_SIZE + threadIdx.x];
        tile_B[threadIdx.y][threadIdx.x] = B[(k * BLOCK_SIZE +
        ↪ threadIdx.y) * N + col];

        __syncthreads();

        for (int n = 0; n < BLOCK_SIZE; ++n)
            value += tile_A[threadIdx.y][n] *
            ↪ tile_B[n][threadIdx.x];

        __syncthreads();
    }

    C[row * N + col] = value;
}
"""

# Constants
BLOCK_SIZE = 16

# Helper function to initialize the matrix
def initialize(N):
    A = np.random.rand(N, N).astype(np.float32)
    B = np.random.rand(N, N).astype(np.float32)
    C = np.zeros((N, N), dtype=np.float32)
    return A, B, C
```

```
# Prepare data
N = 256  # Size of matrix
A, B, C = initialize(N)

# Allocate device memory
A_gpu = cuda.mem_alloc(A.nbytes)
B_gpu = cuda.mem_alloc(B.nbytes)
C_gpu = cuda.mem_alloc(C.nbytes)

# Transfer data to device
cuda.memcpy_htod(A_gpu, A)
cuda.memcpy_htod(B_gpu, B)

# Compile the kernel code
mod = SourceModule(kernel_code.replace("BLOCK_SIZE",
↪   str(BLOCK_SIZE)))
matrixMulShared = mod.get_function("matrixMulShared")

# Execute the kernel
block = (BLOCK_SIZE, BLOCK_SIZE, 1)
grid = (N // BLOCK_SIZE, N // BLOCK_SIZE)
matrixMulShared(A_gpu, B_gpu, C_gpu, np.int32(N), block=block,
↪   grid=grid)

# Retrieve result
cuda.memcpy_dtoh(C, C_gpu)

# Validate result
print("Matrix C (Product of A and B):")
print(C)

# Clean up
A_gpu.free()
B_gpu.free()
C_gpu.free()
```

This code includes vital functions and operations necessary for effective matrix multiplication with shared memory tiling in CUDA:

- The `matrixMulShared` kernel utilizes shared memory for efficient matrix multiplication.

- The `initialize` function generates random matrices for demonstration purposes.

- PyCUDA is used for memory allocation and data transfer between the host and the GPU.

- The kernel execution is configured with specific block and grid dimensions to manage the mapping of threads and tiles.

- The result is validated by printing the resulting matrix, demonstrating the successful execution of the tiled matrix multiplication.

This implementation highlights the efficient use of shared memory and demonstrates improvement in performance over standard global memory operations.

# Chapter 11

# Exploring Warp Behavior and Efficiency

## Warp Scheduling

In CUDA architecture, warps form the fundamental execution units within a Streaming Multiprocessor (SM). Each warp consists of 32 threads, executed in SIMD fashion. The warp scheduler dispatches one warp at a time to functional units for execution.

Let $W$ be a warp, composed of threads $\{t_0, t_1, \ldots, t_{31}\}$. The scheduling efficiency can be defined as:

$$\eta = \frac{\sum_{i=0}^{31} \delta_i}{32}$$

where $\delta_i$ is an indicator function given by:

$$\delta_i = \begin{cases} 1, & \text{if } t_i \text{ executes successfully} \\ 0, & \text{otherwise} \end{cases}$$

The goal is to maximize $\eta$ through effective scheduling, which relies on warp state, availability of operands, and operational dependencies within the threads.

## Conditional Branching

In cases of divergent branching within warps, the execution path splits, which can diminish warp efficiency. Let $B$ denote a branch instruction and $\mathcal{P}$ the set of predicates:

$$B: \quad (P, Q) \in \mathcal{P} \implies \text{Path } P \text{ or } Q$$

Divergent branching within a warp means some predicates result in different execution paths, such that warp $W$ diverges into paths $W_P$ and $W_Q$:

$$W = W_P \cup W_Q$$

The execution time $T$ with divergence can then be expressed by:

$$T_{\text{diverged}} = \max(T_{W_P}, T_{W_Q})$$

Mitigating divergence through the alignment of predicates leads to improved warp execution efficiency.

# Improving Warp Execution Efficiency

## 1 Algorithmic Optimization

Reducing divergence and optimal resource utilization are key to improving warp execution efficiency. Tactics include data coalescing, minimizing conditional branches, and restructuring algorithms for linear execution.

---

**Input:** Task Array $\mathcal{T}$
**Output:** Optimized Task Execution
**for** *All tasks in $\mathcal{T}$* **do**
  Rearrange tasks to align memory access;
  **if** *task dependent branches* **then**
    Encapsulate branches to reduce divergence;

---

## 2 Mathematical Formulation

Warp efficiency can be further quantitatively analyzed by modeling performance. The efficiency $\epsilon$ of executing instructions with $\mathcal{I}$ instructions and $D$ divergent branches is given by:

$$\epsilon = \frac{\mathcal{I} - D}{\mathcal{I}}$$

The aim is to minimize $D$, harnessing memory and computational parallelism to optimize $\epsilon$.

## 3  Latency Management

Latency is managed through effective warp cohort scheduling and balancing workload distribution. A mathematical expression of anticipated latency $\Lambda$ considering computational load $\mathcal{L}$ and scheduling overhead $\Omega$ is:

$$\Lambda = \frac{\mathcal{L} + \Omega}{\eta}$$

Strategically partitioning workloads to reduce overhead $\Omega$ enhances the overall warp latency.

# Advanced Techniques for Warp Synchronization

Warp synchronization is achieved through the usage of specific instructions ensuring all threads complete their current instructions before proceeding. Notably, CUDA provides the `__syncwarp()` primitive:

$$\texttt{\_\_syncwarp()} \implies \forall i, j \in W, \ t_i \to t_j$$

where $i \leq j$, ensuring precise synchronization.

Efficient usage of warp synchronization mechanisms contributes to maintaining high parallelism and minimizing idle cycles.

# Ensuring Consistency in Warp Execution

Ensuring consistency in warp execution encompasses addressing hardware specific divergence handling and employing high-level warp-coherent algorithms. The requirement for maintaining synchronized execution of warps can be represented by the following constraint:

$$C_W = \texttt{warp\_consistency}(W) = \text{TRUE}$$

where the function ensures that state transitions and memory operations remain consistent across warp execution cycles.

By observing these strategies, warp efficiency is reinforced through optimal scheduling, reduced divergence, and coherent memory operations.

# Python Code Snippet

Below is a Python code snippet that takes into account the mathematical expressions from the chapter such as warp scheduling efficiency, execution efficiency, and latency management, as well as algorithms for improving warp execution efficiency. It illustrates how these concepts can be translated into practical CUDA programming using PyCUDA.

```python
import pycuda.autoinit
import pycuda.driver as cuda
from pycuda.compiler import SourceModule
import numpy as np

# Define CUDA kernel as a C string
mod = SourceModule("""
__global__ void calculate_eta(int *warp_results, float *eta) {
    int idx = threadIdx.x;
    __shared__ int results[32];
    results[idx] = warp_results[idx];
    __syncthreads();

    // Calculate the total active threads in warp
    int active_count = 0;
    for (int i = 0; i < 32; i++) {
        active_count += results[i];
    }

    if (idx == 0) {
        eta[0] = active_count / 32.0;
    }
}

__global__ void calculate_execution_efficiency(int
 ↪  total_instructions, int divergent_branches, float *efficiency) {
    efficiency[0] = (total_instructions - divergent_branches) /
     ↪  (float) total_instructions;
}

__global__ void manage_latency(float load, float overhead, float
 ↪  eta, float *latency) {
    latency[0] = (load + overhead) / eta;
}
```

```
__global__ void optimize_tasks(int *task_arr, int n) {
    int idx = threadIdx.x + blockIdx.x * blockDim.x;
    if (idx < n) {
        // Simulated task optimization
        task_arr[idx] = task_arr[idx] * 2; // Dummy operation
    }
}

__global__ void enforce_warp_sync(int *data) {
    int idx = threadIdx.x;
    __syncwarp();
    data[idx] += 1;  // Simulated warp synchronized operation
}
""")

# Task setup
task_arr = np.array([1, 2, 3, 4, 5, 6, 7, 8], dtype=np.int32)
task_arr_gpu = cuda.mem_alloc(task_arr.nbytes)
cuda.memcpy_htod(task_arr_gpu, task_arr)

# Kernel execution
optimize_tasks = mod.get_function("optimize_tasks")
optimize_tasks(task_arr_gpu, np.int32(len(task_arr)), block=(8, 1,
↪ 1), grid=(1, 1))

# Collect results
optimized_task_arr = np.empty_like(task_arr)
cuda.memcpy_dtoh(optimized_task_arr, task_arr_gpu)
print("Optimized Tasks:", optimized_task_arr)

# Calculate warp scheduling efficiency eta
warp_results = np.random.randint(0, 2, size=32).astype(np.int32)
eta = np.zeros(1).astype(np.float32)
warp_results_gpu = cuda.mem_alloc(warp_results.nbytes)
eta_gpu = cuda.mem_alloc(eta.nbytes)
cuda.memcpy_htod(warp_results_gpu, warp_results)
calculate_eta = mod.get_function("calculate_eta")
calculate_eta(warp_results_gpu, eta_gpu, block=(32, 1, 1))
cuda.memcpy_dtoh(eta, eta_gpu)
print("Warp Efficiency ():", eta[0])

# Calculate execution efficiency
execution_efficiency = np.zeros(1).astype(np.float32)
calculate_execution_efficiency =
↪ mod.get_function("calculate_execution_efficiency")
calculate_execution_efficiency(np.int32(100), np.int32(10),
                               cuda.Out(execution_efficiency),
                               ↪ block=(1, 1, 1))
print("Execution Efficiency ():", execution_efficiency[0])

# Manage latency
latency = np.zeros(1).astype(np.float32)
manage_latency = mod.get_function("manage_latency")
```

```
manage_latency(np.float32(500), np.float32(10), eta,
               cuda.Out(latency), block=(1, 1, 1))
print("Latency ():", latency[0])

# Enforce warp synchronization
data = np.arange(32).astype(np.int32)
data_gpu = cuda.mem_alloc(data.nbytes)
cuda.memcpy_htod(data_gpu, data)
enforce_warp_sync = mod.get_function("enforce_warp_sync")
enforce_warp_sync(data_gpu, block=(32, 1, 1))
cuda.memcpy_dtoh(data, data_gpu)
print("Data after sync:", data)
```

This code uses PyCUDA to implement the key concepts discussed in the chapter:

- It defines CUDA kernels for calculating warp efficiency, execution efficiency, and latency, using actual execution on the GPU.

- The `optimize_tasks` kernel illustrates basic task optimization that could align with reduction techniques.

- The `calculate_eta` function computes warp scheduling efficiency $\eta$, aggregating active threads.

- The `calculate_execution_efficiency` kernel computes execution efficiency $\epsilon$ considering the reduction in divergent branches.

- The `manage_latency` kernel provides a computation model for warp-related latency $\Lambda$.

- The `enforce_warp_sync` kernel exemplifies warp synchronization using the `__syncwarp()` intrinsic.

The final part of the code demonstrates these functionalities using randomly initialized inputs, showcasing practical GPU programming with PyCUDA.

# Chapter 12

# Achieving Concurrency with Multiple GPUs

## Parallel Decomposition of Tasks

Consider the decomposition of a computational task $T$ into subtasks $T_1, T_2, \ldots, T_n$. Each subtask is assigned to one of the $m$ available GPUs for concurrent execution. Let $G = \{G_1, G_2, \ldots, G_m\}$ denote the set of GPUs, with $\texttt{assign}(T_i, G_k)$ representing the allocation of subtask $T_i$ to GPU $G_k$. The goal is to maximize the parallel efficiency $\rho$, defined by

$$\rho = \frac{\sum_{i=1}^{n} \frac{1}{t_i}}{\frac{1}{\max(t_1, t_2, \ldots, t_m)}}$$

where $t_i$ is the execution time of subtask $T_i$ on its assigned GPU. Optimal allocation reduces inter-GPU communication overhead $\varphi$, and for highly parallelizable tasks, $\varphi \to 0$.

## Load Balancing Across GPUs

The effective distribution of workload amongst GPUs is central to achieving concurrency. Let $W(T_i)$ be the computational intensity of task $T_i$, modeled as

$$W(T_i) = \mathcal{O}(n_i \cdot \log(n_i))$$

where $n_i$ represents workload size. Optimal load balancing requires

$$\min_{P \in \texttt{Perm}(G)} \max_{G_k \in G} \sum_{T_i \in P(G_k)} W(T_i)$$

where $\texttt{Perm}(G)$ denotes all permutations of task assignments to GPUs, ensuring minimized variance in GPU workload.

## Efficient Inter-GPU Communication

The interconnect architecture critically influences the performance of multi-GPU setups. A full-bandwidth $\beta$ channel between GPUs ensures minimal communication latency. Let $\tau_{ij}$ denote the transfer time of data $D_{ij}$ between $G_i$ and $G_j$, expressible as

$$\tau_{ij} = \frac{|D_{ij}|}{\beta} + \tau_{\text{overhead}}$$

where $\tau_{\text{overhead}}$ accounts for communication protocol overhead. The synchronization time $S$ required for inter-GPU cooperation is approximated by

$$S = \max_{\substack{1 \le i,j \le m \\ i \ne j}} \tau_{ij}$$

Optimizing $\tau_{ij}$ is pivotal to augment concurrent operations.

## Algorithm for Multi-GPU Concurrent Execution

The deployment of an algorithm over multiple GPUs mandates a structured approach to task partitioning and data distribution.

77

**Input:** Global Task $T$
**Output:** Concurrent Execution Across $G$
Decompose $T$ into sub-tasks $\{T_1, T_2, \ldots, T_n\}$;
**for** *All* $G_k \in G$ **do**
    Assign portion of $\mathcal{T}$ according to load balancing
    criterion;
**while** *Any* $T_i$ *incomplete* **do**
    Inter-GPU data exchange as per dependency graph;
    Update GPU states based on computation status;
Perform `sync` to finalize task execution;

# Reducing Execution Bottlenecks

Evaluating and mitigating the bottlenecks in multi-GPU scenarios focuses on resource contention and execution overlap. Denote the bottleneck factor $\lambda$ by

$$\lambda = \frac{\sum_{i=1}^{n} \tau_i}{m \times \text{time\_parallel}}$$

The bottleneck is minimized by optimizing task reassignment post initial evaluation:

$$\texttt{Reassign}(T_i, G_j) \iff \lambda_{new} < \lambda$$

where $\lambda_{new}$ represents the recalculated bottleneck post reassignment, indicating a superior load balance or communication strategy. .

# Utilizing CUDA Streams

Streams facilitate task concurrency within a single GPU, analogous to multi-GPU strategies for complete execution overlap. Consider independent tasks $A$, $B$ where data dependencies are absent. The concurrent strategy employs streams $S_a$, $S_b$:

```
cudaStream_t S_a, S_b;
    cudaStreamCreate(S_a);
    cudaStreamCreate(S_b);
```

Synchronization to enforce execution order allows

$$\text{cudaStreamSynchronize}(S_a);$$

By effectively distributing streams, concurrency is upheld within the confines of CUDA's execution model, enhancing multi-GPU application scalability.

# Python Code Snippet

Below is a Python code snippet illustrating the application of concurrent execution over multiple GPUs leveraging PyCUDA. This involves optimal task allocation, GPU-based computation, and efficient data transfer management.

```python
import pycuda.driver as cuda
import numpy as np
from pycuda.compiler import SourceModule

# Initialize PyCUDA
cuda.init()
num_gpus = cuda.Device.count()

# Check for multiple GPUs
if num_gpus < 2:
    raise RuntimeError("This script requires at least 2 GPUs to
    ↪ run.")

# Context setup for each GPU
contexts = [cuda.Device(i).make_context() for i in range(num_gpus)]

# Kernel code to execute on GPU
kernel_code = """
__global__ void gpu_task(float *data, int n) {
    int idx = blockIdx.x * blockDim.x + threadIdx.x;
    if (idx < n) {
        // Perform some operations
        data[idx] = data[idx] * 2.0;
    }
}
"""

# Compile the kernel
mod = SourceModule(kernel_code)
gpu_task = mod.get_function("gpu_task")

def allocate_and_upload(data):
    gpu_data = cuda.mem_alloc(data.nbytes)
    cuda.memcpy_htod(gpu_data, data)
```

```
    return gpu_data

# Allocate data for each task
task_size = 1024   # Example task size
tasks = [np.random.rand(task_size).astype(np.float32) for _ in
↪    range(num_gpus)]
gpu_data = [allocate_and_upload(task) for task in tasks]

# Execute tasks on each GPU
for i in range(num_gpus):
    contexts[i].push()
    gpu_task(gpu_data[i], np.int32(task_size), block=(256, 1, 1),
↪    grid=(4, 1))
    contexts[i].pop()

# Retrieve results from GPUs
results = []
for i in range(num_gpus):
    result = np.empty_like(tasks[i])
    contexts[i].push()
    cuda.memcpy_dtoh(result, gpu_data[i])
    contexts[i].pop()
    results.append(result)

# Clean up GPU contexts
for context in contexts:
    context.pop()

# Display the results
for i, result in enumerate(results):
    print(f"Result from GPU {i}:")
    print(result[:10])   # Print the first 10 elements of the result
↪    array
```

This code demonstrates efficient parallel computing using Py-
CUDA:

- `allocate_and_upload` prepares data for CUDA execution by
  allocating GPU memory and performing data transfer from
  host to device.

- A GPU kernel `gpu_task` is defined to parallelize data operations across threads, with task execution triggered on specified GPU contexts.

- Proper context management is employed to handle multiple
  GPUs, ensuring tasks are executed on designated devices.

- After computation, data is captured back to the host from
  each GPU for post-processing or further analysis.

80

# Chapter 13

# Dynamic Parallelism in CUDA

## Defining Dynamic Parallelism

Dynamic parallelism in CUDA enables a kernel to directly launch child kernels, enhancing computational flexibility and scalability. Consider a kernel $K : \mathbb{R}^n \to \mathbb{R}^m$ such that $K = \{K_1, K_2, \ldots, K_l\}$, where sub-kernels $K_i$ can dynamically spawn additional kernels during execution. This capacity allows hierarchical parallelization, improving performance for irregular data and control structures.

The mathematical framework supporting dynamic parallelism necessitates handling nested grids and blocks. Let $\mathcal{T} = \{t_1, t_2, \ldots, t_k\}$ be tasks distributed among the parent kernel, each with a potential set of dynamically generated task $\mathcal{D}_i$. The execution timeline can be represented as:

$$T_{\text{total}} = \sum_{i=1}^{k} t_i + \sum_{i=1}^{k} \sum_{j=1}^{d_i} \tilde{t}_{ij}$$

where $\tilde{t}_{ij}$ denotes the execution time of dynamically spawned sub-tasks within $t_i$.

## Kernel Launch Hierarchies

The launch of kernels from within other kernels necessitates managing hierarchical execution dependencies. Within CUDA, a child kernel is invoked through `cudaLaunchKernel()`. Define a hierarchical task execution model as $\mathcal{H} = (\mathcal{P}, \mathcal{C})$ where $\mathcal{P}$ is the set of parent tasks, and $\mathcal{C}$ is the corresponding set of child tasks:

$$\mathcal{P} = \{P_1, P_2, \ldots, P_m\}, \quad \mathcal{C} = \bigcup_{i=1}^{m} \{C_{i1}, C_{i2}, \ldots, C_{ip}\}$$

The dependency relation $D : \mathcal{C} \to \mathcal{P}$ defines which parent task each child task is linked to, ensuring compliance with execution priorities and inter-task dependencies.

# Optimization of Dynamic Kernel Invocations

Minimizing overhead and maximizing throughput in dynamic kernel execution involves careful orchestration of task spawning and resource management. The execution efficiency is quantified by an overhead factor, $\xi$, defined as:

$$\xi = \frac{T_{\text{overhead}}}{T_{\text{execution}}}$$

where $T_{\text{execution}}$ accounts for actual kernel execution time, and $T_{\text{overhead}}$ is the time consumed in managing kernel launches and synchronizations. Strategies for reducing $\xi$ optimize memory allocation, streamline kernel launch parameters, and harmonize disparate kernel grid configurations.

# Algorithm for Dynamic Kernel Management

**Input:** Root Task Set $\mathcal{T}$
**Output:** Hierarchical Task Execution
**foreach** *Parent Task* $t_i \in \mathcal{T}$ **do**
  Execute `Kernel_Launch` for $t_i$;
  **while** *Child Tasks* $\mathcal{D}_i$ *Available* **do**
    Launch $\mathcal{D}_i$ using `dynamicParallelLaunch`;
    Manage synchronization and resource dependencies;

This algorithm encapsulates the dynamic invocation process under CUDA's paradigm, emphasizing runtime task allocation and concurrent kernel launches.

# Mathematical Modeling of Resource Utilization

Efficient resource utilization within a dynamic parallelism context requires balancing computational load across available GPU resources. Assume the availability of processing units such that $R = \{R_1, R_2, \ldots, R_q\}$. The goal is optimal distribution defined by a minimization objective $\hat{\Sigma}$:

$$\hat{\Sigma} = \min \left( \sum_{j=1}^{p} \sum_{k=1}^{q} w_{jk} \times U(R_k) \right)$$

where $w_{jk}$ represents the weight of task allocation to resource $R_k$, and $U(R_k)$ measures the utilization of resource $R_k$. The optimization calls for an adaptable execution strategy that modifies host-side kernel launch intervals and thread prioritization policies dynamically.

In the context of CUDA, leveraging dynamic parallelism efficiently necessitates a profound understanding of the hierarchical kernel execution model, detailed interdependencies, and sophisticated resource management intrinsic to scalable GPU computing architectures.

# Python Code Snippet

Below is a Python code snippet that encompasses the core computational elements mentioned in the chapter, including dynamic kernel management and execution within a PyCUDA environment.

```
import pycuda.driver as cuda
import pycuda.autoinit
from pycuda.compiler import SourceModule
import numpy as np

# CUDA kernel for dynamic parallelism
mod = SourceModule("""
__global__ void parent_kernel() {
```

```
    int idx = threadIdx.x + blockIdx.x * blockDim.x;
    if (idx == 0) {  // Let's assume only one thread launches the
    ↪    child kernel
        child_kernel<<<1, 5>>>(); // Launch a child kernel with 5
        ↪    threads
    }
}

// Simple child kernel
__global__ void child_kernel() {
    int idx = threadIdx.x;
    printf("Child kernel execution from thread %d\\n", idx);
}
""")

parent_kernel = mod.get_function("parent_kernel")

def execute_dynamic_kernel():
    """
    Function to execute the parent kernel, which in turn launches a
    ↪    child kernel using dynamic parallelism.
    """
    block_size = 10
    grid_size = 1   # Single block for demonstration
    parent_kernel(grid_size, block_size)

# Run the dynamic parallelism example
execute_dynamic_kernel()

def calculate_execution_overhead():
    """
    Function to calculate execution overhead for dynamic parallelism
    ↪    example.
    :return: Overhead ratio xi.
    """
    host_start = cuda.Event()
    host_end = cuda.Event()

    # Timing the execution of the parent kernel
    host_start.record()
    execute_dynamic_kernel()
    host_end.record()

    host_end.synchronize()
    total_time = host_start.time_till(host_end)

    # Simulating overhead calculation
    execution_time = 10   # Placeholder for actual execution time in
    ↪    milliseconds
    overhead_time = total_time - execution_time

    xi = overhead_time / execution_time
    print("Execution Overhead xi:", xi)
```

```
# Run the overhead calculation
calculate_execution_overhead()

def optimize_resource_utilization(resource_allocation):
    """
    Function to model resource utilization during kernel execution.
    :param resource_allocation: Dictionary for task allocation to
    ↪    resources.
    :return: Optimal allocation strategy.
    """
    utilization = {resource: allocation / 100 for resource,
    ↪    allocation in resource_allocation.items()}

    # Summing up weighted utilization for a resource optimization
    ↪    model
    utilization_sum = sum(u * w for u, w in
    ↪    zip(utilization.values(), range(1, len(utilization) + 1)))

    print("Resource Utilization:", utilization)
    print("Utilization Sum:", utilization_sum)

    return utilization

# Example resource allocation
resource_allocation = {'R1': 70, 'R2': 50, 'R3': 90}
optimize_resource_utilization(resource_allocation)
```

This code defines several key functions necessary for executing dynamic parallelism within a CUDA context using `PyCUDA`:

- `execute_dynamic_kernel` function manages the launch of a parent kernel which invokes a child kernel using CUDA's dynamic parallelism feature. It demonstrates CUDA kernel execution and the direct invocation of nested kernels.

- `calculate_execution_overhead` calculates the execution overhead by recording the time taken for kernel launches and execution. This method is essential to understand the performance and efficiency of kernel invocations.

- `optimize_resource_utilization` models resource utilization and demonstrates an abstract optimization exercise based on predefined resource allocation schemes, relevant to minimizing overhead in GPU resource management.

The provided code examples and function outlines showcase practical application and methodology for leveraging dynamic parallelism and optimization techniques in CUDA programming.

# Chapter 14

# Using the Thrust Library for High-Level Programming

## Overview of the Thrust Library

The Thrust library provides an interface for high-level parallel programming on CUDA-enabled devices. It abstracts the complexities of CUDA kernel management through a collection of data structures and algorithms similar to the C++ Standard Template Library (STL), enabling efficient manipulation and computation on large datasets.

Let $\mathbf{V}$ be a vector space often represented via Thrust vectors, `thrust::device_vector`, designed to facilitate memory operations on the GPU. Let $v_i \in \mathbf{V}$ denote elements of this space. The operations supported by Thrust for these vectors are crucial for computational efficiency, expressed in terms of transformations such as:

$$v_i' = f(v_i) = v_i + \alpha \cdot g(v_i)$$

where $\alpha$ is a scalar and $g(v_i)$ represents another transformation or operation.

# Parallel Algorithms with Thrust

Thrust's core utility is found in its template functions that support a range of parallel algorithms. An essential aspect is utilizing these algorithms without direct kernel invocation. For example, the operation `thrust::transform` applies a unary or binary function to all elements in a range, reducing the need for explicit thread management in CUDA.

Consider the application of `thrust::reduce` to sum all elements in a vector $\mathbf{V}$:

$$\text{Sum}(\mathbf{V}) = \sum_i v_i =$$

`thrust::reduce(`$\mathbf{V}.begin()$`, `$\mathbf{V}.end()$`, 0, thrust::plus<int>())`

This exploits parallel reduction on the GPU, optimizing performance through concurrent execution.

# Data Structures in Thrust

The Thrust library expands traditional data structures to support efficient device-based computations. A `thrust::device_vector<T>` represents a sequence of elements of type $T$, equipped with capabilities for automated memory management between host and device. This structure is pivotal in high-level operations by encapsulating vector operations such as resizing, sorting, and scanning.

For example, the sorting operation with `thrust::sort` on $\mathbf{V}$ can be expressed as:

$$\texttt{thrust::sort}(\mathbf{V}.begin(), \mathbf{V}.end())$$

This operation arranges elements in non-decreasing order, impacting time complexity according to parallel sorting algorithms.

# Implementing Transform Operations

A key functionality of Thrust, `thrust::transform`, facilitates element-wise operations on vectors. Consider applying a transformation, $f : \mathbb{R} \to \mathbb{R}$, represented in Thrust as:

$$v_i' = \texttt{thrust::transform}(\mathbf{V_1}.begin(), \mathbf{V_1}.end(), \mathbf{V_2}.begin(), \texttt{Operation}())$$

where `Operation` is a functor defining the transformation to be applied across $\mathbf{V_1}$, producing results stored in $\mathbf{V_2}$.

# Algorithmic Example Using Thrust

The utility of Thrust for streamlined implementation of algorithms is underscored by its supportive syntax and abstraction. Below, a high-level pseudocode representation of a computation using Thrust is depicted:

---

**Input:** Device Vector $\mathbf{V}$
**Output:** Transformed Device Vector $\mathbf{V}'$
Initialize vector $\mathbf{U}$ on device;
`thrust::transform` on $\mathbf{V}$ to create $\mathbf{U}$;
`thrust::reduce` over $\mathbf{U}$;
`thrust::copy` result back to host if needed;

---

The algorithm demonstrates the process flow, leveraging Thrust's capabilities to allow a higher abstraction level than raw CUDA programming.

# Performance Considerations

Employing Thrust optimizes computational throughput mainly through efficient memory access patterns and minimized kernel launch overhead. The function `thrust::count` can measure the occurrence of specific values within a dataset, with execution time represented as:

$$T_{\text{count}} = \mathcal{O}\left(\frac{n}{p}\right),$$

where $n$ is the number of elements and $p$ is the number of processors, capitalizing on parallel execution paths.

In summary, the Thrust library serves as a powerful tool for CUDA programmers by refining computational resource usage and simplifying the implementation of parallel algorithms.

# Python Code Snippet

Below is a Python code snippet that encapsulates important calculations and operations involved in using the Thrust library for high-level programming, using the PyCUDA library to directly interact with CUDA capabilities.

```python
import pycuda.autoinit
import pycuda.driver as cuda
import numpy as np
import pycuda.gpuarray as gpuarray
from pycuda.elementwise import ElementwiseKernel

def thrust_like_transform(input_array, scalar, transform_function):
    '''
    Perform a transformation similar to thrust::transform using
    ↪ PyCUDA.
    :param input_array: Input GPU array.
    :param scalar: Scalar multiplier for transformation.
    :param transform_function: Target transform function in CUDA
    ↪ format.
    :return: Transformed GPU array.
    '''
    transform_kernel = ElementwiseKernel(
        "float *out, float *in, float alpha",
        "out[i] = in[i] + alpha * %s(in[i])" % transform_function,
        "transform_kernel")

    output_array = gpuarray.empty_like(input_array)
    transform_kernel(output_array, input_array, np.float32(scalar))
    return output_array

def thrust_like_reduce(input_array):
    '''
    Perform a reduction equivalent to thrust::reduce to sum array
    ↪ elements.
    :param input_array: Input GPU array.
    :return: Sum of the elements.
    '''
    return gpuarray.sum(input_array).get()

def thrust_like_sort(input_array):
    '''
    Perform a sorting operation similar to thrust::sort using
    ↪ PyCUDA.
    :param input_array: Input array for sorting.
    :return: Sorted GPU array.
    '''
    sorted_array = gpuarray.to_gpu(np.sort(input_array.get()))
    return sorted_array

# Initialize data
input_size = 1024
host_data = np.random.randn(input_size).astype(np.float32)

# Copy data to GPU
device_data = gpuarray.to_gpu(host_data)

# Perform thrust-like transform
```

```
transformed_data = thrust_like_transform(device_data, 2.0, "sin")

# Perform thrust-like reduction
sum_result = thrust_like_reduce(transformed_data)

# Perform thrust-like sort
sorted_data = thrust_like_sort(transformed_data)

# Transfer result back to host
transformed_host_data = transformed_data.get()
sorted_host_data = sorted_data.get()

print("Sum Result:", sum_result)
print("Transformed Data (first 5 elements):",
↪   transformed_host_data[:5])
print("Sorted Data (first 5 elements):", sorted_host_data[:5])
```

This code snippet demonstrates how to perform Thrust-like operations using PyCUDA:

- A `thrust_like_transform` function that simulates the `thrust::transform` functionality by applying an element-wise transformation to a GPU array.

- A `thrust_like_reduce` function mimics `thrust::reduce`, summing all elements of a GPU array.

- A `thrust_like_sort` function replicating `thrust::sort`, sorting the elements of a GPU array.

The example uses PyCUDA to perform computations on the GPU, highlighting the practical application and efficiency of CUDA in task parallelization.

# Chapter 15

# Efficient Reduction Operations

## Reduction Operations in Parallel Computing

Reduction operations are fundamental in parallel computing, allowing for the aggregation of elements across a data set into a single summary value. These operations are executed to compute results such as sums, products, or maximum values. Mathematically, given a vector $\mathbf{v} = (v_1, v_2, \ldots, v_n)$, the sum reduction operation can be expressed as:

$$S = \sum_{i=1}^{n} v_i$$

Similarly, the maximum reduction is defined by:

$$M = \max(v_1, v_2, \ldots, v_n)$$

In a parallel computing context, efficiently implementing these operations is crucial for performance gains, particularly on GPU architectures where concurrency can be fully exploited.

# Parallel Sum Reduction on the GPU

The parallel sum reduction on a GPU involves dividing the computation across multiple threads, each processing a segment of the total data. The initial step engages each thread to perform local aggregation, often storing results in shared memory. The local sums are then reduced hierarchically. The operation can be mathematically described as follows for $P$ processors:

$$S = \sum_{p=1}^{P} \left( \sum_{i=1}^{n/P} v_{i,p} \right)$$

where $v_{i,p}$ denotes the elements of the vector handled by processor $p$.

---

**Input:** Vector $\mathbf{v}$ of length $n$
**Output:** Sum $S$
Partition $\mathbf{v}$ among threads;
**for** *each thread $t$* **do**
   ⎿ Compute local sum $S_t$ by summing $\frac{n}{T}$ elements;
Perform parallel reduction on $S_t$ values;
**return** aggregated sum $S$;

---

# Efficient Maximum Reduction

The maximum value computation follows a similar trajectory, where each thread computes local maxima before engaging in a hierarchical reduction to identify the global maximum. Mathematically, this can be represented as:

$$M = \max_{p=1}^{P} \left( \max_{i=1}^{n/P} v_{i,p} \right)$$

To optimize this process, consideration of warp size and the memory hierarchy is crucial to minimize latency and ensure efficient bandwidth utilization.

**Input:** Vector **v** of length $n$
**Output:** Maximum $M$
Partition **v** among threads;
**for** *each thread t* **do**
  Compute local maximum $M_t = \max(v_{1,t}, v_{2,t}, \ldots, v_{\frac{n}{T},t})$;
Perform parallel reduction on $M_t$ values;
**return** global maximum $M$;

# Optimization Techniques

The use of efficient memory access patterns and reduction strategies is imperative for performance. Techniques such as loop unrolling and warp-level primitives streamline execution. The balance of computational load ensures optimal usage of GPU resources. Given that shared memory is faster than global memory, storing intermediate results in shared memory during the reduction phases is advantageous.

An advanced technique involves handling reduction at the warp level using warp intrinsics:

$$v_i' = \texttt{\_\_shfl\_down\_sync}(v_i, 1)$$

This allows the data to be shuffled within a warp, thereby reducing the need for synchronization between threads.

The reduction kernels should align data access optimally according to:

$$T_{\text{parallel}} \leq \frac{T_{\text{serial}}}{n}$$

where $T_{\text{parallel}}$ and $T_{\text{serial}}$ represent the execution times of parallel and serial operations respectively.

# Conclusion

Reduction operations, through orchestrated memory management and parallel processes, can be optimized on the GPU for high performance, essential in computational scenarios demanding efficient data aggregation.

# Python Code Snippet

Below is a Python code snippet that demonstrates the implementation of reduction operations, such as sum and maximum, using PyCUDA on GPU. This code optimizes data parallelism for efficient computation.

```python
import pycuda.autoinit
import pycuda.driver as cuda
from pycuda.compiler import SourceModule
import numpy as np

# CUDA kernel code for parallel reduction
module = SourceModule("""
__global__ void sum_reduce(float *g_idata, float *g_odata, unsigned
↪  int n) {
    extern __shared__ float shared_data[];
    unsigned int tid = threadIdx.x;
    unsigned int i = blockIdx.x * blockDim.x + threadIdx.x;
    shared_data[tid] = (i < n) ? g_idata[i] : 0;
    __syncthreads();

    // do reduction in shared memory
    for (unsigned int s = 1; s < blockDim.x; s *= 2) {
        if (tid % (2 * s) == 0) {
            shared_data[tid] += shared_data[tid + s];
        }
        __syncthreads();
    }

    // write result for this block to global memory
    if (tid == 0) g_odata[blockIdx.x] = shared_data[0];
}

__global__ void max_reduce(float *g_idata, float *g_odata, unsigned
↪  int n) {
    extern __shared__ float shared_data[];
    unsigned int tid = threadIdx.x;
    unsigned int i = blockIdx.x * blockDim.x + threadIdx.x;
    shared_data[tid] = (i < n) ? g_idata[i] : -FLT_MAX;
    __syncthreads();

    // do reduction in shared memory
    for (unsigned int s = 1; s < blockDim.x; s *= 2) {
        if (tid % (2 * s) == 0) {
            shared_data[tid] = fmaxf(shared_data[tid],
            ↪  shared_data[tid + s]);
        }
        __syncthreads();
    }
```

```
            // write result for this block to global memory
            if (tid == 0) g_odata[blockIdx.x] = shared_data[0];
    }
    """)

    sum_reduce = module.get_function("sum_reduce")
    max_reduce = module.get_function("max_reduce")

    def parallel_sum(input_vector):
        n = len(input_vector)
        block_size = 512
        grid_size = (n + block_size - 1) // block_size
        output_size = grid_size

        input_gpu = cuda.mem_alloc(input_vector.nbytes)
        output_gpu = cuda.mem_alloc(output_size *
        ↪   input_vector.dtype.itemsize)

        cuda.memcpy_htod(input_gpu, input_vector)

        sum_reduce(input_gpu, output_gpu, np.uint32(n),
        ↪   block=(block_size, 1, 1), grid=(grid_size, 1),
        ↪   shared=block_size * input_vector.itemsize)

        output_vector = np.empty(output_size, dtype=np.float32)
        cuda.memcpy_dtoh(output_vector, output_gpu)

        total_sum = sum(output_vector)
        return total_sum

    def parallel_max(input_vector):
        n = len(input_vector)
        block_size = 512
        grid_size = (n + block_size - 1) // block_size
        output_size = grid_size

        input_gpu = cuda.mem_alloc(input_vector.nbytes)
        output_gpu = cuda.mem_alloc(output_size *
        ↪   input_vector.dtype.itemsize)

        cuda.memcpy_htod(input_gpu, input_vector)

        max_reduce(input_gpu, output_gpu, np.uint32(n),
        ↪   block=(block_size, 1, 1), grid=(grid_size, 1),
        ↪   shared=block_size * input_vector.itemsize)

        output_vector = np.empty(output_size, dtype=np.float32)
        cuda.memcpy_dtoh(output_vector, output_gpu)

        global_max = max(output_vector)
        return global_max

    # Example usage
```

```
vector = np.random.rand(1024).astype(np.float32)

sum_result = parallel_sum(vector)
max_result = parallel_max(vector)

print("Sum of elements:", sum_result)
print("Maximum element:", max_result)
```

This code includes the necessary GPU kernel functions and host-side Python code to carry out reduction operations:

- The sum_reduce kernel computes the sum of input elements by using a hierarchical reduction approach, leveraging shared memory for intermediate sums.

- The max_reduce kernel finds the maximum element by parallel comparison, similarly utilizing shared memory for efficient access.

- parallel_sum function initializes GPU memory and launches the sum_reduce kernel to compute and return the total sum of the input vector.

- parallel_max function sets up the necessary GPU data transfers and executes the max_reduce kernel to determine the maximum value.

Each function efficiently maps computational tasks to GPU threads and collects results through cudaMemcpy operations. Performance optimizations like shared memory utilization and structured grid and block dimensions ensure high execution efficiency on GPU hardware.

# Chapter 16

# Prefix Sum (Scan) Algorithms

## Introduction to Prefix Sum

The prefix sum, or scan operation, is a pivotal concept in parallel computing, enabling the transformation of an input sequence into a sequence of prefix sums. Mathematically, the prefix sum for a vector $\mathbf{x} = (x_1, x_2, \ldots, x_n)$ is given by:

$$\mathbf{y} = (y_1, y_2, \ldots, y_n) \quad \text{where} \quad y_i = \sum_{j=1}^{i} x_j$$

This operation is instrumental in various applications, including parallel algorithms where cumulative totals need to be calculated efficiently.

## Parallel Prefix Sum Operations

In parallel computing architectures, especially those leveraging Graphics Processing Units (GPU), implementing prefix sums involves partitioning input data across multiple processing units, allowing for concurrent computation.

# 1 Efficient Parallel Prefix Sum

The implementation of a parallel prefix sum algorithm typically operates under the assumption that there are $P$ processors. The input vector $\mathbf{x}$ is evenly divided among the processors.

Mathematically, each processor $p$ computes a local prefix sum $\mathbf{y}_p = (y_{p,1}, y_{p,2}, \ldots, y_{p,k})$ for its segment such that:

$$y_{p,i} = \sum_{j=1}^{i+kp} x_{j+kp}$$

where $k = \frac{n}{P}$ is the number of elements per processor.

---

**Input:** Vector $\mathbf{x}$ of length $n$
**Output:** Prefix sum vector $\mathbf{y}$
Partition $\mathbf{x}$ into sub-vectors $\mathbf{x}_p$ for each processor;
**for** *each processor $p$* **do**
$\quad \lfloor$ Compute local prefix sum $\mathbf{y}_p$;
Perform iterative update across processors for final prefix sum aggregation;
**return** aggregated vector $\mathbf{y}$;

---

# 2 Up-Sweep and Down-Sweep Approach

A common technique for parallel prefix sum is the up-sweep (reduce) and down-sweep (down-scan) approach. The up-sweep phase computes partial sums, while the down-sweep phase compiles the total prefix sum.

- *Up-Sweep Phase:* Each thread calculates partial reductions and stores intermediate results, thereby forming a tree structure.

- *Down-Sweep Phase:* The computation reverses direction, distributing aggregated totals downwards to finalize prefix sums.

This methodology owes its efficiency to the logarithmic reduction in computational depth, leading to a time complexity of $O(\log n)$.

# Mathematical Formalism of Prefix Sum Phases

## 1 Up-Sweep (Reduce) Phase

Let d be the depth in the tree structure and $s = 2^d$. Compute:

$$y[i + s - 1] = y[i + s - 1] + y[i + s/2 - 1] \quad \text{for each } i$$

## 2 Down-Sweep (Down-Scan) Phase

Initialize $y[n - 1] = 0$. For each level:

$$\text{temp} = y[i + s/2 - 1]$$
$$y[i + s/2 - 1] = y[i + s - 1]$$
$$y[i + s - 1] = \text{temp} + y[i + s - 1]$$

# Advanced Implementation Considerations

Optimization of prefix sum algorithms in a parallel environment often involves careful memory access planning and minimizing synchronization points. Usage of shared memory for temporary storage of intermediate values is crucial.

Furthermore, deploying warp-level primitives and leveraging intrinsic functions such as `__shfl_down_sync()` enhances data sharing within a warp, further expediting the scan operation.

Efficient mapping of computation to hardware threads, along with consideration of coalesced memory access patterns, defines proficiency in executing such algorithms on GPU architectures.

# Python Code Snippet

Below is a Python code snippet that implements the parallel prefix sum (scan) algorithm using PyCUDA, demonstrating how to effectively distribute computations across multiple GPU threads to calculate prefix sums efficiently.

```
import numpy as np
import pycuda.driver as cuda
```

```python
import pycuda.autoinit
from pycuda.compiler import SourceModule

# Kernel for up-sweep phase
up_sweep_kernel = """
__global__ void up_sweep(float *data, int n, int step)
{
    int index = threadIdx.x + blockIdx.x * blockDim.x;
    int gap = step << 1;

    if (index < n && (index & (gap - 1)) == 0) {
        data[index + gap - 1] += data[index + step - 1];
    }
}
"""

# Kernel for down-sweep phase
down_sweep_kernel = """
__global__ void down_sweep(float *data, int n, int step)
{
    int index = threadIdx.x + blockIdx.x * blockDim.x;
    int gap = step << 1;

    if (index < n && (index & (gap - 1)) == 0) {
        float temp = data[index + step - 1];
        data[index + step - 1] = data[index + gap - 1];
        data[index + gap - 1] += temp;
    }
}
"""

def gpu_prefix_sum(arr):
    n = len(arr)
    arr = np.array(arr, dtype=np.float32)

    # Allocate memory on GPU and copy input data
    arr_gpu = cuda.mem_alloc(arr.nbytes)
    cuda.memcpy_htod(arr_gpu, arr)

    # Compile the kernels
    mod_up = SourceModule(up_sweep_kernel)
    mod_down = SourceModule(down_sweep_kernel)

    up_sweep = mod_up.get_function("up_sweep")
    down_sweep = mod_down.get_function("down_sweep")

    # Define grid and block size
    block_size = 256
    grid_size = (n + block_size - 1) // block_size

    # Up-sweep phase
    step = 1
    while step < n:
```

```
    up_sweep(arr_gpu, np.int32(n), np.int32(step),
    ↳  block=(block_size, 1, 1), grid=(grid_size, 1))
    step <<= 1

# Set last element to zero for down-sweep
cuda.memset_d32(arr_gpu + (n-1)*arr.itemsize, 0, 1)

# Down-sweep phase
step >>= 1
while step > 0:
    down_sweep(arr_gpu, np.int32(n), np.int32(step),
    ↳  block=(block_size, 1, 1), grid=(grid_size, 1))
    step >>= 1

# Copy result back to host
result = np.empty_like(arr)
cuda.memcpy_dtoh(result, arr_gpu)

return result

# Example usage
input_array = [1.0, 2.0, 3.0, 4.0, 5.0, 6.0, 7.0, 8.0]
output_array = gpu_prefix_sum(input_array)
print("Input Array:", input_array)
print("Prefix Sum (Output Array):", output_array)
```

This code defines a GPU-based implementation using PyCUDA for calculating prefix sums via the up-sweep and down-sweep phases:

- The `up_sweep_kernel` is responsible for computing the partial reductions in the up-sweep phase.

- The `down_sweep_kernel` handles the propagation of partial sums in the down-sweep phase to compute the final prefix sums.

- `gpu_prefix_sum` function drives the entire process, incorporating memory management on the GPU and execution of kernels.

- Example usage demonstrates transforming an input array to its prefix sum using CUDA acceleration.

With this approach, large-scale prefix sums are computed efficiently by making full use of GPU parallelism techniques provided through CUDA architecture.

# Chapter 17

# Working with Texture Memory

## Introduction to Texture Memory

Texture memory in the GPU architecture offers a specialized mechanism for accessing data, providing a caching layer that is notably beneficial for read-only data frequently queried by the processing units. This access pattern invariably enhances performance by utilizing spatial locality and built-in hardware interpolation capabilities. Consider an array $\mathbf{T} = (t_1, t_2, \ldots, t_n)$, which is frequently accessed for read operations. Storing $\mathbf{T}$ in texture memory can considerably reduce memory latency due to its cache mechanism.

## 1 Texture Memory Characteristics

Texture memory is optimized for fetching two-dimensional data patterns, though one-dimensional and three-dimensional textures are also feasible. A critical aspect of texture memory management is the hardware's ability to coalesce memory accesses for adjacent threads, mitigating the latency typically associated with accessing global memory directly. The mapping of a linear array to texture memory can be described by a texture reference, typically utilizing the function:

$$\mathtt{cudaBindTexture}(\&\text{textureRef}, \text{array}, \text{size})$$

where textureRef is the identifier for the bound texture.

# Mathematical Model of Texture Caching

The efficiency of texture memory can be attributed to its inherent caching mechanism which reduces redundant global memory accesses. Texture caching exploits the spatial locality intrinsic to several parallel processing algorithms. Consider a set of texture coordinates $\mathbf{u} = (u_1, u_2, \ldots, u_m)$ accessing texture $\mathbf{T}$:

$$v_i = \texttt{tex1D}(\text{textureRef}, u_i)$$

where $v_i$ denotes the value fetched from texture memory using the one-dimensional texture fetch function $\texttt{tex1D}$.

# Implementing Access Patterns with Texture Memory

## 1 Configuration and Optimization

Efficient utilization of texture memory involves managing its configuration correctly. The texture memory is typically bound to linear memory through the CUDA run-time, forming a linear opaque reference by using:

```
cudaChannelFormatDesc channelDesc = cudaCreateChannelDesc<float>();
cudaBindTexture(NULL, textureRef, d_array, channelDesc);
```

The binding process requires consideration of the texture data type, dimensionality, and memory alignment. Operating within these constraints ensures optimal performance enhancement when accessing data from texture memory.

# Analytical Perspective on Performance

The increased efficiency attributed to texture memory can be quantitatively analyzed. Let $\tau$ symbolize the access latency to global memory, and $\tau_t$ be the reduced access latency when accessing data through texture memory. The performance gain $G$ can be modeled as:

$$G = \frac{\tau}{\tau_t}$$

where $\tau_t < \tau$, thereby quantifying the advantage of using texture memory over traditional global memory access.

# 1 Interpolation Advantage

Texture memory provides built-in interpolation facilities, allowing smooth value extraction for non-integer coordinates, applicable in graphics and computational simulations. This can be mathematically described using bilinear or trilinear interpolation:

$$v(u,v) \approx (1 - \alpha)(1 - \beta)T(i,j) + \alpha(1 - \beta)T(i+1,j)+$$

$$(1 - \alpha)\beta T(i,j+1) + \alpha\beta T(i+1,j+1)$$

where $\alpha = u - \lfloor u \rfloor$ and $\beta = v - \lfloor v \rfloor$ are the fractional parts of the coordinates.

# Algorithmic Utilization

Given a matrix where frequent read-only access is optimal, texture memory provides significant performance gains. Such matrices **A** could be utilized in the computation of convolution operations, described as follows:

---

**Input:** Matrix **A** stored in global memory
**Output:** Transformed matrix leveraging texture memory
        caching
Bind matrix **A** to a 2D texture;
**for** *each element $a_{i,j}$ in **A*** **do**
    Access $a_{i,j}$ using bilinear interpolation through texture
    memory operations;
Apply convolution filters using fetch operations from
  texture memory;

---

The algorithm underscores the feasibility of reducing computational time by leveraging the interpolation capabilities and caching mechanism inherent to texture memory. Such applications are pivotal in image processing and computer vision tasks.

# Python Code Snippet

Below is a Python code snippet that implements the core functionalities of using texture memory in CUDA, including binding and accessing texture memory in a GPU program.

```
import pycuda.driver as cuda
import pycuda.autoinit
import numpy as np
from pycuda.compiler import SourceModule

# Initialize array size and create a random numpy array
array_size = 256
host_array = np.random.rand(array_size).astype(np.float32)

# Allocate device memory and copy host array to device
d_array = cuda.mem_alloc(host_array.nbytes)
cuda.memcpy_htod(d_array, host_array)

# Create a texture reference and bind it to the linear array
mod = SourceModule("""
texture<float, 1, cudaReadModeElementType> tex;

__global__ void tex_fetch(float *output, int n) {
    int idx = threadIdx.x + blockIdx.x * blockDim.x;
    if (idx < n) {
        // Fetch from texture memory
        output[idx] = tex1D(tex, idx);
    }
}
""")

# Allocate output array
output = np.zeros_like(host_array)

# Get function and texture reference from module
texref = mod.get_texref("tex")
texref.set_address(d_array, host_array.nbytes)

# Allocate output in device memory
d_output = cuda.mem_alloc(output.nbytes)

# Bind texture to device array
mod.get_function("tex_fetch")(d_output, np.int32(array_size),
↪   block=(256, 1, 1), grid=(1, 1))

# Copy device output array back to host
cuda.memcpy_dtoh(output, d_output)

print("Input Array:\n", host_array)
print("Output Array after Texture Fetch:\n", output)
```

This code performs several key operations related to texture
memory usage in a CUDA application:

- Allocate and copy 'host_array' to device memory using Py-
  CUDA functions like 'cuda.mem_alloc' and 'cuda.memcpy_htod'.

105

- Set up a CUDA texture reference within a kernel using the 'texture' directive.

- Bind the input array in device memory to the texture reference with 'texref.set_address'.

- Define a CUDA kernel 'tex_fetch' that uses 'tex1D' to access values from texture memory and writes them to an output array.

- Launch the kernel with suitable grid and block dimensions to perform the texture memory fetch.

- Copy the results back to the host using 'cuda.memcpy_dtoh' to verify the operations.

This implementation demonstrates the setup and use of texture memory in a PyCUDA application, leveraging the caching and interpolation features inherent to GPU texture memory to optimize read operations.

# Chapter 18

# Implementing Matrix Multiplication

## Overview of Matrix Multiplication

Matrix multiplication is a fundamental operation in numerous computational tasks, characterized by the mathematical operation $\mathbf{C} = \mathbf{A} \times \mathbf{B}$ where $\mathbf{A}$ is an $m \times n$ matrix, $\mathbf{B}$ is an $n \times p$ matrix, and the resulting matrix $\mathbf{C}$ is of dimension $m \times p$. The individual elements of $\mathbf{C}$ are computed as:

$$c_{i,j} = \sum_{k=1}^{n} a_{i,k} \cdot b_{k,j}$$

This section considers the transformation of this standard mathematical definition into parallel operations suited for execution on a GPU, leveraging the capabilities of CUDA to optimize performance.

## Decomposition Strategy for GPU Execution

The GPU architecture facilitates parallelism by dispatching computations into appropriate blocks and threads. The matrix multiplication task is divided into smaller submatrix operations that can be executed concurrently. By assigning each thread to compute a specific element $c_{i,j}$ of the resulting matrix $\mathbf{C}$, one can effectively utilize the massive parallel processing power of GPUs.

The submatrix operations can be represented as:

$$c_{i,j} = \sum_{k=0}^{n-1}(a_{i,k} \times b_{k,j})$$

An efficient decomposition will exploit the memory hierarchy, including the use of shared memory to minimize global memory accesses. Shared memory, owing to its faster access times compared to global memory, is ideal for storing submatrices of $\mathbf{A}$ and $\mathbf{B}$.

# Algorithm for Parallel Matrix Multiplication

An algorithmic representation using CUDA can be described as follows:

---

**Input:** Matrices $\mathbf{A}_{m \times n}$, $\mathbf{B}_{n \times p}$
**Output:** Matrix $\mathbf{C}_{m \times p}$
Allocate memory on the device for $\mathbf{A}$, $\mathbf{B}$, and $\mathbf{C}$;
cudaMemcpy matrices $\mathbf{A}$ and $\mathbf{B}$ to device memory;
Define grid and block dimensions;
Launch GPU kernel for matrix multiplication;
**for** *each thread* **do**
    Compute single element $c_{i,j}$ using shared memory to store portions of $\mathbf{A}$ and $\mathbf{B}$;
    Accumulate partial results using the shared memory;
cudaMemcpy result matrix $\mathbf{C}$ from device to host memory;

---

Critical to performance is the strategy employed for loading matrix elements into shared memory. This optimization reduces the need for repetitive access to global memory, thus increasing memory throughput.

# Shared Memory and Tiling Technique

Tiling involves partitioning the matrices into smaller submatrices (tiles) that fit into shared memory, improving data locality and coalesced access patterns. Let $T_s$ denote the tile dimension:

$$t_{i,j} = \sum_{k=0}^{T_s-1} a_{ik} \cdot b_{kj}$$

where $i, j \in [0, T_s - 1]$ are local indices within the tile. Each thread evaluates the products of elements in a $T_s \times T_s$ tile, accumulating results for elements of **C**.

The configuration of $T_s$ is pivotal and typically requires empirical tuning to balance between shared memory occupancy and thread concurrency.

# Performance Analysis

The computational complexity remains $O(mnp)$; however, the parallel execution model and reduced memory access latency significantly lower the effective runtime on the GPU. The performance improvements can be quantified using metrics such as achieved bandwidth and computation throughput:

$$\text{Performance} = \frac{2 \times m \times n \times p}{\text{Execution Time}}$$

This analysis elucidates the practical enhancement derived from the GPU's inherent parallel nature for matrix multiplication when utilizing memory hierarchy optimizations through tiling and shared memory.

# Python Code Snippet

Below is a Python code snippet that implements the matrix multiplication algorithm using PyCUDA, featuring the parallel execution strategy, memory management, and tiling optimization as discussed in this chapter.

```python
import numpy as np
import pycuda.driver as cuda
import pycuda.autoinit
from pycuda.compiler import SourceModule

# CUDA kernel for matrix multiplication
mod = SourceModule("""
__global__ void MatrixMulKernel(float *A, float *B, float *C, int m,
    int n, int p) {
```

```
    extern __shared__ float shared[];
    float* sA = shared;
    float* sB = (float*)&sA[n];

    int tx = threadIdx.x, ty = threadIdx.y;
    int row = blockIdx.y * blockDim.y + ty;
    int col = blockIdx.x * blockDim.x + tx;

    float value = 0;

    for (int t = 0; t < (n + blockDim.x - 1) / blockDim.x; t++) {
        if (t * blockDim.x + tx < n && row < m) {
            sA[ty * blockDim.x + tx] = A[row * n + t * blockDim.x +
            ↪   tx];
        } else {
            sA[ty * blockDim.x + tx] = 0;
        }

        if (t * blockDim.x + ty < n && col < p) {
            sB[ty * blockDim.x + tx] = B[(t * blockDim.x + ty) * p +
            ↪   col];
        } else {
            sB[ty * blockDim.x + tx] = 0;
        }

        __syncthreads();

        for (int k = 0; k < blockDim.x; k++) {
            value += sA[ty * blockDim.x + k] * sB[k * blockDim.x +
            ↪   tx];
        }

        __syncthreads();
    }

    if (row < m && col < p) {
        C[row * p + col] = value;
    }
}
""")

# Host code
def matrix_multiply(A, B):
    m, n = A.shape
    n, p = B.shape

    # Allocate memory on the device
    A_gpu = cuda.mem_alloc(A.nbytes)
    B_gpu = cuda.mem_alloc(B.nbytes)
    C_gpu = cuda.mem_alloc(A.shape[0] * B.shape[1] * A.itemsize)

    # Transfer input matrices to device
    cuda.memcpy_htod(A_gpu, A)
```

```
cuda.memcpy_htod(B_gpu, B)

# Define block and grid dimensions
block_size = 16   # Assume a block size
block = (block_size, block_size, 1)
grid = ((p + block[0] - 1) // block[0], (m + block[1] - 1) //
↪   block[1])

# Launch Kernel
matrixmul = mod.get_function("MatrixMulKernel")
matrixmul(A_gpu, B_gpu, C_gpu, np.int32(m), np.int32(n),
↪   np.int32(p), block=block, grid=grid)

# Allocate memory to store the result
C = np.empty((m, p), dtype=np.float32)

# Transfer result from device to host
cuda.memcpy_dtoh(C, C_gpu)

return C

# Example usage
A = np.random.randn(1024, 1024).astype(np.float32)
B = np.random.randn(1024, 1024).astype(np.float32)

# Perform matrix multiplication on GPU
C = matrix_multiply(A, B)
print("Matrix C shape:", C.shape)
```

This code defines the core functions necessary for executing matrix multiplication on a GPU using PyCUDA:

- `MatrixMulKernel` is a CUDA kernel that performs matrix multiplication using a tiling technique and shared memory to optimize global memory access.

- `matrix_multiply` function orchestrates the device memory allocation, kernel execution, and result retrieval.

- The example usage demonstrates generating random matrices and computing their product on a GPU.

The parallel computation model in the CUDA kernel utilizes the GPU's fast shared memory to store submatrices of **A** and **B**, optimizing the data throughput and computation efficiency significantly.

# Chapter 19

# CUDA Libraries and Tools Overview

## CUDA Libraries for Optimized Computation

The CUDA ecosystem is enriched by an array of libraries designed to harness the power of GPU computing for diverse computational tasks. These libraries provide pre-optimized, high-performance functions for data processing, linear algebra, signal processing, and more, serving as essential tools for developers seeking to leverage CUDA's potential without delving into low-level programming.

## 1   cuBLAS: Basic Linear Algebra Subprograms

The cuBLAS library offers GPU-accelerated routines for operations on vectors and matrices, mirroring those in the standard BLAS (Basic Linear Algebra Subprograms) library. These routines include vector-vector, matrix-vector, and matrix-matrix operations. For instance, matrix multiplication using cuBLAS can be expressed as:

$$\mathbf{C} = \alpha \cdot \texttt{cuBLAS\_gemm}(\mathbf{A}, \mathbf{B}) + \beta \cdot \mathbf{C}$$

where $\mathbf{A}$, $\mathbf{B}$, and $\mathbf{C}$ are matrices, and $\alpha$ and $\beta$ are scalar coefficients.

## 2  cuFFT: Fast Fourier Transforms

The `cuFFT` library is engineered to compute Fourier transforms efficiently, a fundamental operation in numerous scientific and engineering applications. The transformation is defined by:

$$X_k = \sum_{n=0}^{N-1} x_n \cdot e^{-2\pi i k n / N}$$

`cuFFT` provides routines to compute both the forward and inverse transforms with complexity $O(N \log N)$, optimized for execution on NVIDIA GPUs.

## 3  cuRAND: Random Number Generation

`cuRAND` is utilized for generating high-quality pseudorandom and quasirandom numbers optimized for parallel processing. Random number generation of a scalar $x$ is succinctly expressed as:

$$x \sim U(a, b)$$

where $U(a, b)$ denotes the uniform distribution over the interval $[a, b]$. `cuRAND` supports multiple distributions to meet a range of application needs.

# CUDA Development Tools

Alongside libraries, CUDA offers a suite of tools to enhance development efficiency, including debugging and profiling utilities that are critical for optimizing GPU performance.

## 1  NVIDIA Nsight Systems

NVIDIA Nsight Systems provides insights into application behavior, enabling developers to identify bottlenecks related to both the CPU and GPU. By visualizing application performance over time, it allows for pinpointing inefficiencies using event tracing and profiling.

## 2  NVIDIA Nsight Compute

NVIDIA Nsight Compute is intended for kernel profiling, offering a detailed analysis of runtime behavior and performance metrics for individual kernels. Through metrics such as throughput, memory usage, and stall reasons, developers can refine their code for optimal performance:

$$\text{Efficiency} = \frac{\text{Useful Throughput}}{\text{Total Throughput}}$$

This ratio serves as a measure for guiding optimization efforts.

---

**Input:** Kernel to be profiled
**Output:** Performance metrics and stall analysis
Initialize-`NsightComputeProfiler`;
Load-Kernel← Load(`Kernel`);
`Collect Metrics`;
**while** *Profiling* **do**

    `Analyze Memory Access Patterns`;
    ;

Output Results;

---

# 3 CUDA-GDB: Debugger

CUDA-GDB provides a means for debugging GPU code, employing an interface familiar to developers experienced with GDB. This tool supports breakpoint setting, stack trace retrieval, and variable inspection at both the host and device levels, facilitating the correction of logical and runtime errors within CUDA applications.

# 4 CUDA-MEMCHECK: Memory Debugging

CUDA-MEMCHECK is utilized to diagnose memory errors that commonly plague CUDA applications, such as out-of-bounds accesses and misaligned memory operations. These issues can manifest in erroneous computations and crashes, which CUDA-MEMCHECK can help prevent by conducting a thorough memory access analysis, reported as:

$$\text{Error Rate} = \frac{\text{Faulty Memory Accesses}}{\text{Total Memory Operations}}$$

# Integrative Use of Libraries and Tools

Optimizing CUDA application performance necessitates a comprehensive approach, integrating the use of the libraries and tools outlined. The coordinated use of CUDA libraries yields considerable gains in computational efficiency, while development tools offer the insights needed to fine-tune performance metrics. These resources form the backbone of a robust CUDA development environment, supporting both the creation and optimization of high-performance applications.

# Python Code Snippet

Below is a Python code snippet that encompasses the core computational elements of the CUDA libraries and tools discussed in this chapter, including the use of cuBLAS for matrix multiplication, cuFFT for Fourier transforms, cuRAND for random number generation, and CUDA profiling using PyCUDA.

```python
import pycuda.autoinit
import pycuda.driver as cuda
import numpy as np
import skcuda.linalg as culinalg
import skcuda.fft as cu_fft
from skcuda import rand

culinalg.init()

# Example: Using cuBLAS for matrix multiplication
A = np.random.rand(3, 3).astype(np.float32)
B = np.random.rand(3, 3).astype(np.float32)
A_gpu = cuda.mem_alloc(A.nbytes)
B_gpu = cuda.mem_alloc(B.nbytes)
C_gpu = cuda.mem_alloc(A.nbytes)

cuda.memcpy_htod(A_gpu, A)
cuda.memcpy_htod(B_gpu, B)

C_gpu = culinalg.dot(A_gpu, B_gpu)

C = np.empty_like(A)
cuda.memcpy_dtoh(C, C_gpu)

print("Matrix A:", A)
print("Matrix B:", B)
print("Result of A * B with cuBLAS:", C)

# Example: Using cuFFT for Fourier transform
N = 1024
x = np.random.rand(N).astype(np.complex64)
x_gpu = cuda.mem_alloc(x.nbytes)
```

```
cuda.memcpy_htod(x_gpu, x)

fft_plan = cu_fft.Plan(x.shape, np.complex64, np.complex64)
y_gpu = cuda.mem_alloc(x.nbytes)
cu_fft.fft(x_gpu, y_gpu, fft_plan)

y = np.empty_like(x)
cuda.memcpy_dtoh(y, y_gpu)

print("Input signal for FFT:", x[:10])
print("Output signal after cuFFT:", y[:10])

# Example: Using cuRAND for random number generation
n = 1000
rand_handle =
↪   rand.curand_create_generator(rand.CURAND_RNG_PSEUDO_MTGP32)
rand.curand_generate_uniform(rand_handle, y_gpu, n)

random_numbers = np.empty(n, dtype=np.float32)
cuda.memcpy_dtoh(random_numbers, y_gpu)

print("Random Numbers generated with cuRAND:", random_numbers[:10])

rand.curand_destroy_generator(rand_handle)
cuda.Context.synchronize()
```

This code defines several key functions necessary for leveraging CUDA's high-performance computation libraries using PyCUDA:

- Using `culinalg.dot` from the cuBLAS library for efficient matrix multiplication on the GPU. The matrices **A** and **B** are multiplied and the result is stored in **C**.

- Utilizing `cu_fft.fft` from the cuFFT library to compute the Fast Fourier Transform of a complex signal array efficiently.

- Implementing `rand.curand_generate_uniform` from cuRAND to generate high-quality pseudorandom numbers optimized for GPU execution.

These examples illustrate how to implement core computational tasks leveraging GPU strengths, providing a starting point for developing high-performance applications in various domains.

116

# Chapter 20

# Debugging CUDA Applications

## Types of Bugs in CUDA Applications

In CUDA programming, bugs predominantly arise from incorrect memory operations, improper synchronization, and erroneous kernel launches. These can generally be categorized as:

1. Memory-related errors, 2. Synchronization issues, 3. Logical errors.

## 1  Memory-Related Errors

Memory-related bugs in CUDA applications typically manifest as illegal memory access or incorrect data transfer between host and device. The relevant conditions involve incorrect allocation, misaligned accesses, and out-of-bounds memory operations. In mathematical form, if $\mathbf{A}$ is an array indexed by $i$, an illegal access may occur when:

$$i < 0 \quad \text{or} \quad i \geq \text{size}(\mathbf{A})$$

To ensure correct memory handling, the following invariants must be preserved:

$$\text{address}(\mathbf{A}[i]) = \text{base\_address}(\mathbf{A}) + i \times \text{element\_size}$$

117

# 2 Synchronization Issues

Synchronization errors occur when threads do not coordinate appropriately, resulting in race conditions. These involve data races or deadlocks around shared resources. In a race condition, the order of execution affects the correctness:

Consider threads performing:

$$\mathbf{Z}[i] = f(\mathbf{X}[i]) + g(\mathbf{Y}[i])$$

Without proper synchronization, each thread's result may depend on another thread's execution order, violating deterministic execution assumptions. Synchronization primitives, such as `__syncthreads()`, are crucial:

$$\texttt{\_\_syncthreads()} \implies \forall i,j: \quad T_i \leq T_j \vee T_j \leq T_i$$

where $T_i$ and $T_j$ denote thread execution sequences.

# Debugging Tools in CUDA

## 1 CUDA-GDB: A Parallel Debugger

CUDA-GDB provides a comprehensive interface for debugging CUDA applications, analogous to GDB for serial code. This tool supports debugger commands such as setting breakpoints, inspecting variables, and stepping through code. Consider a typical debug session:

```
break <kernel_name>
```

Followed by:

```
run
```

to initiate execution until the kernel's entry.

## 2 CUDA-MEMCHECK: Memory Checking

CUDA-MEMCHECK aids in diagnosing memory discrepancies, reporting erroneous operations through memory access validation. An error rate metric is defined as:

$$\text{Error Rate} = \frac{\text{Invalid Memory Accesses}}{\text{Total Memory Operations}}$$

118

This tool iterates over memory transactions, capturing mismatches in expected versus actual operations, crucial for mitigating silent data corruption.

---

**Input:** Memory trace logs
**Output:** List of memory errors
Initialize Error Counter;
**foreach** *entry in memory trace logs* **do**
⎢ **if** *entry indicates invalid access* **then**
⎢ ⎢ Increment Error Counter;
⎢ ⎣ Mark Access Location;

Output Error Count;

---

## 3   Profiling for Bottleneck Identification

Profiling tools, such as NVIDIA Nsight Systems and Nsight Compute, provide visibility into CUDA application performance, identifying bottlenecks via temporal and spatial analysis. Consider a computational workload represented by:

$$\text{Execution Time} = \text{Kernel Launch Overhead} +$$

$$\text{Computation} + \text{Data Transfer}$$

Profiling decomposes total execution into these constituents, isolating bottlenecks as increases in any term. The efficiency of kernel operations can be further scrutinized via metrics:

$$\text{Efficiency} = \frac{\text{Actual Performance}}{\text{Theoretical Peak Performance}}$$

This informs whether computational or data transfer bandwidth contributes predominantly to delays.

# Best Practices for Debugging CUDA Applications

Experts deploy strategic methodologies to systematically debug applications, emphasizing the delineation between computational errors and memory/synchronization faults. An expert approach involves:

1. Verifying individual kernel logic through unit testing,

2. Employing conditional synchronization checks,

3. Utilizing assertions for boundary conditions.

These practices integrate the mathematical understanding of CUDA's concurrency model, mitigating error introduction stemming from concurrent execution complexities.

# Python Code Snippet

Below is a Python code snippet that implements the core concepts from this chapter, including memory checking, synchronization handling in PyCUDA, and debugging techniques for CUDA applications.

```python
import pycuda.autoinit
import pycuda.driver as cuda
import numpy as np
from pycuda.compiler import SourceModule

# Define kernel for illustrative purposes
kernel_code = """
__global__ void vector_add(float *a, float *b, float *c, int n) {
    int tid = blockIdx.x * blockDim.x + threadIdx.x;
    if (tid < n)
        c[tid] = a[tid] + b[tid];
}
"""

# Compile kernel code
mod = SourceModule(kernel_code)
vector_add = mod.get_function("vector_add")

# Initialize host data
n = 1024
a = np.random.randn(n).astype(np.float32)
b = np.random.randn(n).astype(np.float32)
c = np.zeros_like(a)

# Allocate memory on device
a_gpu = cuda.mem_alloc(a.nbytes)
b_gpu = cuda.mem_alloc(b.nbytes)
c_gpu = cuda.mem_alloc(c.nbytes)

# Transfer data to device
cuda.memcpy_htod(a_gpu, a)
cuda.memcpy_htod(b_gpu, b)

# Set grid and block dimensions
```

```python
block_size = (256, 1, 1)
grid_size = (int(np.ceil(n / block_size[0])), 1)

# Launch the kernel
vector_add(a_gpu, b_gpu, c_gpu, np.int32(n), block=block_size,
↪    grid=grid_size)

# Copy the result back to host
cuda.memcpy_dtoh(c, c_gpu)

# Verify results
assert np.allclose(c, a + b), "Result does not match expected
↪    output"

# Debug section: Simulating checking for a specific issue
def check_synchronization(a, b, c):
    '''
    Mock function to simulate checking for synchronization errors.
    '''
    if not np.allclose(c, a + b):
        print("Synchronization Error Detected!")
    else:
        print("No Synchronization Issues.")

# Example of using the function
check_synchronization(a, b, c)

# Memory checking algorithm
def memory_check(a, b, c, n):
    '''
    Checking the integrity of memory operations.
    '''
    error_count = 0
    for idx in range(n):
        if not np.isfinite(a[idx] + b[idx]):
            error_count += 1

    if error_count > 0:
        print(f"Memory Check Failed with {error_count} errors.")
    else:
        print("Memory Check Passed.")

memory_check(a, b, c, n)
```

This Python code implements several key debugging and synchronization best practices demonstrated previously in the chapter:

- The 'vector_add' kernel is an example of a simple element-wise vector addition function using CUDA.

- The 'check_synchronization' function serves to illustrate how one might look for synchronization errors and errors due to incorrect execution order.

- The 'memory_check' function simulates memory validation, checking whether each element was processed correctly and resulted in a finite value.

- These debugging strategies help ensure that memory operations, thread synchronizations, and computations are correct and efficient.

# Chapter 21

# Profiling and Optimization Strategies

## Profiling CUDA Applications

Profiling is a critical step in identifying performance bottlenecks in CUDA applications. It involves measuring various aspects of the application's execution to determine where optimizations are most needed. Key metrics include execution time, memory throughput, and kernel occupancy.

The total execution time $T_{\text{total}}$ of a CUDA application can be expressed as:

$$T_{\text{total}} = T_{\text{setup}} + T_{\text{data\_transfer}} + T_{\text{computation}}$$

where $T_{\text{setup}}$ represents task setup time, $T_{\text{data\_transfer}}$ is the time dedicated to data migrations between host and device, and $T_{\text{computation}}$ denotes the computational workload execution time on the GPU.

Memory throughput, $\Gamma_{\text{memory}}$, can be measured as:

$$\Gamma_{\text{memory}} = \frac{\text{total bytes transferred}}{T_{\text{data\_transfer}}}$$

Kernel occupancy, $\mathcal{O}$, a measure of how efficiently the GPU resources are utilized, is defined as:

$$\mathcal{O} = \frac{\text{active warps per multiprocessor}}{\text{maximum warps per multiprocessor}}$$

Profilers such as `Nsight Systems` and `Nsight Compute` provide these metrics, facilitating analysis of application behavior over time and across different CUDA kernels.

# Optimization Strategies in CUDA

Optimization in CUDA involves strategies to improve memory access patterns, increase kernel occupancy, and reduce overhead. The primary areas of focus include memory hierarchies, computation workloads, and concurrent execution.

## 1  Memory Optimization

Efficient use of memory hierarchies can dramatically affect CUDA performance. Memory alignment, coalescing, and usage of shared memory are crucial for optimal memory bandwidth utilization.

Given a memory access pattern:

$$\text{address} = \text{base\_address} + i \times \text{element\_size}$$

For coalesced memory access, all threads in a warp should access contiguous memory locations. Shared memory usage minimizes global memory access latency. Bank conflicts in shared memory are avoided by ensuring:

$$\text{bank\_index} = \frac{\text{address}}{\text{bank\_size}}$$

## 2  Increasing Kernel Occupancy

Kernel occupancy improvements can be achieved through optimal register and shared memory usage, enabling a higher number of active warps. If register count is unoptimized, the effective active warps per multiprocessor $W_{\text{active}}$ is reduced:

$$W_{\text{active}} = \min\left(\frac{\text{total registers available}}{\text{registers per thread}}, \frac{\text{shared memory available}}{\text{shared memory per block}}\right)$$

Adjusting block size block_size can affect occupancy, where:

124

$$block\_size = \frac{\text{threads per block}}{\text{warps per block}}$$

# 3 Reducing Overhead

Reducing overhead involves minimizing data transfer and kernel launch latency. Overlapping data transfers and computation using streams:

$$T_{\text{exec}} = \max(T_{\text{transfer}}, T_{\text{comp}})$$

where concurrent streams allow overlapping of $T_{\text{transfer}}$ and $T_{\text{comp}}$, decreasing the total execution time.

---

**Input:** Tasks $\mathcal{T}_1, \ldots, \mathcal{T}_n$
**Output:** Optimized execution times
Initialize streams;
**foreach** *task* $\in \mathcal{T}_i$ **do**
  Allocate memory asynchronously;
  `cudaStreamSynchronize`;
  Launch kernels in streams;
  `Synchronize streams`;

---

Implementing these strategies allows for efficient usage of hardware resources, achieving performance nearer the theoretical peak.

# Python Code Snippet

Below is a Python code snippet implementing key concepts from this chapter using `PyCUDA`. It illustrates profiling and optimization strategies included in our discussion, encompassing the setup of CUDA context, performing data transfers, executing optimized kernels, and measuring kernel occupancy and memory throughput.

```python
import pycuda.autoinit
import pycuda.driver as cuda
from pycuda.compiler import SourceModule
import numpy as np

# Sample kernel code to demonstrate basic computation
kernel_code = """
__global__ void sampleKernel(float *a, float *b, float *c, int n) {
    int idx = threadIdx.x + blockDim.x * blockIdx.x;
```

```python
    if (idx < n) {
        c[idx] = a[idx] + b[idx];
    }
}
"""

# Compile the kernel code and get the function
mod = SourceModule(kernel_code)
sampleKernel = mod.get_function("sampleKernel")

# Initialize host data
n = 1024 * 1024
a_host = np.random.randn(n).astype(np.float32)
b_host = np.random.randn(n).astype(np.float32)
c_host = np.zeros_like(a_host)

# Allocate device memory and transfer host data to device
a_device = cuda.mem_alloc(a_host.nbytes)
b_device = cuda.mem_alloc(b_host.nbytes)
c_device = cuda.mem_alloc(c_host.nbytes)

cuda.memcpy_htod(a_device, a_host)
cuda.memcpy_htod(b_device, b_host)

# Execute kernel and profile execution time
block_size = 256
grid_size = (n + block_size - 1) // block_size

start = cuda.Event()
end = cuda.Event()

start.record()
sampleKernel(a_device, b_device, c_device, np.int32(n),
↪    block=(block_size, 1, 1), grid=(grid_size, 1))
end.record()
end.synchronize()

exec_time = start.time_till(end) * 1e-3
print(f"Execution Time: {exec_time} seconds")

# Calculate memory throughput
total_bytes = a_host.nbytes + b_host.nbytes + c_host.nbytes
memory_throughput = total_bytes / exec_time
print(f"Memory Throughput: {memory_throughput / (1024 ** 3)} GB/s")

# Retrieve result
cuda.memcpy_dtoh(c_host, c_device)

# Verify result
assert np.allclose(c_host, a_host + b_host)

# Calculate kernel occupancy
device = cuda.Device(0)
```

```
max_threads_per_multiprocessor = device.get_attribute(
cuda.device_attribute.MAX_THREADS_PER_MULTIPROCESSOR)
active_warps = (block_size * grid_size) // 32
max_warps = max_threads_per_multiprocessor // 32
occupancy = active_warps / max_warps
print(f"Kernel Occupancy: {occupancy}")

# Clean up
a_device.free()
b_device.free()
c_device.free()
```

This Python code snippet leverages the power of PyCUDA to execute a simple CUDA kernel that adds two vectors. It demonstrates several key profiling and optimization operations:

- Setup and transfer of data between host and device, utilizing cuda.mem_alloc and cuda.memcpy.

- Measurement of execution time using CUDA events, allowing precise timing of kernel launches.

- Calculation of memory throughput, providing insights into bandwidth utilization during kernel execution.

- Assessment of kernel occupancy, crucial for understanding how well the hardware resources are utilized.

This code serves as a practical demonstration of obtaining and evaluating important performance metrics for optimizing CUDA applications effectively.

# Chapter 22

# Parallel Sorting Algorithms

## Introduction to Parallel Sorting

Sorting is a fundamental operation in computer science with various applications across computational tasks. In the pursuit of efficient sorting with large datasets, parallel algorithms offer significant advantages by distributing the workload across multiple processing units. Sorting algorithms can be optimized for parallel execution on modern architectures such as GPUs, leveraging concurrent operations.

## Overview of Parallel Sorting Techniques

Parallel sorting algorithms aim to reduce the complexity of sorting by dividing the problem into smaller subproblems and solving them concurrently. Among the most notable algorithms is the `Bitonic Sort`, which provides a basis for constructing sorting networks suitable for parallel execution.

## 1  Bitonic Sort

Bitonic Sort operates by recursively forming bitonic sequences and merging them. A sequence is considered bitonic if it consists of two monotonic sub-sequences. The construction of these sequences and their subsequent sorting can exploit parallelism to achieve efficient data sorting.

The merging process within a bitonic sequence is represented mathematically as follows:

$$\sigma(i,j) = \begin{cases} 1, & \text{if } a[i] > a[j] \\ 0, & \text{otherwise} \end{cases}$$

where $a[i]$ and $a[j]$ denote elements in the sequence and $\sigma$ is the swap indicator.

The entire sorting process can be orchestrated through a recursive procedure:

---

**Input:** Array $A$ of length $n$
**Output:** Sorted array $A$
**Function** BitonicSort($A$, *start, end, direction*):
   if *end* − *start* > 1 **then**
      $mid = (start + end)/2$;
      BitonicSort($A$, *start, mid,* 1);
      BitonicSort($A$, *mid, end,* 0);
      BitonicMerge$A$, *start, end, direction*;

**Function** BitonicMerge($A$, *start, end, direction*):
   if *end* − *start* > 1 **then**
      **for** $i = start$ **to** $end/2$ **do**
         **if** $(A[i] > A[i + n/2]) ==$ *direction* **then**
            swap(A[i], A[i + n/2]);
      $mid = (start + end)/2$;
      BitonicMerge($A$, *start, mid, direction*);
      BitonicMerge($A$, *mid, end, direction*);

---

The computational cost of Bitonic Sort is $O(n \log^2 n)$, indicating its suitability for parallel execution environments.

## 2 Other Parallel Sorting Methods

Parallel Quicksort and Merge Sort expand upon traditional algorithms by partitioning the dataset across multiple processors. These methods utilize divide-and-conquer strategies, enhancing data locality and reducing synchronization costs.

Parallel Quicksort can be described with its deterministic partitioning method adjusted for multi-threaded execution. Denoting the index positions within an array $P(i, j)$, the partitioning step is:

$$P(i, j) = \begin{cases} \text{increment left,} & \text{if } A[i] \leq \text{pivot} \\ \text{decrement right,} & \text{otherwise} \end{cases}$$

Tasks are recursively distributed over processors, maintaining concurrency and minimizing idle time.

# Implementation Considerations

The implementation of parallel sorting algorithms must account for architecture-specific optimizations, including memory bandwidth utilization and minimizing synchronization overhead. Efficient memory access patterns and cache hierarchies play a critical role.

Optimal block sizes and warp-level parallelism in GPU architectures can affect sorting performance significantly. The choice of algorithm is influenced by the input data characteristics, with algorithms such as `Parallel Bitonic Sort` preferred for uniformly distributed datasets, while `Quicksort` can provide benefits for datasets exhibiting non-uniform distributions.

Sort functions such as `thrust::sort` leverage these insights and are built on the CUDA platform to accommodate varying data sizes and distributions, providing both robustness and performance.

Through understanding these principles, one can harness the computational capabilities of parallel sorting, achieving significant performance improvements in large-scale data processing tasks.

# Python Code Snippet

Below is a Python code snippet that comprises the core components related to parallel sorting algorithms using PyCUDA, facilitating the use of GPUs for sorting tasks.

```python
import pycuda.autoinit
import pycuda.driver as cuda
import numpy as np
from pycuda.compiler import SourceModule

def bitonic_sort(input_array):
    '''
    Perform bitonic sort on the input array using GPU.
    :param input_array: Input array to be sorted.
    :return: Sorted array.
```

```python
    '''
    n = len(input_array)
    # Ensure n is a power of two
    assert n & (n - 1) == 0, "Input size must be a power of 2"

    # Create a numpy array and copy it to device memory
    a = np.array(input_array, dtype=np.float32)
    a_gpu = cuda.mem_alloc(a.nbytes)
    cuda.memcpy_htod(a_gpu, a)

    # Define CUDA kernel
    mod = SourceModule("""
    __global__ void bitonic_sort(float *a, int j, int k) {
        unsigned int i, ixj;
        i = threadIdx.x + blockDim.x * blockIdx.x;
        ixj = i^j;

        if (ixj > i) {
            if ((i&k) == 0) {
                if (a[i] > a[ixj]) {
                    float temp = a[i];
                    a[i] = a[ixj];
                    a[ixj] = temp;
                }
            }
            if ((i&k) != 0) {
                if (a[i] < a[ixj]) {
                    float temp = a[i];
                    a[i] = a[ixj];
                    a[ixj] = temp;
                }
            }
        }
    }
    """)

    # Kernel function from module
    bitonic_sort_kernel = mod.get_function("bitonic_sort")

    # Prepare threads and blocks
    threads_per_block = 512
    blocks = int(np.ceil(n / threads_per_block))

    # Run the bitonic sort
    k = 2
    while k <= n:
        j = k // 2
        while j > 0:
            bitonic_sort_kernel(a_gpu, np.int32(j), np.int32(k),
                                block=(threads_per_block, 1, 1),
                          ↪ grid=(blocks, 1))
            j //= 2
        k *= 2
```

```python
    # Copy result back to host
    cuda.memcpy_dtoh(a, a_gpu)
    return a

# Test the bitonic_sort function
input_array = [3.0, 7.0, 2.0, 6.0, 4.0, 1.0, 5.0, 8.0]
sorted_array = bitonic_sort(input_array)

print("Original array:", input_array)
print("Sorted array:", sorted_array)

def partition_data(array, low, high):
    '''
    Partition the array for quicksort.
    :param array: The array to partition.
    :param low: Starting index.
    :param high: Ending index.
    :return: Partition index.
    '''

    pivot = array[high]
    i = low - 1
    for j in range(low, high):
        if array[j] <= pivot:
            i += 1
            array[i], array[j] = array[j], array[i]
    array[i + 1], array[high] = array[high], array[i + 1]
    return i + 1

def quicksort(array, low, high):
    '''
    Perform parallelized quicksort on the array.
    :param array: The array to sort.
    :param low: Starting index.
    :param high: Ending index.
    :return: None (sorts array in place).
    '''
    if low < high:
        pi = partition_data(array, low, high)
        quicksort(array, low, pi - 1)
        quicksort(array, pi + 1, high)

# Test the quicksort function
array = [10, 80, 30, 90, 40, 50, 70]
quicksort(array, 0, len(array) - 1)

print("Quicksorted array:", array)
```

This code defines the following key functions for parallel sorting using PyCUDA:

- `bitonic_sort` performs a bitonic sort utilizing the GPU,

demonstrating the parallel computing capabilities of GPUs effectively for sorting tasks.

- `partition_data` is used within the quicksort algorithm to partition the data array about a pivot.

- `quicksort` applies the recursive quicksort algorithm using the partition function to sort the data in a divide-and-conquer manner.

These functions highlight the usage of parallel algorithm strategies with CUDA to enhance data processing speed and efficiency in sorting tasks.

# Chapter 23

# Implementing Graph Algorithms

## Parallel Graph Algorithms on GPUs

Graph algorithms are central to numerous computational and scientific endeavors. Harnessing the power of GPUs to perform complex operations, such as Breadth-First Search (BFS) and Dijkstra's algorithm, allows for significant performance improvements on large graphs, benefiting from massive parallelization capabilities.

## 1  Breadth-First Search (BFS) Implementation

Breadth-First Search is utilized to traverse or search in layered graph structures. Its parallel implementation leverages the concurrent exploration of multiple vertices using a frontier approach. The vertex set is partitioned, with new frontiers formed in each iteration.

The BFS process can be mathematically described as:

$$\mathbf{d}[v] = \min\left(\mathbf{d}[u] + 1 \mid (u, v) \in E\right)$$

Here, $\mathbf{d}[v]$ represents the distance from the source node $s$ to node $v$, and $E$ is the set of edges. In a parallel setting, multiple $(u, v)$ pairs are evaluated simultaneously.

---
**Input:** Graph $G = (V, E)$, Source vertex $s$
**Output:** Array $\mathbf{d}[v]$ containing shortest distances
**foreach** $v \in V$ **do**
 $\lfloor$ $\mathbf{d}[v] \leftarrow \infty$;
$\mathbf{d}[s] \leftarrow 0$; frontier $\leftarrow \{s\}$; **while** *frontier* $\neq \emptyset$ **do**
 $\quad$ next_frontier $\leftarrow \emptyset$ **foreach** $u \in$ *frontier* **do**
 $\quad\quad$ **foreach** $(u, v) \in E$ **do**
 $\quad\quad\quad$ **if** $\boldsymbol{d}[v] = \infty$ **then**
 $\quad\quad\quad\quad$ $\lfloor$ $\mathbf{d}[v] \leftarrow \mathbf{d}[u] + 1$; add v to next_frontier;

 $\quad$ frontier $\leftarrow$ next_frontier;
---

The CUDA-enabled BFS involves parallelizing the above steps by mapping vertices to GPU threads, allowing concurrent updates to the frontier.

## 2 Dijkstra's Algorithm on GPUs

Dijkstra's algorithm computes the shortest paths from a single source vertex to all other vertices in a graph with non-negative edge weights. Its parallelization on a GPU involves concurrent vertex exploration and priority queue updates.

The principal update rule in Dijkstra's algorithm is given by:

$$\mathbf{d}[v] = \min\left(\mathbf{d}[v], \mathbf{d}[u] + w(u, v)\right)$$

where $w(u, v)$ denotes the weight of edge $(u, v)$.

---
**Input:** Graph $G = (V, E)$, Source vertex $s$, Edge weights
 $\quad w$
**Output:** Array $\mathbf{d}[v]$ containing shortest distances
Initialize priority queue $\mathcal{Q}$; **foreach** $v \in V$ **do**
 $\lfloor$ $\mathbf{d}[v] \leftarrow \infty$;
$\mathbf{d}[s] \leftarrow 0$; $\mathcal{Q} \leftarrow \{(0, s)\}$; **while** $\mathcal{Q} \neq \emptyset$ **do**
 $\quad$ $(dist, u) \leftarrow$ extract-min$(\mathcal{Q})$; **foreach** $(u, v) \in E$ **do**
 $\quad\quad$ **if** $\boldsymbol{d}[v] > \boldsymbol{d}[u] + w(u, v)$ **then**
 $\quad\quad\quad$ $\lfloor$ $\mathbf{d}[v] \leftarrow \mathbf{d}[u] + w(u, v)$; decrease-key$(\mathcal{Q}, \mathbf{d}[v])$;
---

Parallelization occurs by decomposing the graph into chunks handled by different processing units and utilizing concurrent read and update operations on the distance array $\mathbf{d}$.

Both BFS and Dijkstra's algorithm adapt to GPUs by overcoming traditional dependencies and synchronizations, instead implementing a frontier or wavefront-based approach and accepting possible edge relaxation conflicts that are resolved post-process through synchronization barriers.

# Python Code Snippet

Below is a Python code snippet that implements both the Breadth-First Search (BFS) and Dijkstra's algorithm using PyCUDA to leverage GPU acceleration.

```python
import pycuda.autoinit
import pycuda.gpuarray as gpuarray
from pycuda.compiler import SourceModule
import numpy as np

# GPU kernel for BFS
bfs_kernel_code = """
__global__ void bfs_kernel(int *d, int *edges, int *frontier, int
   *next_frontier, bool *change, int num_vertices) {
    int idx = blockIdx.x * blockDim.x + threadIdx.x;

    if (idx < num_vertices && frontier[idx]) {
        frontier[idx] = 0;
        int edge_start = edges[idx * 2];
        int edge_end = edges[idx * 2 + 1];

        for (int i = edge_start; i < edge_end; ++i) {
            int neighbor = edges[i];
            if (d[neighbor] == -1) {
                d[neighbor] = d[idx] + 1;
                next_frontier[neighbor] = 1;
                *change = true;
            }
        }
    }
}
"""

# GPU kernel for Dijkstra's
dijkstra_kernel_code = """
__global__ void dijkstra_kernel(float *distances, int *edges, float
   *weights, int *priority_queue, bool *processed, int
   num_vertices) {
    int idx = threadIdx.x + blockIdx.x * blockDim.x;
    if (idx >= num_vertices) return;

    if (!processed[idx]) {
```

136

```
            processed[idx] = true;
            int start_edge = edges[idx * 2];
            int end_edge = edges[idx * 2 + 1];

            for (int i = start_edge; i < end_edge; ++i) {
                int neighbor = edges[i];
                float weight = weights[i];

                float new_distance = distances[idx] + weight;
                if (new_distance < distances[neighbor]) {
                    distances[neighbor] = new_distance;
                    priority_queue[neighbor] = 1;   // Mark for
                    ↪   processing
                }
            }
        }
    }
}
"""


def run_bfs_gpu(edges, source, num_vertices):
    distances = -1 * np.ones(num_vertices, dtype=np.int32)
    distances[source] = 0

    frontier = np.zeros(num_vertices, dtype=np.int32)
    frontier[source] = 1

    next_frontier = np.zeros(num_vertices, dtype=np.int32)
    change = np.array([True], dtype=np.bool)

    edges_gpu = gpuarray.to_gpu(edges)
    d_gpu = gpuarray.to_gpu(distances)
    frontier_gpu = gpuarray.to_gpu(frontier)
    next_frontier_gpu = gpuarray.to_gpu(next_frontier)
    change_gpu = gpuarray.to_gpu(change)

    bfs_module = SourceModule(bfs_kernel_code)
    bfs_kernel = bfs_module.get_function("bfs_kernel")

    while change[0]:
        change[0] = False
        change_gpu.set(change)

        bfs_kernel(d_gpu, edges_gpu, frontier_gpu,
        ↪   next_frontier_gpu, change_gpu, np.int32(num_vertices),
        ↪   block=(256, 1, 1), grid=((num_vertices + 255) // 256,
        ↪   1))

        frontier_gpu.set(next_frontier_gpu.get())
        next_frontier_gpu.fill(0)

    return d_gpu.get()

def run_dijkstra_gpu(edges, weights, source, num_vertices):
```

```
    distances = np.full(num_vertices, np.inf, dtype=np.float32)
    distances[source] = 0

    priority_queue = np.zeros(num_vertices, dtype=np.int32)
    priority_queue[source] = 1

    processed = np.zeros(num_vertices, dtype=np.bool)

    edges_gpu = gpuarray.to_gpu(edges)
    weights_gpu = gpuarray.to_gpu(weights)
    distances_gpu = gpuarray.to_gpu(distances)
    priority_queue_gpu = gpuarray.to_gpu(priority_queue)
    processed_gpu = gpuarray.to_gpu(processed)

    dijkstra_module = SourceModule(dijkstra_kernel_code)
    dijkstra_kernel =
    ↪   dijkstra_module.get_function("dijkstra_kernel")

    while np.any(priority_queue):
        dijkstra_kernel(distances_gpu, edges_gpu, weights_gpu,
        ↪   priority_queue_gpu, processed_gpu,
        ↪   np.int32(num_vertices), block=(256, 1, 1),
        ↪   grid=((num_vertices + 255) // 256, 1))

        priority_queue.fill(0)
        priority_queue_gpu.set(priority_queue)

    return distances_gpu.get()

# Example graph representation
edges = np.array([0, 2, 2, 5, 3, 4, 4, 7, 5, 6], dtype=np.int32)   #
↪   Example edges for BFS
weights = np.array([1.0, 1.5, 2.0, 0.5, 1.2], dtype=np.float32)   #
↪   Example weights for Dijkstra's

source_vertex = 0
num_vertices = 5

# Run BFS
bfs_result = run_bfs_gpu(edges, source_vertex, num_vertices)
print("BFS shortest paths from source:", bfs_result)

# Run Dijkstra's
dijkstra_result = run_dijkstra_gpu(edges, weights, source_vertex,
↪   num_vertices)
print("Dijkstra's shortest paths from source:", dijkstra_result)
```

This code defines Python implementations of both the Breadth-
First Search (BFS) and Dijkstra's algorithm using PyCUDA to take
advantage of GPU acceleration:

- The BFS implementation calculates shortest paths in an un-

138

weighted graph by leveraging parallel exploration of vertices.

- The Dijkstra's algorithm calculates shortest paths in a graph with non-negative weights using concurrent updates of the priority queue.

- Both algorithms define kernels written in CUDA C, which are executed within the Python environment, demonstrating the integration of CPU and GPU computations.

- The example demonstrates how to organize data transfer between host and device, manage GPU memory, and synchronize operations to achieve parallelism.

# Chapter 24

# Image Processing with CUDA

## Introduction to Image Processing Techniques

Image processing encompasses a variety of operations for enhancing and analyzing visual data. Among these operations, filtering and transformations are crucial for applications such as noise reduction, edge detection, and image enhancement. Utilizing the compute capabilities of CUDA significantly accelerates these tasks via parallel implementation.

## CUDA Acceleration of Filtering Operations

Filtering in image processing often involves manipulating pixel values based on a predefined kernel. Convolution is a common filtering operation, defined mathematically as:

$$g(x,y) = \sum_{i=-k}^{k} \sum_{j=-k}^{k} f(x+i, y+j) \cdot h(i,j)$$

where $f(x,y)$ is the input image, $h(i,j)$ is the filter kernel, and $g(x,y)$ is the filtered image. The task of convolution can be parallelized by assigning each pixel computation to a separate GPU thread.

# Implementation of Convolution using CUDA

The implementation of a convolution operation on CUDA involves parallel processing, where each thread computes the convolution for a specific pixel of the output image.

```
Input: Input image f, Kernel h
Output: Output image g
Initialize CUDA memory for input image d_f,
 kernel d_h, and output image d_g
Copy f and h to device memory
dim3 dimBlock(BLOCK_SIZE, BLOCK_SIZE)
dim3 dimGrid((width + dimBlock.x - 1) /
 dimBlock.x, (height + dimBlock.y - 1) /
 dimBlock.y)
convolutionKernel<<<dimGrid, dimBlock>>>(d_f, d_h,
 d_g, width, height)
Copy d_g back to host memory
```

CUDA threads execute the convolution kernel function in parallel, expressing concurrent pixel-wise operations, and store results in the output image.

# Image Transformation Utilizing CUDA

Image transformations involve performing operations that modify the geometry of images. Common transformations include scaling, rotation, and translation, quantified by transformation matrices. A generic transformation can be represented as:

$$\begin{bmatrix} x' \\ y' \\ 1 \end{bmatrix} = \begin{bmatrix} a & b & t_x \\ c & d & t_y \\ 0 & 0 & 1 \end{bmatrix} \begin{bmatrix} x \\ y \\ 1 \end{bmatrix}$$

The coordinates $(x', y')$ are derived from $(x, y)$ using transformation matrix elements $a, b, c, d, t_x, t_y$.

# 1 CUDA Implementation of Image Scaling

Image scaling requires adjusting the size of the image by interpolation or decimation. Utilizing CUDA, the scaling operation can achieve significant performance gains by assigning interpolation calculations for subgroups of pixels to individual threads.

# Edge Detection via Parallel Computing

Edge detection identifies changes in intensity within an image, often utilizing gradient operations such as the Sobel filter, which is calculated as:

$$G_x = \begin{bmatrix} -1 & 0 & 1 \\ -2 & 0 & 2 \\ -1 & 0 & 1 \end{bmatrix} \quad G_y = \begin{bmatrix} -1 & -2 & -1 \\ 0 & 0 & 0 \\ 1 & 2 & 1 \end{bmatrix}$$

The gradient magnitude and direction are then calculated as:

$$G = \sqrt{G_x^2 + G_y^2}$$

$$\theta = \arctan\left(\frac{G_y}{G_x}\right)$$

Parallelization is achieved by distributing gradient calculations across multiple threads, with each thread computing the gradient for a pixel or block of pixels.

# 1 Algorithm for Parallel Edge Detection

---

**Input:** Input image f
**Output:** Edge-detected image g
Initialize CUDA memory for images d_f and d_g
Copy f to device memory
dim3 dimBlock(BLOCK_SIZE, BLOCK_SIZE)
dim3 dimGrid((width + dimBlock.x - 1) /
dimBlock.x, (height + dimBlock.y - 1) /
dimBlock.y)
sobelKernel≪<dimGrid, dimBlock≫>(d_f, d_g, width,
height)
Copy d_g back to host memory

---

The edge detection procedure is seamlessly parallelized over CUDA threads, accelerating the processing time on high-resolution images.

Through these methodologies, CUDA serves as a powerful tool to perform image processing efficiently, handling large data volumes with ease and precision.

# Python Code Snippet

Below is a Python code snippet that encompasses the core computational elements of image processing using CUDA for convolution and edge detection, showcasing parallelized implementations with PyCUDA.

```python
import numpy as np
import pycuda.driver as cuda
import pycuda.autoinit
from pycuda.compiler import SourceModule

# CUDA kernel for convolution
convolution_kernel = """
__global__ void convolution(float *input, float *kernel, float
↪ *output, int width, int height, int k_size) {
    int x = blockIdx.x * blockDim.x + threadIdx.x;
    int y = blockIdx.y * blockDim.y + threadIdx.y;
    int half_k = k_size / 2;
    float sum = 0.0;

    if (x < width && y < height) {
        // Iterate over the kernel
        for (int i = -half_k; i <= half_k; i++) {
            for (int j = -half_k; j <= half_k; j++) {
                int x_index = min(max(x + i, 0), width - 1);
                int y_index = min(max(y + j, 0), height - 1);
                sum += input[y_index * width + x_index] * kernel[(i
↪ + half_k) * k_size + (j + half_k)];
            }
        }
        // Assign result to the output
        output[y * width + x] = sum;
    }
}
"""

# Define image dimensions and kernel size
width = 512
height = 512
kernel_size = 3
```

```python
# Create random input image and kernel
input_image = np.random.rand(height, width).astype(np.float32)
kernel = np.array([[1, 2, 1], [0, 0, 0], [-1, -2, -1]],
↪   dtype=np.float32).flatten()

# Allocate device memory
input_gpu = cuda.mem_alloc(input_image.nbytes)
kernel_gpu = cuda.mem_alloc(kernel.nbytes)
output_gpu = cuda.mem_alloc(input_image.nbytes)

# Copy data to device
cuda.memcpy_htod(input_gpu, input_image)
cuda.memcpy_htod(kernel_gpu, kernel)

# Compile and get the kernel function
module = SourceModule(convolution_kernel)
convolution = module.get_function("convolution")

# Define block and grid sizes
block_size = (16, 16, 1)
grid_size = (int(np.ceil(width / block_size[0])), int(np.ceil(height
↪   / block_size[1])), 1)

# Execute the convolution kernel
convolution(input_gpu, kernel_gpu, output_gpu, np.int32(width),
↪   np.int32(height), np.int32(kernel_size),
            block=block_size, grid=grid_size)

# Transfer output back to host
output_image = np.empty_like(input_image)
cuda.memcpy_dtoh(output_image, output_gpu)

# Display result
print("Output Image (Convolution):", output_image)
```

This code defines several key components for the implementation of convolution using CUDA:

- `convolution_kernel` CUDA C function performs the convolution operation over an input image with a filter kernel.

- Device memory is allocated using PyCUDA to store input, kernel, and output data.

- Data transfer from the host to the device, kernel execution, and transfer back to the host are conducted using PyCUDA's functionality.

- The variable `block_size` defines the dimension of threads

144

per block, while `grid_size` determines the number of blocks needed to cover the entire image.

Through this implementation, PyCUDA allows efficient handling of image processing tasks leveraging GPU acceleration.

# Chapter 25

# Numerical Simulations and Modeling

## Numerical Solutions to Partial Differential Equations

In numerical computations, partial differential equations (PDEs) are often employed to model various physical phenomena. These equations involve functions of several variables and their partial derivatives. The general form of a PDE is given by:

$$F(x_1, x_2, \ldots, x_n, u, u_{x_1}, u_{x_2}, \ldots, u_{x_n}, \ldots, u_{x_1 x_2}, \ldots) = 0$$

where $u$ is the unknown function, and $u_{x_i}$ denotes partial derivatives with respect to the respective variables.

## 1 Finite Difference Methods

Finite difference methods are employed for approximating solutions to PDEs. Given a differential equation, its corresponding finite difference approximation can be represented as:

$$\frac{\partial u}{\partial x} \approx \frac{u(x + \Delta x) - u(x)}{\Delta x}$$

and

$$\frac{\partial^2 u}{\partial x^2} \approx \frac{u(x + \Delta x) - 2u(x) + u(x - \Delta x)}{\Delta x^2}$$

These discretization techniques are parallelizable, making them suitable for GPUs.

# Fluid Dynamics Simulations

For fluid dynamics, the Navier-Stokes equations describe the motion of fluid substances. In vector form, these are expressed as:

$$\rho \left( \frac{\partial \vec{v}}{\partial t} + (\vec{v} \cdot \nabla)\vec{v} \right) = -\nabla p + \mu \nabla^2 \vec{v} + \vec{f}$$

where $\vec{v}$ represents velocity, $\rho$ is fluid density, $p$ is pressure, $\mu$ is dynamic viscosity, and $\vec{f}$ denotes body forces.

## 1 GPU Acceleration Techniques for Navier-Stokes

Implementing the Navier-Stokes equations requires solving large systems of linear equations, typically through iterative solvers such as Jacobi, Gauss-Seidel, or Conjugate Gradient methods.

---

**Input:** Initial velocity field v0
**Output:** Updated velocity field v
Initialize CUDA memory for grids v_d, p_d
Define kernel configuration dimBlock, dimGrid
**while** *not converged* **do**
  pressureSolveKernel≪<dimGrid, dimBlock≫>(v_d,
  p_d)
  velocityUpdateKernel≪<dimGrid, dimBlock≫>(v_d,
  p_d)

---

The equations are divided across blocks and threads, optimizing computations for the GPU architecture.

# Physical Modeling for Dynamic Systems

Models of physical systems often require simulation over time and space. Newton's second law,

$$m\frac{d^2 \vec{x}}{dt^2} = \vec{F}$$

forms the basis for many simulations, where $m$ is mass and $\vec{F}$ is the resultant force vector acting on the body.

# 1    Discrete Element Methods

Discrete element method (DEM) simulates the behavior of assemblies of particles, often applicable in granular material simulations. The interaction between particles is calculated using:

$$\vec{F}_{ij} = k_n \delta_n \hat{n} + k_t \delta_t \hat{t}$$

where $k_n$ and $k_t$ are the normal and tangential stiffness, $\delta_n$ and $\delta_t$ are normal and tangential displacements respectively.

---

**Input:** Particle positions `pos`, velocities `vel`
**Output:** Updated positions `pos`, velocities `vel`
```
Initialize CUDA memory for arrays pos_d, vel_d
Calculate forces using CUDA kernels
Update particle states in parallel
```

---

GPU parallelism significantly accelerates DEM simulations by distributing particle interactions across threads.

# Heat Transfer Simulations

The heat equation, a PDE representing heat distribution, is expressed by:

$$\frac{\partial u}{\partial t} = \alpha \nabla^2 u$$

where $\alpha$ denotes thermal diffusivity. GPU-based solvers employ techniques to efficiently handle the numerical convergence of these processes.

# 1    Parallel Implementation Using CUDA

The finite difference method is suitable for simulating heat conduction, with GPU thread blocks evaluating temperature changes across grid points:

> **Input:** Initial temperature distribution T0
> **Output:** Temperature distribution T
> Define block and grid configurations
> **while** *simulation not complete* **do**
> | heatKernel«<gridDim, blockDim»>(T_d)
> | Update host memory from T_d

Parallel computation of the diffusion process enhances simulation velocities, offering real-time performance improvements for large domains.

This approach enables detailed and rapid exploration of physical scenarios leveraging GPU efficiencies.

# Python Code Snippet

The following Python code snippet contains core computational functions leveraging PyCUDA for GPU acceleration of numerical computations relevant to simulation and modeling of dynamic systems as described in this chapter.

```python
import numpy as np
import pycuda.autoinit
import pycuda.driver as cuda
from pycuda.compiler import SourceModule

mod = SourceModule("""
__global__ void finite_diff(float *u, float *u_next, int n)
{
    int idx = blockIdx.x * blockDim.x + threadIdx.x;
    if(idx > 0 && idx < n - 1) {
        u_next[idx] = u[idx + 1] - 2 * u[idx] + u[idx - 1];
    }
}

__global__ void navier_stokes(float *v, float *p, int n)
{
    int idx = blockIdx.x * blockDim.x + threadIdx.x;
    if(idx < n) {
        float pressure_force = p[idx] - p[idx + 1];
        v[idx] += pressure_force;
    }
}

__global__ void dem(float *pos, float *vel, float *forces, int n)
{
    int idx = blockIdx.x * blockDim.x + threadIdx.x;
```

```
    if(idx < n) {
        // Calculate forces between particles (simplified)
        float force = forces[idx];
        vel[idx] += force;
        pos[idx] += vel[idx];
    }
}
""")

finite_diff = mod.get_function("finite_diff")
navier_stokes = mod.get_function("navier_stokes")
dem = mod.get_function("dem")

# Setting up arrays and initial conditions
n = 1024
u = np.random.randn(n).astype(np.float32)
u_next = np.zeros_like(u)
v = np.random.randn(n).astype(np.float32)
p = np.zeros_like(v)
pos = np.random.randn(n).astype(np.float32)
vel = np.zeros_like(pos)
forces = np.random.randn(n).astype(np.float32)

# Copy data to CUDA device
u_gpu = cuda.mem_alloc(u.nbytes)
u_next_gpu = cuda.mem_alloc(u_next.nbytes)
v_gpu = cuda.mem_alloc(v.nbytes)
p_gpu = cuda.mem_alloc(p.nbytes)
pos_gpu = cuda.mem_alloc(pos.nbytes)
vel_gpu = cuda.mem_alloc(vel.nbytes)
forces_gpu = cuda.mem_alloc(forces.nbytes)

cuda.memcpy_htod(u_gpu, u)
cuda.memcpy_htod(v_gpu, v)
cuda.memcpy_htod(p_gpu, p)
cuda.memcpy_htod(pos_gpu, pos)
cuda.memcpy_htod(vel_gpu, vel)
cuda.memcpy_htod(forces_gpu, forces)

# Define block and grid size
block_size = 256
grid_size = (n + block_size - 1) // block_size

# Launch kernels
finite_diff(u_gpu, u_next_gpu, np.int32(n), block=(block_size, 1,
↪  1), grid=(grid_size, 1))
navier_stokes(v_gpu, p_gpu, np.int32(n), block=(block_size, 1, 1),
↪  grid=(grid_size, 1))
dem(pos_gpu, vel_gpu, forces_gpu, np.int32(n), block=(block_size, 1,
↪  1), grid=(grid_size, 1))

# Retrieve results from device
cuda.memcpy_dtoh(u_next, u_next_gpu)
```

150

```
cuda.memcpy_dtoh(v, v_gpu)
cuda.memcpy_dtoh(pos, pos_gpu)

print("Updated finite difference array:", u_next)
print("Updated velocity array:", v)
print("Updated position array:", pos)
```

This code includes several key functions necessary for GPU-accelerated computations using PyCUDA:

- `finite_diff` function implements a simple finite difference calculation, useful for numerically solving PDEs.

- `navier_stokes` handles a simplified update for velocity fields using the Navier-Stokes equations in a pressure-driven flow context.

- `dem` simulates particle interactions via the Discrete Element Method, updating positions and velocities of particles.

Each of these GPU kernel functions is launched with appropriate block and grid configurations for efficient parallel computation of large-scale numerical simulations. The script prints out the updated results to verify the calculations from the device arrays.

# Chapter 26

# Real-time Ray Tracing Applications

## Ray Tracing Model

Ray tracing simulates the way rays of light interact with surfaces within a scene. Each ray is traced from an observer's eye through a virtual screen and into the scene to determine visibility and shading. The fundamental equation for ray tracing can be formulated as:

$$\mathbf{R}(t) = \mathbf{O} + t\mathbf{D}$$

where $\mathbf{R}(t)$ represents the ray as a function of parameter $t$, $\mathbf{O}$ is the ray origin, and $\mathbf{D}$ is the direction vector. Intersection tests determine the first object hit by each ray if any.

## Ray-Surface Intersection

### 1   Sphere Intersection

For a sphere defined by its center $\mathbf{C}$ and radius $r$, the ray-sphere intersection is defined by solving:

$$(\mathbf{R}(t) - \mathbf{C}) \cdot (\mathbf{R}(t) - \mathbf{C}) = r^2$$

which simplifies to the quadratic equation:

$$\mathbf{D} \cdot \mathbf{D} \cdot t^2 + 2\mathbf{D} \cdot (\mathbf{O} - \mathbf{C}) \cdot t + (\mathbf{O} - \mathbf{C}) \cdot (\mathbf{O} - \mathbf{C}) - r^2 = 0$$

The discriminant $\Delta$ determines the nature of intersection:

$$\Delta = b^2 - 4ac$$

where $a = \mathbf{D} \cdot \mathbf{D}$, $b = 2\mathbf{D} \cdot (\mathbf{O} - \mathbf{C})$, and $c = (\mathbf{O} - \mathbf{C}) \cdot (\mathbf{O} - \mathbf{C}) - r^2$. If $\Delta \geq 0$, there exists at least one real intersection point.

## 2 Plane Intersection

For plane intersection, given a plane defined by point $\mathbf{P}_0$ and normal $\mathbf{N}$, the intersection is determined by:

$$t = \frac{(\mathbf{P}_0 - \mathbf{O}) \cdot \mathbf{N}}{\mathbf{D} \cdot \mathbf{N}}$$

provided $\mathbf{D} \cdot \mathbf{N} \neq 0$, which ensures the ray is not parallel to the plane.

# Ray Tracing with CUDA

## 1 Parallelization Strategy

The parallelizable nature of ray tracing makes it highly amenable to GPU acceleration using CUDA. Each thread processes a single ray's path, necessitating efficient kernel launches and memory accesses.

---

**Input:** Scene data, camera parameters
**Output:** Rendered image
```
Initialize CUDA memory for scene, image buffer
Define grid/block configuration
rayTraceKernel<<gridDim, blockDim>>(scene, image)
```

---

Each `rayTraceKernel` invocation computes the color contribution for individual pixels by tracing the associated rays and reflecting the resultant interactions with scene surfaces.

## 2 Memory Management

Efficient use of shared memory within each CUDA block enhances the stored intermediate computations, minimizing global memory access latency:

```
__shared__ float3 sharedMemory[];
```

This aids in reducing costly data transfers and synchronizes operations efficiently within the block.

# Rendering Equation

The rendering equation captures the equilibrium of radiance leaving a point in the scene:

$$L_o(\mathbf{x}, \omega_o) = L_e(\mathbf{x}, \omega_o) + \int_{\Omega} f_r(\mathbf{x}, \omega_i, \omega_o) L_i(\mathbf{x}, \omega_i)(\omega_i \cdot \mathbf{n}) \, d\omega_i$$

where $L_o$ is the outgoing radiance, $L_e$ is the emitted radiance, $\omega_o$ is the outgoing direction, $f_r$ is the bidirectional reflectance distribution function (BRDF), $L_i$ is incoming radiance, and $\mathbf{n}$ is the surface normal.

## 1   Monte Carlo Integration

Monte Carlo integration is applied to approximate solutions to the rendering equation, particularly where analytical solutions are intractable. The approximation is computed as:

$$L_o \approx \frac{1}{N} \sum_{i=1}^{N} \frac{f_r(\mathbf{x}, \omega_i, \omega_o) L_i(\mathbf{x}, \omega_i)(\omega_i \cdot \mathbf{n})}{p(\omega_i)}$$

where $N$ is the number of samples and $p(\omega_i)$ is the probability density function.

# Photon Mapping and Denoising

Photon mapping is a two-pass algorithmic approach involving photon tracing and radiance estimation, enhancing global illumination effects. Furthermore, denoising techniques refine the final image quality, reducing variance in Monte Carlo simulation outputs.

**Input:** Photons, camera parameters
**Output:** Denoised image
```
Trace photons and store in photon map
Estimate radiance using photon map and kernel
Apply denoising filters to final render
```

Using CUDA streamlining to handle parallel ray dispatch, data structures, and complex arithmetic operations, real-time ray tracing enables the simulation of highly realistic scenes with physically based lighting dynamics.

# Python Code Snippet

Below is a Python code snippet that demonstrates the implementation of core elements used in CUDA-accelerated ray tracing applications. It includes the ray tracing kernel setup, ray-sphere and ray-plane intersection, and associated utility functions using the PyCUDA library.

```python
import pycuda.autoinit
import pycuda.driver as cuda
import numpy as np
from pycuda.compiler import SourceModule

# Ray tracing kernel code
kernel_code = """
#include <math.h>

__device__ bool intersect_sphere(float3 O, float3 D, float3 C, float
↪   r, float &t) {
    float3 OC = O - C;
    float b = dot(D, OC);
    float c = dot(OC, OC) - r * r;
    float discriminant = b * b - c;
    if (discriminant > 0) {
        t = -b - sqrt(discriminant);
        return true;
    }
    return false;
}

__device__ bool intersect_plane(float3 O, float3 D, float3 P0,
↪   float3 N, float &t) {
    float denom = dot(N, D);
    if (fabs(denom) > 1e-6) {
        t = dot(P0 - O, N) / denom;
        return t >= 0;
```

```
    }
    return false;
}

__global__ void ray_trace_kernel(float3 *image, float3 O, float3 D,
↪    float3 sphere_center, float sphere_radius) {
    int x = blockIdx.x * blockDim.x + threadIdx.x;
    int y = blockIdx.y * blockDim.y + threadIdx.y;
    int idx = y * gridDim.x * blockDim.x + x;

    float t;
    float3 color = make_float3(0, 0, 0);

    if(intersect_sphere(O, D, sphere_center, sphere_radius, t)) {
        color = make_float3(1, 0, 0); // Red color for intersection
    }

    image[idx] = color;
}
"""

# Compile the kernel code
mod = SourceModule(kernel_code)

# Allocate space for the image buffer
image_size = (800, 600)
image = np.zeros((image_size[0] * image_size[1], 3),
↪    dtype=np.float32)
image_gpu = cuda.mem_alloc(image.nbytes)

# Set up ray tracing parameters
O = np.array([0.0, 0.0, 0.0], dtype=np.float32)    # Ray origin
D = np.array([0.0, 0.0, -1.0], dtype=np.float32)    # Ray direction
sphere_center = np.array([0.0, 0.0, -5.0], dtype=np.float32)
sphere_radius = np.float32(1.0)

# Get the kernel function
ray_trace_kernel = mod.get_function("ray_trace_kernel")

# Define block and grid size
block = (16, 16, 1)
grid = (image_size[0] // block[0], image_size[1] // block[1], 1)

# Perform ray tracing in parallel
ray_trace_kernel(
    cuda.Out(image),
    cuda.In(O),
    cuda.In(D),
    cuda.In(sphere_center),
    cube_radius,
    block=block,
    grid=grid
)
```

```
# Retrieve the image from the GPU
cuda.memcpy_dtoh(image, image_gpu)

# Example post-processing
# Simple print to verify output (In practice, you can use
↪   visualization tools)
print("Traced Image:", image[:10])   # Print the first 10 pixels for
↪   verification
```

This code defines the following critical elements for ray tracing using CUDA:

- `intersect_sphere` function checks for ray-sphere intersection, returning true if the ray intersects the sphere at a valid distance.

- `intersect_plane` performs ray-plane intersection tests, providing intersection parameters used in rendering.

- `ray_trace_kernel` is the CUDA kernel that performs ray tracing across a grid of threads, determining the image color at each pixel.

- Host-side setup code, including device memory allocation, kernel compilation using PyCUDA, and configuration for parallel execution.

The final segment showcases how these foundational operations are utilized in conjunction with CUDA for efficient real-time ray tracing.

# Chapter 27

# Deep Learning and Neural Networks

## Overview of Deep Neural Networks

Deep neural networks (DNNs) consist of multiple layers of neurons, each performing linear and nonlinear transformations on inputs to learn hierarchical representations. The mathematical representation of a layer, for an input $\mathbf{x}$, is:

$$\mathbf{h}^{(l)} = \sigma(\mathbf{W}^{(l)}\mathbf{h}^{(l-1)} + \mathbf{b}^{(l)})$$

where $\mathbf{h}^{(l)}$ is the output of layer $l$, $\mathbf{W}^{(l)}$ represents the weight matrix, $\mathbf{b}^{(l)}$ is the bias vector, and $\sigma(\cdot)$ is a nonlinear activation function such as ReLU, sigmoid, or tanh.

## CUDA Acceleration in Deep Learning

CUDA's architecture allows for significant acceleration of training and inference in DNNs by leveraging the parallel processing capabilities of GPUs. This is achieved primarily through matrix operations and convolutions, which can be parallelized efficiently.

## 1 Matrix Multiplication

Matrix multiplication, a key operation in forward and backward propagation, is naturally parallelizable. For two matrices $\mathbf{A}$ and

**B**, the element $(i, j)$ of the resultant matrix **C** is expressed as:

$$c_{ij} = \sum_k a_{ik} \cdot b_{kj}$$

CUDA facilitates the computation by launching threads for each element $c_{ij}$, aggregating results efficiently in parallel.

## 2  Convolutional Operations

Convolutional layers utilize kernels to scan inputs, crucial for feature extraction in DNNs, especially within CNNs. The operation is defined as:

$$y(i, j) = \sum_m \sum_n x(i + m, j + n) \cdot k(m, n)$$

CUDA parallelizes this by concurrently computing outputs $y(i, j)$ across different regions of the input **x**.

# Training Deep Networks with CUDA

The training process involves iterative optimization of DNN parameters through algorithms such as stochastic gradient descent (SGD). CUDA expedites this via concurrent evaluations of gradients and updates.

## 1  Backpropagation Algorithm

The backpropagation algorithm calculates gradients of the loss function with respect to each weight. For a neural network parameter $\Theta$, the update rule using learning rate $\eta$ is:

$$\Theta \leftarrow \Theta - \eta \nabla_\Theta \mathcal{L}$$

where $\nabla_\Theta \mathcal{L}$ is the gradient of the loss $\mathcal{L}$. CUDA's parallel computing allows for simultaneous calculation of partial derivatives, thereby reducing computational time significantly.

---

**Input:** Network parameters $\Theta$, training data $\mathbf{X}, \mathbf{Y}$,
   learning rate $\eta$
**Output:** Updated parameters $\Theta$
**foreach** *mini-batch* $(\mathbf{X}_b, \mathbf{Y}_b)$ **do**

   Forward_Pass($\mathbf{X}_b$)
   Compute_Loss($\mathbf{Y}_b$)
   Backward_Pass()
   Update_Parameters($\Theta, \eta$)

---

# Inference and Deployment

## 1   Efficient Batch Processing

During inference, batch processing improves throughput by sending multiple inputs simultaneously through the network. Utilizing CUDA, matrix operations scale efficiently across the batch dimension, enhancing both latency and throughput.

## 2   Model Optimization Techniques

Techniques such as quantization and pruning reduce the computational footprint of DNNs, making them more suitable for deployment on edge devices. Specifically, quantization approximates model weights to a lower precision, while pruning removes non-essential connections:

$$w \leftarrow \mathrm{round}(w \times \mathrm{scale\_factor})/\mathrm{scale\_factor}$$

Incorporating these techniques within a CUDA framework leverages its parallelism to maintain efficiency despite reduced precision and complexity.

# Conclusion

The application of CUDA in the sphere of deep neural networks significantly enhances training and deployment efficiency by fully utilizing the parallel computational capabilities of modern GPUs. These improvements manifest through accelerated matrix computations, optimized backpropagation processes, and efficient model inference workflows.

# Python Code Snippet

Below is a Python code snippet that encompasses the core computational elements of deep learning with CUDA, utilizing matrix multiplication, convolution operations, backpropagation, and model inference optimization.

```python
import pycuda.autoinit
import pycuda.driver as drv
import numpy as np
from pycuda.compiler import SourceModule

mod = SourceModule("""
__global__ void MatMulKernel(float *A, float *B, float *C, int N) {
    int tx = threadIdx.x;
    int ty = threadIdx.y;
    float value = 0;
    for (int k = 0; k < N; ++k) {
        value += A[ty * N + k] * B[k * N + tx];
    }
    C[ty * N + tx] = value;
}


__global__ void ConvolutionKernel(float *input, float *kernel, float
↪   *output,
                                   int N, int kernel_size) {
    int x = blockIdx.x * blockDim.x + threadIdx.x;
    int y = blockIdx.y * blockDim.y + threadIdx.y;
    float value = 0;
    for (int i = 0; i < kernel_size; i++) {
        for (int j = 0; j < kernel_size; j++) {
            value += input[(y + i) * N + x + j] * kernel[i *
            ↪   kernel_size + j];
        }
    }
    output[y * N + x] = value;
}


__global__ void BackpropagationKernel(float *gradients, float
↪   *weights,
                                       float *update, int N, float
                                       ↪   eta) {
    int idx = blockIdx.x * blockDim.x + threadIdx.x;
    if (idx < N) {
        update[idx] = gradients[idx] * eta;
        weights[idx] -= update[idx];
    }
}
""")


def matrix_multiplication(A, B, N):
```

```
"""
Matrix multiplication using CUDA.
"""
A_gpu = drv.mem_alloc(A.nbytes)
B_gpu = drv.mem_alloc(B.nbytes)
C_gpu = drv.mem_alloc(A.nbytes)
drv.memcpy_htod(A_gpu, A)
drv.memcpy_htod(B_gpu, B)

func = mod.get_function("MatMulKernel")
block_size = (16, 16, 1)
grid_size = (N // block_size[0], N // block_size[1], 1)
func(A_gpu, B_gpu, C_gpu, np.int32(N), block=block_size,
↪    grid=grid_size)

C = np.empty_like(A)
drv.memcpy_dtoh(C, C_gpu)
return C

def convolution_operation(input_array, kernel, N, kernel_size):
    """
    Convolution operation using CUDA.
    """
    input_gpu = drv.mem_alloc(input_array.nbytes)
    kernel_gpu = drv.mem_alloc(kernel.nbytes)
    output_gpu = drv.mem_alloc(input_array.nbytes)
    drv.memcpy_htod(input_gpu, input_array)
    drv.memcpy_htod(kernel_gpu, kernel)

    func = mod.get_function("ConvolutionKernel")
    block_size = (16, 16, 1)
    grid_size = (N // block_size[0], N // block_size[1], 1)
    func(input_gpu, kernel_gpu, output_gpu, np.int32(N),
↪       np.int32(kernel_size),
           block=block_size, grid=grid_size)

    output = np.empty_like(input_array)
    drv.memcpy_dtoh(output, output_gpu)
    return output

def backpropagation_update(gradients, weights, eta, N):
    """
    Backpropagation weight update using CUDA.
    """
    gradients_gpu = drv.mem_alloc(gradients.nbytes)
    weights_gpu = drv.mem_alloc(weights.nbytes)
    update_gpu = drv.mem_alloc(weights.nbytes)
    drv.memcpy_htod(gradients_gpu, gradients)
    drv.memcpy_htod(weights_gpu, weights)

    func = mod.get_function("BackpropagationKernel")
    block_size = (256, 1, 1)
    grid_size = (N // block_size[0] + 1, 1, 1)
```

```
func(gradients_gpu, weights_gpu, update_gpu, np.int32(N),
→  np.float32(eta),
    block=block_size, grid=grid_size)

updated_weights = np.empty_like(weights)
drv.memcpy_dtoh(updated_weights, weights_gpu)
return updated_weights

# Initialize matrices and arrays for testing
N = 16
A = np.random.rand(N, N).astype(np.float32)
B = np.random.rand(N, N).astype(np.float32)
input_array = np.random.rand(N, N).astype(np.float32)
kernel = np.random.rand(3, 3).astype(np.float32)
weights = np.random.rand(N).astype(np.float32)
gradients = np.random.rand(N).astype(np.float32)
eta = 0.01

C = matrix_multiplication(A, B, N)
output = convolution_operation(input_array, kernel, N, 3)
updated_weights = backpropagation_update(gradients, weights, eta, N)

print("Matrix Multiplication Result:\n", C)
print("Convolution Operation Result:\n", output)
print("Updated Weights After Backpropagation:\n", updated_weights)
```

This code defines several key functions necessary for implementing deep learning models using CUDA:

- `matrix_multiplication` utilizes PyCUDA to perform matrix multiplication, a fundamental operation in deep learning.

- `convolution_operation` encompasses efficient convolution computations essential for extracting features in convolutional neural networks.

- `backpropagation_update` demonstrates parallelized updates of neural network parameters during backpropagation using CUDA.

The final block of code executes these operations, demonstrating their effectiveness in leveraging GPU parallelism for deep learning tasks.

# Chapter 28

# CUDA for Financial Analytics

## Introduction to Financial Computing

The application of CUDA (Compute Unified Device Architecture) has profoundly impacted the field of financial analytics, enabling the rapid computation of extensive datasets through parallel processing. Financial models, often requiring substantial computational resources, benefit from CUDA's capacity to execute concurrent operations efficiently.

## Monte Carlo Simulations

Monte Carlo simulations play a critical role in financial calculations, particularly in the valuation of derivatives and risk assessment. The fundamental task is to simulate random paths of underlying asset prices, frequently modeled using stochastic differential equations (SDEs). The basic form of a geometric Brownian motion, used to model stock prices, can be expressed as:

$$dS_t = \mu S_t \, dt + \sigma S_t \, dW_t$$

where $S_t$ represents the stock price at time $t$, $\mu$ is the drift coefficient, $\sigma$ is the volatility coefficient, and $W_t$ is a Wiener process. Monte Carlo methods compute expectations by generating a large number of random paths and averaging the results, a process that is inherently parallelizable.

---

**Input:** Initial stock price $S_0$, drift $\mu$, volatility $\sigma$, time horizon $T$, number of steps $N$, number of paths $P$
**Output:** Simulated asset paths
**foreach** *path* $p \leftarrow 1$ *to* $P$ **do**
$\quad$ Initialize $S_0$
$\quad$ **foreach** *step* $n \leftarrow 1$ *to* $N$ **do**
$\quad\quad$ Generate `random` $\Delta W_n \sim \mathcal{N}(0, \sqrt{\Delta t})$
$\quad\quad$ Update $S_n = S_{n-1} + \mu S_{n-1}\Delta t + \sigma S_{n-1}\Delta W_n$

---

CUDA accelerates this process by employing a sufficient number of threads to compute multiple paths simultaneously, utilizing thousands of CUDA cores on a modern GPU.

# Option Pricing Models

Option pricing, foundational in quantitative finance, often requires the numerical solution of partial differential equations (PDEs), such as the Black-Scholes equation. The computational load is substantial, especially in evaluating complex options like barrier options. The Black-Scholes PDE is expressed as:

$$\frac{\partial V}{\partial t} + \frac{1}{2}\sigma^2 S^2 \frac{\partial^2 V}{\partial S^2} + rS\frac{\partial V}{\partial S} - rV = 0$$

where $V$ is the option value, $r$ is the risk-free interest rate, and $S$ is the underlying asset price. CUDA is particularly advantageous for grid-based numerical methods such as finite difference methods, allowing for parallel updates of each grid point.

## 1 Parallel Binomial Trees

Binomial tree models, simpler than PDE methods, use discrete time steps to model price evolution. The tree consists of nodes where prices can either move up or down with a certain probability. The option value is recursively calculated backwards from expiration:

$$V_i = \frac{1}{1 + r\Delta t}(pV_u + (1 - p)V_d)$$

165

where $p$ is the probability of an up movement, and $V_u$ and $V_d$ are option values at the subsequent nodes. CUDA facilitates this by assigning each node computation to a separate thread.

# Risk Management

Risk management, incorporating measures such as Value at Risk (VaR) and Conditional Value at Risk (CVaR), is critical for financial institutions. These metrics are computed via large data samples to assess potential portfolio losses. The relationship between asset returns $\mathbf{R}$ and portfolio loss $L$ is expressed as:

$$L = w^{\mathbf{R}}$$

where $w$ represents the vector of portfolio weights. Calculating VaR and CVaR involves creating a distribution of $L$ from simulated returns and finding quantiles, tasks that benefit from parallel batch evaluations using CUDA.

# Backtesting Strategies

Backtesting evaluates the performance of trading strategies by applying them to historical data. The key computation involves the re-evaluation of a strategy over multiple past time periods, determining its profitability and risk levels. CUDA can rapidly iterate over these periods by parallelizing the task across GPUs.

# High-Frequency Trading Algorithms

In high-frequency trading (HFT), decisions must be made in microseconds, necessitating the need for advanced computational power. CUDA assists by enabling the parallel processing of market data feeds and decision algorithms, reducing latency and optimizing execution speed.

## 1   Order Book Dynamics

Order book models analyze the supply and demand dynamics of financial instruments over time. This often involves processing millions of entries to capture market depth and liquidity. CUDA provides the needed computational capability to evaluate these models, updating states with each new order and cancellation in parallel.

$$OBD(S, t) = f(\text{limit order, market order, cancellation, etc.})$$

where OBD represents the evolving state of the order book and $f$ encompasses the complex interactions.

By integrating CUDA, financial analytics processes from valuation to risk assessment achieve tangible improvements in speed and efficiency, empowering institutions to handle unprecedented volumes of data and perform intricate computations with greater efficacy.

# Python Code Snippet

Below is a comprehensive Python code snippet implementing key algorithms for CUDA-assisted financial analytics, leveraging the PyCUDA library to perform parallel computations in the procedures discussed earlier.

```python
import pycuda.autoinit
import pycuda.driver as drv
import numpy as np
from pycuda.compiler import SourceModule

# CUDA kernel for Monte Carlo simulation
monte_carlo_kernel_code = """
__global__ void monte_carlo(int num_paths, int num_steps, float *dS,
↪    float *d_results,
                            float S0, float mu, float sigma, float
                            ↪    dt){
    int tid = blockIdx.x * blockDim.x + threadIdx.x;
    if(tid < num_paths){
        float S = S0;
        float z;
        for(int i=0; i<num_steps; i++){
            z = curand_normal(&state);
            S += mu * S * dt + sigma * S * z * sqrt(dt);
        }
        d_results[tid] = S;
    }
}
"""

# Compile the kernel code
```

```python
mod = SourceModule(monte_carlo_kernel_code)
monte_carlo = mod.get_function("monte_carlo")

def run_monte_carlo(S0, mu, sigma, T, num_steps, num_paths):
    """
    Run Monte Carlo simulations on the GPU.
    :param S0: Initial stock price.
    :param mu: Drift coefficient.
    :param sigma: Volatility coefficient.
    :param T: Time horizon.
    :param num_steps: Number of time steps.
    :param num_paths: Number of simulation paths.
    :return: A numpy array with the simulated terminal stock prices.
    """
    dt = T / num_steps
    dS = np.zeros(num_paths).astype(np.float32)
    d_results = np.zeros(num_paths).astype(np.float32)

    monte_carlo(drv.In(np.array([num_paths, num_steps],
    ↪   dtype=np.int32)),
                drv.InOut(dS), drv.Out(d_results),
                np.float32(S0), np.float32(mu), np.float32(sigma),
                ↪   np.float32(dt),
                block=(128, 1, 1), grid=(num_paths//128 + 1, 1))

    return d_results

# Parameters
S0, mu, sigma, T = 100, 0.05, 0.2, 1
num_paths, num_steps = 10000, 252

# Run simulation
simulated_prices = run_monte_carlo(S0, mu, sigma, T, num_steps,
↪   num_paths)

# Simple Output
print("Sample of simulated end prices:", simulated_prices[:10])

# Option pricing kernel using parallel binomial tree model
binomial_tree_kernel_code = """
__global__ void binomial_tree(float *prices, float *option_values,
                              float S0, float K, float r, float T,
                              ↪   int num_steps){
    int tid = blockIdx.x * blockDim.x + threadIdx.x;
    if(tid < num_steps+1){
        float dt = T / num_steps;
        float up = exp(sigma * sqrt(dt));
        float p = (exp(r * dt) - 1/up) / (up - 1/up);
        float discount = exp(-r * dt);

        // Calculate stock price at nodes
        for(int i=0; i<num_steps; i++){
            prices[tid] *= (i % 2 == 0) ? up : 1/up;
```

```
        }

        // Calculate option value at nodes
        float C0 = max(prices[tid] - K, 0.0);
        option_values[tid] = discount * (p * C0 + (1 - p) *
        ↪   (prices[tid] - K));
    }
}
"""

# Compile the kernel code
mod_bt = SourceModule(binomial_tree_kernel_code)
binomial_tree = mod_bt.get_function("binomial_tree")

def run_binomial_tree(S0, K, r, T, sigma, num_steps):
    """
    Compute European call option prices using a parallel binomial
    ↪   tree model.
    :param S0: Initial stock price.
    :param K: Strike price.
    :param r: Risk-free rate.
    :param T: Expiration time.
    :param sigma: Volatility.
    :param num_steps: Number of time steps/nodes.
    :return: A numpy array with the option values at each node.
    """
    prices = np.array([S0] * (num_steps + 1), dtype=np.float32)
    option_values = np.zeros(num_steps + 1, dtype=np.float32)

    binomial_tree(drv.InOut(prices), drv.Out(option_values),
                  np.float32(S0), np.float32(K), np.float32(r),
                  ↪   np.float32(T), np.int32(num_steps),
                  block=(128, 1, 1), grid=(num_steps//128 + 1, 1))

    return option_values

# Parameters for binomial tree
K, r, sigma = 100, 0.05, 0.2

# Run binomial tree pricing
option_prices = run_binomial_tree(S0, K, r, T, sigma, num_steps)

# Output sample option prices
print("Sample of computed option values:", option_prices[:10])
```

This comprehensive Python code leverages CUDA utilization for essential computations in financial analytics:

- The `monte_carlo` kernel performs stochastic path simulations for asset price modeling.

169

- The `run_monte_carlo` function executes Monte Carlo simulations using GPU parallelism.

- An additional `binomial_tree` kernel evaluates the European call option values through a parallel binomial tree model.

- The `run_binomial_tree` function calculates option prices by harnessing CUDA's parallel processing abilities.

These code snippets demonstrate how CUDA accelerates complex financial analytics through efficient parallel computations, enhancing decision-making capabilities in the field.

# Chapter 29

# Signal Processing Techniques

## Fast Fourier Transform (FFT) on GPUs

The Fast Fourier Transform (FFT) is a critical component in modern signal processing tasks. By leveraging the parallel processing capabilities of GPUs via CUDA, FFT computations are significantly accelerated. The FFT algorithm transforms data between time (or spatial) domain and frequency domain, and its computational complexity is $O(N \log N)$, where $N$ denotes the data sample size.

## 1 Discrete Fourier Transform (DFT) Definition

The Discrete Fourier Transform (DFT) of a sequence $x[n]$ of length $N$ is given by

$$X[k] = \sum_{n=0}^{N-1} x[n] e^{-j\frac{2\pi}{N}kn}$$

where $j$ is the imaginary unit, and $k$ represents the frequency index. The inverse transform is defined by

$$x[n] = \frac{1}{N} \sum_{k=0}^{N-1} X[k] e^{j\frac{2\pi}{N}kn}$$

171

These operations, central to signal analysis, are optimized using FFT when implemented on CUDA-enabled GPUs.

## 2  CUDA Implementation of FFT

CUDA facilitates the decomposition of FFT into multiple stages, each computed by separate threads, exploiting the massive parallelism of GPUs. The Cooley-Tukey algorithm is typically employed:

---

**Input:** Signal data $x[n]$, number of data points $N$
**Output:** Frequency data $X[k]$
cudaMalloc memory for input and output sequences.
**for** *each stage* $m \leftarrow 1$ *to* $\log_2 N$ **do**
    |   launch **kernel** to compute FFT for stage $m$.

cudaFree memory.

---

The kernel leverages shared memory and $O(\log N)$ synchronization steps per stage to efficiently compute the FFT.

# Convolution Operations on GPUs

Convolution is another fundamental operation in signal processing, primarily used for filtering and transforming signals. The discrete convolution of a signal $x[n]$ with a filter $h[n]$ is mathematically expressed as

$$y[n] = \sum_{m=-\infty}^{\infty} x[m]h[n-m]$$

For digital signals of finite duration, it is often constrained to

$$y[n] = \sum_{m=0}^{M-1} x[m]h[n-m]$$

where $M$ is the length of the filter.

## 1  Efficient Convolution through CUDA

The CUDA-based implementation of convolution utilizes shared memory to accelerate data access patterns. Shared memory enables faster reads and writes compared to global memory, significantly reducing the time complexity for large datasets.

Kernel functions are crafted to partition data into tiles, each processed by a block of threads. This approach improves memory coalescing and minimizes redundant data transfers.

Maximizing occupancy through careful resource allocation and overlapping data transfers via CUDA streams ameliorates convolution execution performance further.

# Applications in Signal Processing

## 1  Spectral Analysis

In spectral analysis, FFT is employed to evaluate the frequency spectrum of time-domain signals, standard in audio and electromagnetic spectrum analysis. The accelerated computation permits real-time spectrum adjustments and anomaly detection.

## 2  Filtering and Image Processing

Convolution operations are pivotal in filtering applications, including smoothing, sharpening, and edge detection in images. Efficient GPU-accelerated convolutions facilitate these tasks by rapidly processing high-resolution images or video streams. The improved execution pace allows for practical deployment in scenarios demanding low-latency performance such as real-time image enhancement and object recognition.

## 3  Time-Frequency Analysis

Time-frequency representations, typified by spectrograms, necessitate multiple FFTs applied to signal segments. Through GPU acceleration, complex algorithms like the Short-Time Fourier Transform (STFT) become viable for examining non-stationary signals effectively. This capability underpins applications such as feature extraction in speech and sonar systems.

The versatility of GPUs in executing parallelized signal processing tasks underscores their indispensable role in contemporary computing solutions. By adopting CUDA, signal processing workloads exploit increased computational throughput, thereby achieving enhanced efficiency and scalability.

# Python Code Snippet

Below is a Python code snippet that encompasses the core computational elements of signal processing techniques using CUDA for Fast Fourier Transform (FFT) and convolution on GPUs.

```python
import pycuda.autoinit
import pycuda.driver as cuda
import numpy as np
from pycuda.compiler import SourceModule
import cufft

# Example data
N = 1024
data = np.random.rand(N).astype(np.complex64)

# GPU memory allocation
data_gpu = cuda.mem_alloc(data.nbytes)
cuda.memcpy_htod(data_gpu, data)

# FFT using cuFFT
plan = cufft.Plan1d(N, cufft.CUFFT_C2C, 1)
cufft.cufftExecC2C(plan, data_gpu, data_gpu, cufft.CUFFT_FORWARD)

# Retrieve the result from GPU
result = np.empty_like(data)
cuda.memcpy_dtoh(result, data_gpu)

def convolution_gpu(signal, kernel):
    '''
    Perform convolution using CUDA on the GPU.
    :param signal: Input signal array.
    :param kernel: Convolution kernel array.
    :return: Convolved signal.
    '''
    signal_len = len(signal)
    kernel_len = len(kernel)
    output_len = signal_len + kernel_len - 1

    # Allocate memory
    signal_gpu = cuda.mem_alloc(signal.nbytes)
    kernel_gpu = cuda.mem_alloc(kernel.nbytes)
    result_gpu = cuda.mem_alloc(output_len * signal.dtype.itemsize)

    # Copy to device
    cuda.memcpy_htod(signal_gpu, signal)
    cuda.memcpy_htod(kernel_gpu, kernel)

    # CUDA Kernel
    mod = SourceModule("""
```

```
__global__ void convolution(float *signal, float *kernel, float
↪   *result, int signal_length, int kernel_length) {
    int idx = blockIdx.x * blockDim.x + threadIdx.x;
    if (idx < signal_length + kernel_length - 1) {
        float conv_sum = 0.0;
        for (int k = 0; k < kernel_length; ++k) {
            if (idx - k >= 0 && idx - k < signal_length) {
                conv_sum += signal[idx - k] * kernel[k];
            }
        }
        result[idx] = conv_sum;
    }
}
""")

convolution = mod.get_function("convolution")
block_size = 256
grid_size = (output_len + block_size - 1) // block_size
convolution(signal_gpu, kernel_gpu, result_gpu,
↪   np.int32(signal_len), np.int32(kernel_len),
↪   block=(block_size, 1, 1), grid=(grid_size, 1))

result = np.empty(output_len, dtype=signal.dtype)
cuda.memcpy_dtoh(result, result_gpu)
return result

# Initialize kernel and perform convolution
kernel = np.array([1, 0, -1], dtype=np.float32)
input_signal = np.random.rand(10).astype(np.float32)
convolved_result = convolution_gpu(input_signal, kernel)

print("FFT Result:", result)
print("Convolved Result:", convolved_result)
```

This code defines several key functions necessary for performing Fast Fourier Transform and convolution using CUDA:

- The Fast Fourier Transform (FFT) is computed using the `cufft` library, which efficiently computes FFTs on the GPU using CUDA.

- The `convolution_gpu` function carries out convolution of a signal with a kernel on the GPU, employing a custom CUDA kernel for parallel computation.

- The examples given show how to perform these operations on a simple set of data using CUDA and PyCUDA to harness the power of GPUs.

The final block of code provides examples of computing FFT and convolution results using random data.

175

# Chapter 30

# Molecular Dynamics Simulations

## Introduction to Molecular Dynamics

Molecular dynamics (MD) is a computational simulation method used to study the physical movements of atoms and molecules. By applying Newton's equations of motion, MD provides insights into the dynamical evolution of systems at the atomic scale. The fundamental equation governing particle motion in an MD simulation is:

$$F_i = m_i \frac{d^2 r_i}{dt^2}$$

where $F_i$ is the force experienced by the $i$-th atom, $m_i$ is its mass, and $r_i$ is its position vector.

## Force Calculations and Interaction Potentials

In molecular dynamics, forces between atoms are derived from interaction potentials, commonly described by empirical models. A widely used potential is the Lennard-Jones potential, expressed as:

$$V_{LJ}(r) = 4\epsilon \left[ \left( \frac{\sigma}{r} \right)^{12} - \left( \frac{\sigma}{r} \right)^{6} \right]$$

where $\epsilon$ is the depth of the potential well, $\sigma$ is the finite distance at which the inter-particle potential is zero, and $r$ is the distance between particles. The force $F_{ij}$ between particles $i$ and $j$ is computed as:

$$F_{ij} = -\nabla V_{LJ}(r_{ij})$$

# Equations of Motion

The integration of Newton's equations of motion is crucial for updating particle positions and velocities. The velocity Verlet algorithm is often employed due to its stability and time-reversibility properties:

---

**Input:** Positions $r_i(t)$, velocities $v_i(t)$, forces $F_i(t)$, and timestep $\Delta t$
**Output:** Updated positions $r_i(t + \Delta t)$ and velocities $v_i(t + \Delta t)$
Compute new positions:
$r_i(t + \Delta t) = r_i(t) + v_i(t)\Delta t + \frac{1}{2m_i}F_i(t)(\Delta t)^2$
Update forces: compute $F_i(t + \Delta t)$
Compute new velocities:
$v_i(t + \Delta t) = v_i(t) + \frac{1}{2m_i}[F_i(t) + F_i(t + \Delta t)]\Delta t$

---

# CUDA Implementation of Molecular Dynamics

Massive parallelism of GPUs can be exploited for MD simulations using the CUDA programming model. The computation of inter-particle forces is parallelized by assigning different threads to calculate force contributions for each particle pair.

## 1 Parallel Force Computation

In a CUDA-based MD simulation, the force computation is distributed across threads, making extensive use of shared and global memory to optimize data access patterns. The integration step might involve computing partial forces within each thread block:

$$\text{partial\_force}[thread\_id] = \sum_j F_{ij}$$

Summation across all thread blocks yields the total force on each particle.

## 2 Data Structures and Memory Management

Effective memory management is critical for maximizing computational throughput. Positions, velocities, and forces are allocated in global memory, while shared memory is used for storing local particle lists within thread blocks to minimize data transfer latency.

$$cudaMalloc((void**)d\_positions,$$

$$N \times \texttt{sizeof}(\texttt{float3}))$$

# Temperature Control: The Nosé-Hoover Thermostat

Temperature control in MD is often necessary to maintain desired thermodynamic states. The Nosé-Hoover thermostat method introduces a heat bath with a fictitious mass $Q$, affecting the system dynamics through a coupling term:

$$\frac{d\eta}{dt} = \frac{1}{Q}\left[\sum_i \frac{m_i v_i^2}{k_B T} - 1\right]$$

where $\eta$ is the thermostat variable, $k_B$ is the Boltzmann constant, and $T$ is the target temperature.

# Performance Considerations

Optimization of MD simulations on GPUs involves balancing computational and memory operations. Strategies include employing fast mathematics intrinsic functions, optimizing data alignment for coalesced memory access, and minimizing kernel launch overhead.

The collective capabilities of GPUs, when utilized effectively with CUDA, substantially accelerate the execution of molecular dynamics simulations, allowing the detailed study of atomic and molecular behaviors over time.

# Python Code Snippet

Below is a Python code snippet implementing molecular dynamics force calculations and integration using PyCUDA. This snippet focuses on initial setup without undertaking full simulation.

```python
import pycuda.autoinit
import pycuda.driver as cuda
import numpy as np
from pycuda.compiler import SourceModule

# Number of particles
N = 1024

# Initialize positions, velocities, and forces as numpy arrays
positions = np.random.rand(N, 3).astype(np.float32)
velocities = np.zeros_like(positions)
forces = np.zeros_like(positions)

# CUDA kernel for force computation using Lennard-Jones potential
lj_kernel = SourceModule("""
__global__ void compute_forces(float3 *positions, float3 *forces,
↪ int N, float epsilon, float sigma) {
    int i = threadIdx.x + blockIdx.x * blockDim.x;
    if (i < N) {
        float3 pos_i = positions[i];
        float3 force = make_float3(0.0, 0.0, 0.0);
        for (int j = 0; j < N; ++j) {
            if (i != j) {
                float3 pos_j = positions[j];
                float3 r;
                r.x = pos_i.x - pos_j.x;
                r.y = pos_i.y - pos_j.y;
                r.z = pos_i.z - pos_j.z;
                float dist2 = r.x * r.x + r.y * r.y + r.z * r.z;
                float invDist2 = 1.0f / dist2;
                float invDist6 = invDist2 * invDist2 * invDist2;
                float f = 48.0f * epsilon * invDist6 * (invDist6 -
                ↪ 0.5f) * invDist2;
                force.x += f * r.x;
                force.y += f * r.y;
                force.z += f * r.z;
            }
        }
        forces[i] = force;
    }
}
""")

# Allocate device memory and transfer data to GPU
d_positions = cuda.mem_alloc(positions.nbytes)
```

179

```
d_forces = cuda.mem_alloc(forces.nbytes)

cuda.memcpy_htod(d_positions, positions)
cuda.memcpy_htod(d_forces, forces)

# Kernel function and its execution
compute_forces = lj_kernel.get_function("compute_forces")
block_size = 256
grid_size = (N + block_size - 1) // block_size

# Parameters for Lennard-Jones potential
epsilon = np.float32(0.1)
sigma = np.float32(1.0)

compute_forces(d_positions, d_forces, np.int32(N), epsilon, sigma,
↪    block=(block_size, 1, 1), grid=(grid_size, 1))

# Copy back the forces from device to host
cuda.memcpy_dtoh(forces, d_forces)

# Example of integrating using velocity Verlet algorithm
def velocity_verlet(positions, velocities, forces, dt=0.01):
    """
    Update positions, velocities, and forces for one time step using
    ↪    the Velocity Verlet integration.
    :param positions: array of particle positions
    :param velocities: array of particle velocities
    :param forces: array of particle forces
    :param dt: time step
    """
    positions += velocities * dt + 0.5 * forces * dt**2
    velocities += forces * dt  # Assuming force update happens
    ↪    before this in a full implementation
    return positions, velocities

# Integrating one step
positions, velocities = velocity_verlet(positions, velocities,
↪    forces)

# Free CUDA device memory
d_positions.free()
d_forces.free()
```

This code defines functions and implementations essential for the core of molecular dynamics simulations:

- CUDA kernel for `compute_forces` calculates inter-particle forces using the Lennard-Jones potential.

- GPU memory allocation with `mem_alloc` and data transfer using `memcpy_htod` and `memcpy_dtoh` for efficient computation on the device.

- The `velocity_verlet` function updates particle positions and velocities based on force calculations, illustrating the integration of equations of motion.

- Ensures cleanup of device resources with `free` calls on allocated memory.

This setup prepares the system for executing molecular dynamics simulations while utilizing the massive parallelism provided by GPU resources through CUDA.

# Chapter 31

# Optimizing Sparse Matrix Operations

## Introduction to Sparse Matrices

Sparse matrices are matrices predominantly populated with zero elements, which arise in numerous computational applications ranging from scientific computing to machine learning. Efficient storage and manipulation of sparse matrices can significantly enhance computational performance. This chapter delves into techniques for optimizing operations involving sparse matrices, maintaining a focus on computational efficiency for large-scale applications.

## Sparse Matrix Storage Formats

Sparse matrices leverage compact storage schemes to reduce memory usage and improve access speed. Common formats include Compressed Sparse Row (CSR), Compressed Sparse Column (CSC), and Coordinate (COO) format. These are defined as follows:

### 1 Compressed Sparse Row (CSR)

The CSR format stores a matrix using three arrays: `values`, `col_index`, and `row_ptr`. The non-zero elements are stored in `values`, their corresponding column indices are stored in `col_index`, and `row_ptr` stores the cumulative count of non-zero elements by row:

$$\text{values}[k] = A_{i,j}, \quad \text{col\_index}[k] = j, \quad \text{row\_ptr}[i] \leq k < \text{row\_ptr}[i+1]$$

## 2 Compressed Sparse Column (CSC)

Analogous to CSR, but focused on columns, the CSC format stores a matrix using three arrays: `values`, `row_index`, and `col_ptr`. Here, `row_index` provides the row indices for `values`, while `col_ptr` contains pointers to the start of each column in `values`.

## 3 Coordinate (COO)

In COO format, each non-zero element is explicitly stored with its row and column indices. Three parallel arrays `values`, `row`, and `col` can describe the matrix:

$$\text{values}[k] = A_{row[k],col[k]}$$

# Efficient Sparse Matrix-Vector Multiplication

Sparse Matrix-Vector Multiplication (SpMV) serves as a pivotal operation in many applications like iterative solvers. The CSR format is particularly well-suited for this operation. Efficient SpMV implementations maximize data locality and minimize computational load by leveraging vectorization. The SpMV for a matrix $\mathbf{A}$ with vector $\mathbf{x}$ is described mathematically as:

$$y_i = \sum_{j \in \text{row\_ptr}[i]...\text{row\_ptr}[i+1]-1} \text{values}[j] \cdot x_{\text{col\_index}[j]}$$

Algorithmically, the sparse matrix-vector product can be expressed using the `algorithm2e` package for clarification:

> **Input:** CSR representation (`values`, `col_index`,
> `row_ptr`) of matrix **A** and vector **x**
> **Output:** Result vector **y**
> **for** $i \leftarrow 0$ **to** $n - 1$ **do**
> $\quad y[i] \leftarrow 0$
> $\quad$ **for** $j \leftarrow row\_ptr[i]$ **to** $row\_ptr[i+1] - 1$ **do**
> $\quad\quad y[i] \mathrel{+}= \text{values}[j] \times x[\text{col\_index}[j]]$

# Optimization Strategies for Sparse Operations

Enhancing the performance of sparse matrix operations is achieved through various optimization strategies. These optimizations take advantage of both hardware capabilities and algorithmic improvements.

## 1  Data Preprocessing

Converting sparse matrices to an optimal format tailored to the specific operation can improve performance. This step often includes permuting rows and columns to cluster non-zero elements, enhancing data locality.

## 2  Blocking Techniques

Blocking or tiling strategies partition the matrix into submatrices that fit into processor caches, decreasing memory latency and increasing bandwidth usage efficiency. For sparse matrices, reordering and partitioning help improve data access patterns, effectively utilizing the sparse structure.

## 3  Parallelization

GPU architectures, particularly CUDA-enabled devices, afford substantial parallelism for sparse matrix computations. By assigning matrix elements or blocks to computational threads, processes such as SpMV can be significantly accelerated. CUDA kernels are designed to optimize memory transactions and leverage shared memory for faster access.

# Numerical Stability in Sparse Computations

Sparse matrix computations are susceptible to numerical instability due to the irregular distribution of elements. Strategies for ensuring stability include regularization techniques and the use of robust algorithms for continuation and pivoting. The impact of round-off errors on numerical methods should be minimized, maintaining precise arithmetic across floating-point operations.

The profound complexity of optimizing sparse matrix operations requires in-depth understanding of underlying mathematical principles and computational strategies.

# Python Code Snippet

Below is a Python code snippet that encompasses the core computational elements for optimizing sparse matrix operations using PyCUDA. This includes the setup for efficient Sparse Matrix-Vector Multiplication (SpMV) using the CSR format, represented in the code.

```python
import pycuda.autoinit
import pycuda.driver as cuda
import numpy as np
from pycuda.compiler import SourceModule

# Kernel for Sparse Matrix-Vector Multiplication in CSR format
kernel_code = """
__global__ void spmv_csr(float *values, int *col_index, int
    *row_ptr, float *x, float *y, int num_rows)
{
    int row = blockIdx.x * blockDim.x + threadIdx.x;

    if (row < num_rows) {
        float dot = 0;
        int row_start = row_ptr[row];
        int row_end = row_ptr[row+1];

        for (int j = row_start; j < row_end; j++) {
            dot += values[j] * x[col_index[j]];
        }

        y[row] = dot;
    }
}
```

```
"""

mod = SourceModule(kernel_code)
spmv_csr = mod.get_function("spmv_csr")

# Example sparse matrix in CSR format
values = np.array([1, 4, 2, 6, 9, 3, 7, 1, 5], dtype=np.float32)
col_index = np.array([0, 1, 0, 2, 2, 3, 1, 3, 4], dtype=np.int32)
row_ptr = np.array([0, 2, 3, 4, 7, 9], dtype=np.int32)
x = np.array([1, 2, 3, 4, 5], dtype=np.float32)

# Prepare result vector
num_rows = len(row_ptr) - 1
y = np.zeros(num_rows, dtype=np.float32)

# Transfer data to GPU
values_gpu = cuda.mem_alloc(values.nbytes)
col_index_gpu = cuda.mem_alloc(col_index.nbytes)
row_ptr_gpu = cuda.mem_alloc(row_ptr.nbytes)
x_gpu = cuda.mem_alloc(x.nbytes)
y_gpu = cuda.mem_alloc(y.nbytes)

cuda.memcpy_htod(values_gpu, values)
cuda.memcpy_htod(col_index_gpu, col_index)
cuda.memcpy_htod(row_ptr_gpu, row_ptr)
cuda.memcpy_htod(x_gpu, x)

# Launch kernel
block_size = 256
grid_size = (num_rows + block_size - 1) // block_size

spmv_csr(values_gpu, col_index_gpu, row_ptr_gpu, x_gpu, y_gpu,
↪  np.int32(num_rows), block=(block_size, 1, 1), grid=(grid_size,
↪  1))

# Copy result from GPU to host
cuda.memcpy_dtoh(y, y_gpu)

print("Resultant vector y after SpMV:", y)
```

This code defines several key components necessary for efficient execution of Sparse Matrix-Vector Multiplication using the CSR storage format on CUDA-enabled hardware:

- `spmv_csr` kernel computes the dot product for each row of the sparse matrix using PyCUDA for efficient parallel execution.

- Memory allocations for the sparse matrix and vector are handled through `cuda.mem_alloc` to ensure data resides on the GPU for fast access.

- Transfers between host and device are conducted with `cuda.memcpy_htod` and `cuda.memcpy_dtoh`, ensuring data integrity across operations.

- The block size and grid size are dynamically set to accommodate the matrix dimensions, allowing for scalable execution.

The final block of code demonstrates the execution of the sparse matrix-vector multiplication, showcasing CUDA's capability to handle large-scale computations effectively.

# Chapter 32

# Implementing Fractal Generation Algorithms

## Mathematical Foundations of Fractals

Fractals are intricate mathematical sets exhibiting self-similar patterns at every scale. Complex dynamics and iterative functions characterize fractals, often yielding visually fascinating structures. The Mandelbrot and Julia sets are prominent examples, defined within the complex plane.

## 1  Mandelbrot Set

Given a complex function $f_c(z) = z^2 + c$, the Mandelbrot set consists of all complex numbers $c$ for which the sequence $z_{n+1} = f_c(z_n)$ remains bounded as $n \to \infty$. Mathematically, the set can be expressed as:

$$M = \{c \in \mathbb{C} \mid \limsup_{n \to \infty} |z_n| < \infty, \; z_0 = 0\}$$

The boundary of $M$ is a fractal that emerges through the application of iterative algorithms, evaluating the stability of each $c$ in the complex plane.

## 2  Julia Set

For a given complex constant $c$, the Julia set $J(c)$ is the set of initial points $z_0$ where the sequence defined by:

$$z_{n+1} = z_n^2 + c$$

remains bounded. It is the locus of points whose trajectories do not escape to infinity. The mathematical formulation is:

$$J(c) = \{z_0 \in \mathbb{C} \mid \limsup_{n \to \infty} |z_n| < \infty\}$$

Each $c$ produces a uniquely structured fractal, revealing the recursive complexity inherent to Julia sets.

# Parallel Computing of Fractals on GPUs

Fractal generation benefits significantly from high parallelism, a feature efficiently realizable on Graphics Processing Units (GPUs). Utilizing CUDA, the generation of both Mandelbrot and Julia sets can be accelerated by evaluating fractal iterations across the complex plane concurrently.

## 1 CUDA Implementation of Mandelbrot Set

The GPU facilitates parallel computation of the escape time algorithm, estimating the bounded nature directly suited for fractal calculation. The algorithm, defined below, implements parallel execution across complex points:

---

**Input:** Complex plane parameters: `min_x`, `max_x`, `min_y`, `max_y`, `max_iterations`
**Output:** Mandelbrot image **I**
**for** *each pixel* $(x, y)$ *in image* **do**
  $c \leftarrow \text{complex}(x, y)$
  $z \leftarrow 0$
  `iteration` $\leftarrow 0$
  **while** $|z| \leq 2$ *and* `iteration` < `max_iterations` **do**
    $z \leftarrow z^2 + c$
    `iteration` += 1
  $\mathbf{I}[x, y] \leftarrow$ `iteration`

---

The kernel dispatches computations for each fractal point, using GPU threads to concurrently evaluate escape conditions across a substantial grid.

## 2 CUDA Implementation of Julia Set

A similar kernel applies to the Julia set generation, albeit iterating over initial values $z_0$, with each calculation thread determining if an initial point belongs to a given Julia set:

$$\text{Given } c,$$
$$\text{For each } z_0 \in \text{complex plane}:$$
$$z_{n+1} = z_n^2 + c,$$

---

**Input:** Complex constant c, complex plane parameters,
        `max_iterations`
**Output:** Julia set image **J**
**for** *each pixel* $(x, y)$ *in image* **do**
$\quad$ $z \leftarrow \text{complex}(x, y)$
$\quad$ `iteration` $\leftarrow 0$
$\quad$ **while** $|z| \leq 2$ *and* `iteration` $<$ `max_iterations` **do**
$\quad\quad$ $z \leftarrow z^2 + c$
$\quad\quad$ `iteration` $+= 1$
$\quad$ $\mathbf{J}[x, y] \leftarrow$ `iteration`

---

Each thread evaluates a point's stability and accumulates results to form the visual representation of $J(c)$.

# Optimization Strategies

The precise fractal rendering necessitates optimized computation paths, leveraging CUDA's provisions for high-performance computing.

## 1 Memory Coalescing and Shared Memory

Fractal computation, particularly within CUDA, can benefit from memory coalescing. By aligning memory accesses within CUDA warps, the execution efficiency is elevated. Shared memory usage in CUDA enhances data reuse among threads, lowering latency for image reconstruction tasks.

## 2 Adaptive Rendering Techniques

Adaptive algorithms refine fractal depiction by dynamically adjusting computational detail, using recursion and iterative refinement methods. Crucially, focusing resources on areas of higher interest and omitting irrelevant regions augments performance.

## 3 Load Balancing

Dynamic workload balancing across the CUDA architecture ensures full utilization of GPU cores. Implementing load balancing significantly improves performance, especially in regions of fractal boundary where computation intensity varies.

Crucial to these optimizations is an acute understanding of the fractal's mathematical properties blended with computational resources, enabling efficient and expressive fractal algorithm implementations.

# Python Code Snippet

Below is a Python code snippet that demonstrates the CUDA-based implementation of fractal generation algorithms for the Mandelbrot and Julia sets, leveraging the capabilities of PyCUDA for parallel computation:

```python
import numpy as np
import pycuda.autoinit
import pycuda.driver as cuda
from pycuda.compiler import SourceModule
import matplotlib.pyplot as plt

# CUDA kernel code for computing the Mandelbrot set
mandelbrot_kernel = """
__global__ void mandelbrot(float *output, float min_x, float max_x,
↪  float min_y,
                           float max_y, int max_iterations, int
                               ↪  width, int height) {
    int px = blockIdx.x * blockDim.x + threadIdx.x;
    int py = blockIdx.y * blockDim.y + threadIdx.y;

    if (px >= width || py >= height) return;

    float x0 = min_x + px * (max_x - min_x) / width;
    float y0 = min_y + py * (max_y - min_y) / height;
    float x = 0.0;
    float y = 0.0;
    int iteration = 0;

    while (x*x + y*y <= 4.0 && iteration < max_iterations) {
        float temp = x*x - y*y + x0;
```

```
        y = 2.0*x*y + y0;
        x = temp;
        iteration++;
    }

    output[py * width + px] = iteration;
}
"""

# CUDA kernel code for computing the Julia set
julia_kernel = """
__global__ void julia(float *output, float c_re, float c_im, float
↪  min_x, float max_x,
                      float min_y, float max_y, int max_iterations,
                      ↪  int width, int height) {
    int px = blockIdx.x * blockDim.x + threadIdx.x;
    int py = blockIdx.y * blockDim.y + threadIdx.y;

    if (px >= width || py >= height) return;

    float x = min_x + px * (max_x - min_x) / width;
    float y = min_y + py * (max_y - min_y) / height;
    int iteration = 0;

    while (x*x + y*y <= 4.0 && iteration < max_iterations) {
        float temp = x*x - y*y + c_re;
        y = 2.0*x*y + c_im;
        x = temp;
        iteration++;
    }

    output[py * width + px] = iteration;
}
"""


# Parameters for both fractals
width, height = 800, 800
max_iterations = 256

# Allocate space on the device
output_mandelbrot = cuda.mem_alloc(width * height *
↪  np.float32().itemsize)
output_julia = cuda.mem_alloc(width * height *
↪  np.float32().itemsize)

# Compile the kernel code
mandelbrot_mod = SourceModule(mandelbrot_kernel)
julia_mod = SourceModule(julia_kernel)

# Get the functions from the compiled module
mandelbrot_function = mandelbrot_mod.get_function("mandelbrot")
julia_function = julia_mod.get_function("julia")
```

```
# Set up grid and block dimensions
block = (16, 16, 1)
grid = (width // block[0] + 1, height // block[1] + 1)

# Parameters for Mandelbrot set
min_x, max_x = -2.0, 1.0
min_y, max_y = -1.5, 1.5

# Launch Mandelbrot kernel
mandelbrot_function(output_mandelbrot, np.float32(min_x),
↪   np.float32(max_x),
                    np.float32(min_y), np.float32(max_y),
                    ↪   np.int32(max_iterations),
                    np.int32(width), np.int32(height), block=block,
                    ↪   grid=grid)

# Parameters for a sample Julia set
c_re, c_im = -0.7, 0.27015

# Launch Julia kernel
julia_function(output_julia, np.float32(c_re), np.float32(c_im),
↪   np.float32(min_x),
               np.float32(max_x), np.float32(min_y),
               ↪   np.float32(max_y),
               np.int32(max_iterations), np.int32(width),
               ↪   np.int32(height),
               block=block, grid=grid)

# Retrieve and visualize the result
result_mandelbrot = np.empty((height, width), dtype=np.float32)
result_julia = np.empty((height, width), dtype=np.float32)

cuda.memcpy_dtoh(result_mandelbrot, output_mandelbrot)
cuda.memcpy_dtoh(result_julia, output_julia)

# Plot to visualize
plt.figure(figsize=(12, 6))
plt.subplot(1, 2, 1)
plt.title("Mandelbrot Set")
plt.imshow(result_mandelbrot, extent=(min_x, max_x, min_y, max_y),
↪   cmap="hot")

plt.subplot(1, 2, 2)
plt.title("Julia Set")
plt.imshow(result_julia, extent=(min_x, max_x, min_y, max_y),
↪   cmap="hot")

plt.show()
```

This code implements the fractal generation of the Mandelbrot and Julia sets using PyCUDA to leverage GPU parallelism:

- The Mandelbrot and Julia sets are computed by kernels `mandelbrot` and `julia`, which run on CUDA-enabled devices.

- `pycuda.autoinit` is used to initialize a CUDA context.

- Functions `mandelbrot_function` and `julia_function` manage the execution of CUDA kernels with defined parameters.

- The kernels perform parallel computations for each pixel in the image, checking escape conditions and recording iteration counts.

- Visualization is performed using `matplotlib.pyplot`, which generates a graphical display of the computed fractals.

- The use of efficiently aligned data and grid/block dimensions ensures optimized performance on compatible devices.

This example serves as a reference for applying PyCUDA to implement mathematical fractals in a parallel computing framework.

# Chapter 33

# Physics Simulations with Particle Systems

## Mathematical Formulation of Particle Systems

Particle systems serve as a crucial computational model in simulating diverse physical phenomena, encompassing fluid dynamics, astrophysical processes, and granular flows. The particles, as fundamental entities, enable the approximation of continuous fields through discrete representations.

## 1 Equations of Motion

The governing dynamics of particles in a system are described by Newton's second law. For a particle $i$, the equation of motion is given by:

$$m_i \frac{d^2 \mathbf{r}_i}{dt^2} = \mathbf{F}_i$$

where $m_i$ is the mass, $\mathbf{r}_i$ is the position vector, and $\mathbf{F}_i$ represents the total force acting on the particle. The force $\mathbf{F}_i$ can be decomposed into external and inter-particle forces:

$$\mathbf{F}_i = \sum_{j \neq i} \mathbf{F}_{ij} + \mathbf{F}_{\text{ext},i}$$

In the context of gravitational simulations or point-based approximations, the inter-particle forces $\mathbf{F}_{ij}$ derive typically from potentials $V(r_{ij})$, where $r_{ij} = |\mathbf{r}_i - \mathbf{r}_j|$.

## 2 Time Integration Schemes

Efficient and accurate simulation of particle systems hinges on robust integration schemes. The Velocity Verlet algorithm serves widely in molecular dynamics due to its favorable balance of simplicity, stability, and time-reversibility. Its integration is articulated as:

$$\mathbf{r}_i(t + \Delta t) = \mathbf{r}_i(t) + \mathbf{v}_i(t)\Delta t + \frac{1}{2}\mathbf{a}_i(t)(\Delta t)^2,$$

$$\mathbf{v}_i(t + \Delta t) = \mathbf{v}_i(t) + \frac{1}{2}\left(\mathbf{a}_i(t) + \mathbf{a}_i(t + \Delta t)\right)\Delta t,$$

where $\mathbf{a}_i(t) = \mathbf{F}_i(t)/m_i$ represents the acceleration.

# GPU-based Simulation Techniques

The advent of GPU computing radically advances the simulation of particle systems, primarily owing to the GPU's substantial parallelism which aligns well with the independent updates of particles. CUDA provides a robust framework for implementing such high-performance simulations.

## 1 Parallel Computation of Interactions

A canonical challenge in simulating particle systems is calculating pairwise interactions efficiently. The naive $\mathcal{O}(N^2)$ complexity can become prohibitive. Employing spatial partitioning strategies, such as Verlet lists or cell lists, ameliorates this to $\mathcal{O}(N)$. CUDA kernels effectively parallelize this computational workload.

**Input:** Particle data: positions $\mathbf{r}[i]$, velocities $\mathbf{v}[i]$, forces
  $\mathbf{F}[i]$
**Output:** Updated positions and velocities
compute_forces(positions $\mathbf{r}[i]$)
**for** *each particle $i$* **do**
  $\mathbf{v}[i] \mathrel{+}= \mathbf{F}[i]/m_i \cdot \Delta t$
  $\mathbf{r}[i] \mathrel{+}= \mathbf{v}[i] \cdot \Delta t$
  update forces $\mathbf{F}[i]$

The compute_forces function invokes the CUDA kernel, distributing inter-particle force computation across threads, leveraging shared memory to optimize data reuse.

## 2  Handling Collision and Boundary Conditions

Handling particle collisions and boundary constraints necessitates a tailored approach in CUDA. Implementing boundary handling leverages conditional logic within kernels:

$$\mathbf{v}_i = -\mathbf{v}_i, \qquad \text{if } \mathbf{r}_i \text{ crosses boundary}$$
$$\text{reset } \mathbf{r}_i, \qquad \text{to enforce periodic boundaries.}$$

Collisions are often resolved using impulse-based methods, maintaining computational efficiency by bounding calculations within GPU memory constraints.

## 3  Data Structures and Memory Management

CUDA's parallel architecture benefits from optimized data structures, especially efficiency gained through coalesced global memory access patterns. Structure of Arrays (SoA) format is favorable over Array of Structures (AoS):

- float3 arrays for position, velocity, and force vectors,

- Unified memory to simplify memory management, reducing transfer overhead between host and device.

197

# Optimizations for Performance Enhancement

To harness the potent computational abilities of GPUs, several optimization strategies are pertinent:

## 1 Computational Load Balancing

Balancing the computational load across GPU threads mitigates divergence and enhances overall throughput. This involves dynamically adjusting thread assignments based on particle concentration, prioritizing dense regions.

## 2 Leveraging Shared and Constant Memory

Utilizing shared memory within CUDA blocks can mitigate costly global memory accesses. For constant parameters shared across blocks, constant memory provides rapid data access, reducing overhead.

## 3 Optimization using Warp-Level Primitives

Employing warp-level primitives enhances performance by minimizing warp divergence issues. Operations like `__shfl_sync` allow efficient cross-lane data exchanges within GPU warps, particularly useful for reductions in force calculations.

The application of these advanced techniques accelerates particle simulations, significantly broadening the scale and complexity of physical systems computationally tractable using contemporary GPU technology.

# Python Code Snippet

Below is a Python code snippet that demonstrates the core computational elements for simulating particle systems using PyCUDA. This includes the setup for particle interaction computation, CUDA kernel implementation, and updating particles' positions and velocities.

```
import pycuda.autoinit
import pycuda.driver as cuda
```

```python
from pycuda.compiler import SourceModule
import numpy as np

# Simulation parameters
num_particles = 1024
timesteps = 100
dt = 0.01

# Initialize particle data
masses = np.ones(num_particles, dtype=np.float32)
positions = np.random.rand(num_particles, 3).astype(np.float32)
velocities = np.zeros_like(positions, dtype=np.float32)
forces = np.zeros_like(positions, dtype=np.float32)

# CUDA kernel for particle force computation
kernel_code = """
__global__ void compute_forces(float *positions, float *forces, int
↪   num_particles) {
    int idx = blockIdx.x * blockDim.x + threadIdx.x;
    if (idx >= num_particles) return;

    float fx = 0.0, fy = 0.0, fz = 0.0;
    float3 pos_i = make_float3(positions[3*idx], positions[3*idx+1],
    ↪   positions[3*idx+2]);

    for (int j = 0; j < num_particles; ++j) {
        if (j == idx) continue;
        float3 pos_j = make_float3(positions[3*j], positions[3*j+1],
        ↪   positions[3*j+2]);
        float3 diff = make_float3(pos_j.x - pos_i.x, pos_j.y -
        ↪   pos_i.y, pos_j.z - pos_i.z);
        float dist = sqrt(diff.x * diff.x + diff.y * diff.y + diff.z
        ↪   * diff.z);
        float force_magnitude = 1.0 / (dist * dist + 1e-15);
        fx += force_magnitude * diff.x;
        fy += force_magnitude * diff.y;
        fz += force_magnitude * diff.z;
    }

    forces[3*idx] = fx;
    forces[3*idx+1] = fy;
    forces[3*idx+2] = fz;
}

__global__ void update_positions(float *positions, float
↪   *velocities, float *forces, float *masses, float dt, int
↪   num_particles) {
    int idx = blockIdx.x * blockDim.x + threadIdx.x;
    if (idx >= num_particles) return;

    float inv_mass = 1.0 / masses[idx];
    velocities[3*idx] += forces[3*idx] * inv_mass * dt;
    velocities[3*idx+1] += forces[3*idx+1] * inv_mass * dt;
```

```
    velocities[3*idx+2] += forces[3*idx+2] * inv_mass * dt;

    positions[3*idx] += velocities[3*idx] * dt;
    positions[3*idx+1] += velocities[3*idx+1] * dt;
    positions[3*idx+2] += velocities[3*idx+2] * dt;
}
"""

module = SourceModule(kernel_code)
compute_forces = module.get_function("compute_forces")
update_positions = module.get_function("update_positions")

# Allocate memory on the device
d_positions = cuda.mem_alloc(positions.nbytes)
d_velocities = cuda.mem_alloc(velocities.nbytes)
d_forces = cuda.mem_alloc(forces.nbytes)
d_masses = cuda.mem_alloc(masses.nbytes)

# Copy data to device
cuda.memcpy_htod(d_positions, positions)
cuda.memcpy_htod(d_velocities, velocities)
cuda.memcpy_htod(d_forces, forces)
cuda.memcpy_htod(d_masses, masses)

# Run simulation
block_size = 256
grid_size = (num_particles + block_size - 1) // block_size

for _ in range(timesteps):
    compute_forces(d_positions, d_forces, np.int32(num_particles),
    ↪   block=(block_size, 1, 1), grid=(grid_size, 1))
    update_positions(d_positions, d_velocities, d_forces, d_masses,
    ↪   np.float32(dt), np.int32(num_particles), block=(block_size,
    ↪   1, 1), grid=(grid_size, 1))

# Copy results back to host
cuda.memcpy_dtoh(positions, d_positions)
cuda.memcpy_dtoh(velocities, d_velocities)

print("Final positions:", positions)
print("Final velocities:", velocities)
```

This code implements several key functions necessary for simulating particle systems:

- **compute_forces**: A CUDA kernel that calculates inter-particle forces provided an array of particle positions.

- **update_positions**: A CUDA kernel that updates particle positions and velocities based on calculated forces.

- Initialization of particle data includes setting random initial positions and zero initial velocities.

- The simulation loop invokes these kernels over specified timesteps to simulate particle dynamics iteratively.

The Python snippet illustrates setting up GPU memory, defining kernels, transferring data to and from the GPU, and executing particle interaction calculations effectively.

# Chapter 34

# Bioinformatics Applications

## Genome Sequencing Acceleration

Genome sequencing is a critical task in bioinformatics, often involving the alignment of short DNA fragments to a reference genome. CUDA enables parallel processing, significantly enhancing the throughput of these computationally intensive tasks.

## 1 Sequence Alignment Algorithms

The Smith-Waterman algorithm is widely used for local sequence alignment. Given sequences $A$ and $B$ of lengths $m$ and $n$ respectively, the dynamic programming matrix $H$ is defined by the recurrence relation:

$$
H(i, j) = \max \begin{cases} 0, \\ H(i-1, j-1) + s(A_i, B_j), \\ H(i-1, j) - d, \\ H(i, j-1) - d \end{cases}
$$

where $s(A_i, B_j)$ denotes the substitution score and $d$ is a linear gap penalty. CUDA can parallelize this computation by processing multiple matrix cells concurrently.

## 2  Implementing Parallel Smith-Waterman

In the CUDA implementation, each thread computes a cell of the matrix $H$. The data dependencies form a wavefront pattern, making it suitable for parallelism. Shared memory is utilized for sub-matrices to minimize global memory access overhead.

---

**Input:** DNA sequences $A$, $B$, substitution matrix $S$, gap
      penalty $d$
**Output:** Alignment score $H(m, n)$
initialize kernel(substitution matrix $S$, $d$)
for *each submatrix tile* do
    load tile into shared memory
    compute $H(i, j)$ using CUDA threads
    update global matrix

---

# Protein Folding Simulations

Protein folding prediction is a complex problem involving the determination of a protein's three-dimensional structure from its amino acid sequence. Accelerating these computations is crucial for understanding biological processes.

## 1  Energy Minimization Models

The energy state of a protein configuration is often modeled by the Lennard-Jones potential:

$$E(r_{ij}) = 4\epsilon \left[ \left( \frac{\sigma}{r_{ij}} \right)^{12} - \left( \frac{\sigma}{r_{ij}} \right)^6 \right]$$

where $\epsilon$ is the depth of the potential well, $\sigma$ is the finite distance at which the inter-particle potential is zero, and $r_{ij}$ is the distance between particles $i$ and $j$.

## 2  Parallel Folding Using CUDA

CUDA can accelerate protein folding by parallelizing the computation of pairwise forces and energy. The CUDA kernels calculate the forces acting on each atom concurrently, updating their positions according to the steepest descent method:

$$\mathbf{F}_{ij} = -\nabla E(r_{ij}),$$

$$\mathbf{x}_i(t + \Delta t) = \mathbf{x}_i(t) + \Delta t \left( \frac{\mathbf{F}_i(t)}{m_i} \right)$$

---

**Input:** Initial atomic positions **x**, energy model
   parameters $\epsilon, \sigma$
**Output:** Folded protein structure
initialize positions and forces
**while** *energy not minimized* **do**
|   invoke CUDA kernel for pairwise force
|   computation
|   update atomic positions in parallel
|_  recompute energy

---

# CUDA Memory Management

Efficient memory management is crucial to leveraging CUDA's parallelism in bioinformatics applications. Ensuring coalesced memory access patterns and utilizing shared memory can significantly optimize performance.

## 1   Memory Coalescing

In genome sequencing and protein folding, arranging data in a Structure of Arrays (SoA) format rather than an Array of Structures (AoS) can lead to improved memory coalescence. For instance, storing positions and forces in separate contiguous arrays allows multiple threads to access data efficiently.

## 2   Shared Memory Utilization

Shared memory provides a high-speed buffer for CUDA threads within the same block. In sequence alignment, portions of the dynamic programming matrix can be loaded into shared memory, decreasing global memory accesses:

$$H_{\text{shared}}[i, j] = \text{load}(H[i, j])$$

Managing memory efficiently in these computational workflows is essential for exploiting the complete potential of GPU acceleration in bioinformatics tasks.

# Python Code Snippet

Below is a Python code snippet that encompasses the core computational elements of bioinformatics applications such as sequence alignment and protein folding using the PyCUDA library for GPU acceleration.

```python
import numpy as np
import pycuda.autoinit
import pycuda.driver as cuda
from pycuda.compiler import SourceModule

# CUDA kernel for Smith-Waterman sequence alignment algorithm
smith_waterman_kernel = """
__global__ void smith_waterman(int *H, const char *A, const char *B,
    int *S, int m, int n, int d) {
    int i = blockIdx.y * blockDim.y + threadIdx.y;
    int j = blockIdx.x * blockDim.x + threadIdx.x;

    if (i >= m || j >= n) return;

    int match = (A[i - 1] == B[j - 1]) ? S[i * n + j] : -S[i * n +
        j];
    int score = 0;
    __shared__ int H_shared[BLOCK_SIZE][BLOCK_SIZE];

    if (i > 0 && j > 0) {
        score = max(0, max(H[(i-1) * n + j-1] + match,
                        H[(i-1) * n + j] - d,
                        H[i * n + j-1] - d));
    }

    H_shared[threadIdx.y][threadIdx.x] = score;
    __syncthreads();
    H[i * n + j] = score;
}

#define BLOCK_SIZE 16
"""

# Function to initialize and invoke the Smith-Waterman kernel
def smith_waterman_cuda(seqA, seqB, substitution_matrix,
    gap_penalty):
    m, n = len(seqA) + 1, len(seqB) + 1
```

```
# Allocate memory for sequences and scoring matrix
A = np.array(list(map(ord, seqA)), dtype=np.int32)
B = np.array(list(map(ord, seqB)), dtype=np.int32)
H = np.zeros((m, n), dtype=np.int32)
S = np.array(substitution_matrix, dtype=np.int32)

# Allocate GPU memory
A_gpu = cuda.mem_alloc(A.nbytes)
B_gpu = cuda.mem_alloc(B.nbytes)
H_gpu = cuda.mem_alloc(H.nbytes)
S_gpu = cuda.mem_alloc(S.nbytes)

# Copy to GPU memory
cuda.memcpy_htod(A_gpu, A)
cuda.memcpy_htod(B_gpu, B)
cuda.memcpy_htod(H_gpu, H)
cuda.memcpy_htod(S_gpu, S)

# Compile CUDA kernel
mod = SourceModule(smith_waterman_kernel)
func = mod.get_function("smith_waterman")

# Launch kernel
block = (16, 16, 1)
grid = (int(np.ceil(n / block[0])), int(np.ceil(m / block[1])),
 ↪ 1)
func(H_gpu, A_gpu, B_gpu, S_gpu, np.int32(m), np.int32(n),
 ↪ np.int32(gap_penalty), block=block, grid=grid)

# Copy result back to host
cuda.memcpy_dtoh(H, H_gpu)
return H

# Example usage for sequence alignment
seqA = "ACGTTGAC"
seqB = "ACGTCGAC"
substitution_matrix = np.identity(256)  # Simplified example
 ↪ substitution matrix
gap_penalty = 2

alignment_score_matrix = smith_waterman_cuda(seqA, seqB,
 ↪ substitution_matrix, gap_penalty)
print("Alignment Score Matrix:", alignment_score_matrix)
```

---

This code defines several key functions necessary for the implementation of bioinformatics applications using CUDA:

- The `smith_waterman_kernel` CUDA function implements the core logic for computing the Smith-Waterman alignment matrix by utilizing parallel threads to calculate scores for sequence alignment efficiently.

- The `smith_waterman_cuda` function initializes required data structures, invokes the CUDA kernel, and manages data transfer between host and device memory.

- The example usage demonstrates aligning two DNA sequences using the Smith-Waterman algorithm, highlighting CUDA's capability to speed up computation-intensive tasks in bioinformatics.

The final block of code provides an example of computing the alignment score matrix for two sequences using a simplified substitution matrix and a defined gap penalty.

# Chapter 35

# Implementing Game Physics

## Collision Detection and Response

The implementation of collision detection is vital in the realm of game physics to ensure realistic interactions between objects. The problem can be approached using bounding volumes such as axis-aligned bounding boxes (AABB) or bounding spheres. Given objects $i$ and $j$, the condition for intersection using AABB can be expressed as:

$$\text{AABB}(i) \cap \text{AABB}(j) \neq \emptyset$$
$$\iff (x_i^{\min} < x_j^{\max} \wedge x_i^{\max} > x_j^{\min})$$
$$\wedge (y_i^{\min} < y_j^{\max} \wedge y_i^{\max} > y_j^{\min})$$
$$\wedge (z_i^{\min} < z_j^{\max} \wedge z_i^{\max} > z_j^{\min})$$

Upon detection of a collision, the response can be modeled by the impulse-based approach. The impulse $\mathbf{J}$ applied upon collision depends on the relative velocity $\mathbf{v}_{ij}$ and the masses $m_i$ and $m_j$ of the objects:

$$\mathbf{J} = \frac{-(1+e)(\mathbf{v}_{ij} \cdot \mathbf{n})}{\frac{1}{m_i} + \frac{1}{m_j}}$$

where $e$ denotes the coefficient of restitution, and $\mathbf{n}$ is the collision normal.

# Rigid Body Dynamics

The simulation of rigid body dynamics is governed by Newton-Euler equations. The linear motion is described by:

$$m\frac{d\mathbf{v}}{dt} = \mathbf{F}$$

where $m$ is the mass, $\mathbf{v}$ is velocity, and $\mathbf{F}$ is the sum of forces acting on the body. For rotational dynamics, Euler's equation is:

$$\mathbf{I}\frac{d\boldsymbol{\omega}}{dt} = \mathbf{T} - \boldsymbol{\omega} \times (\mathbf{I}\boldsymbol{\omega})$$

with $\mathbf{I}$ representing the inertia tensor, $\boldsymbol{\omega}$ the angular velocity, and $\mathbf{T}$ the applied torque.

---

**Input:** Initial position $\mathbf{x}_0$, velocity $\mathbf{v}_0$, angular velocity $\boldsymbol{\omega}_0$, timestep $\Delta t$
**Output:** Updated position $\mathbf{x}_t$ and orientation at time $t$
for *each timestep* $[0, T]$ do

> apply forces and torque
> integrate linear motion: $\mathbf{v} \leftarrow \mathbf{v} + \frac{\mathbf{F}}{m}\Delta t$,
> $\mathbf{x} \leftarrow \mathbf{x} + \mathbf{v}\Delta t$
> integrate rotational motion:
> $\boldsymbol{\omega} \leftarrow \boldsymbol{\omega} + \mathbf{I}^{-1} \cdot (\mathbf{T} - \boldsymbol{\omega} \times (\mathbf{I}\boldsymbol{\omega}))\Delta t$; update
> orientation

---

# Particle Systems

Particle systems are employed to simulate phenomena such as fire, smoke, or explosions. The behavior of an individual particle is dictated by forces applied, such as gravity and drag.

The governing equations of motion for each particle are:

$$\mathbf{F}_{\text{gravity}} = m \cdot \mathbf{g}$$
$$\mathbf{F}_{\text{drag}} = -c_d \cdot \mathbf{v}$$

where $\mathbf{g}$ is the gravitational acceleration and $c_d$ the drag coefficient. The motion equation is:

$$m\frac{d\mathbf{v}}{dt} = \mathbf{F}_{\text{gravity}} + \mathbf{F}_{\text{drag}}$$

Utilizing CUDA, each thread can simulate the dynamics of an independent particle, allowing for scalable and efficient simulation of large particle systems.

# Using CUDA for Real-time Physics

In leveraging the CUDA architecture, game physics simulations can be parallelized, thus reducing computational time significantly. This is particularly beneficial for collision detection and response, rigid body dynamics, and particle system simulations where concurrent compute threads can perform operations like broad-phase collision checks and force accumulations in parallel.

By allocating one CUDA thread per AABB pair or rigid body, and utilizing shared memory to store intermediate results, simulation of game physics can achieve high throughput and real-time performance required in gaming applications.

# Python Code Snippet

Below is a Python code snippet that encompasses the core computational elements of collision detection and response, rigid body dynamics simulation, and particle system dynamics using PyCUDA.

```
import pycuda.autoinit
import pycuda.driver as cuda
import numpy as np
from pycuda.compiler import SourceModule

# PyCUDA kernel for collision detection using AABB
collision_detection_kernel = """
__global__ void detect_collision(float *x_min, float *x_max, float
↪  *y_min, float *y_max, float *z_min, float *z_max, int
↪  *collision_flags, int num_objects) {
    int i = blockIdx.x * blockDim.x + threadIdx.x;
    if (i < num_objects) {
        for (int j = i + 1; j < num_objects; j++) {
            if (x_min[i] < x_max[j] && x_max[i] > x_min[j] &&
                y_min[i] < y_max[j] && y_max[i] > y_min[j] &&
                z_min[i] < z_max[j] && z_max[i] > z_min[j]) {
                collision_flags[i * num_objects + j] = 1;
                collision_flags[j * num_objects + i] = 1;
            }
        }
    }
}
```

```
"""

# PyCUDA kernel for particle system simulation
particle_system_kernel = """
__global__ void update_particle_system(float *pos, float *vel, float
↪ *masses, float *forces, float dt, int num_particles) {
    int idx = threadIdx.x + blockDim.x * blockIdx.x;
    if (idx < num_particles) {
        float mass = masses[idx];

        // Update velocity based on forces
        vel[idx * 3 + 0] += forces[idx * 3 + 0] / mass * dt;
        vel[idx * 3 + 1] += forces[idx * 3 + 1] / mass * dt;
        vel[idx * 3 + 2] += forces[idx * 3 + 2] / mass * dt;

        // Update position based on velocity
        pos[idx * 3 + 0] += vel[idx * 3 + 0] * dt;
        pos[idx * 3 + 1] += vel[idx * 3 + 1] * dt;
        pos[idx * 3 + 2] += vel[idx * 3 + 2] * dt;
    }
}
"""


def simulate_collision_detection(num_objects, h_x_min, h_x_max,
↪ h_y_min, h_y_max, h_z_min, h_z_max):
    # Allocate memory on GPU
    d_x_min = cuda.mem_alloc(h_x_min.nbytes)
    d_x_max = cuda.mem_alloc(h_x_max.nbytes)
    d_y_min = cuda.mem_alloc(h_y_min.nbytes)
    d_y_max = cuda.mem_alloc(h_y_max.nbytes)
    d_z_min = cuda.mem_alloc(h_z_min.nbytes)
    d_z_max = cuda.mem_alloc(h_z_max.nbytes)
    d_collision_flags = cuda.mem_alloc(num_objects * num_objects *
    ↪ np.int32().nbytes)

    # Copy data from host to device
    cuda.memcpy_htod(d_x_min, h_x_min)
    cuda.memcpy_htod(d_x_max, h_x_max)
    cuda.memcpy_htod(d_y_min, h_y_min)
    cuda.memcpy_htod(d_y_max, h_y_max)
    cuda.memcpy_htod(d_z_min, h_z_min)
    cuda.memcpy_htod(d_z_max, h_z_max)

    # Initialize collision flags to zero on the host
    h_collision_flags = np.zeros((num_objects, num_objects),
    ↪ dtype=np.int32)

    # Copy collision flags to device
    cuda.memcpy_htod(d_collision_flags, h_collision_flags)

    # Launch kernel
    mod = SourceModule(collision_detection_kernel)
    detect_collision = mod.get_function("detect_collision")
```

```
        detect_collision(d_x_min, d_x_max, d_y_min, d_y_max, d_z_min,
        ↪  d_z_max, d_collision_flags,
                        np.int32(num_objects), block=(num_objects, 1,
                        ↪  1), grid=(1, 1))

        # Copy the results back to host
        cuda.memcpy_dtoh(h_collision_flags, d_collision_flags)

        return h_collision_flags

def simulate_particle_system(num_particles, h_positions,
↪  h_velocities, h_masses, h_forces, dt):
    # Allocate memory on the GPU
    d_positions = cuda.mem_alloc(h_positions.nbytes)
    d_velocities = cuda.mem_alloc(h_velocities.nbytes)
    d_masses = cuda.mem_alloc(h_masses.nbytes)
    d_forces = cuda.mem_alloc(h_forces.nbytes)

    # Copy data from host to device
    cuda.memcpy_htod(d_positions, h_positions)
    cuda.memcpy_htod(d_velocities, h_velocities)
    cuda.memcpy_htod(d_masses, h_masses)
    cuda.memcpy_htod(d_forces, h_forces)

    # Launch kernel
    mod = SourceModule(particle_system_kernel)
    update_particle_system =
    ↪  mod.get_function("update_particle_system")
    update_particle_system(d_positions, d_velocities, d_masses,
    ↪  d_forces, np.float32(dt),
                        np.int32(num_particles),
                        ↪  block=(num_particles, 1, 1), grid=(1,
                        ↪  1))

    # Copy the results back to host
    cuda.memcpy_dtoh(h_positions, d_positions)
    cuda.memcpy_dtoh(h_velocities, d_velocities)

    return h_positions, h_velocities

# Simulation parameters
num_objects = 10
num_particles = 100
dt = 0.01

# Random test data
h_x_min = np.random.rand(num_objects).astype(np.float32)
h_x_max = h_x_min + 1
h_y_min = np.random.rand(num_objects).astype(np.float32)
h_y_max = h_y_min + 1
h_z_min = np.random.rand(num_objects).astype(np.float32)
h_z_max = h_z_min + 1
```

212

```
h_positions = np.random.rand(num_particles * 3).astype(np.float32)
h_velocities = np.random.rand(num_particles * 3).astype(np.float32)
↪    * 0.1
h_masses = np.ones(num_particles).astype(np.float32)
h_forces = (np.random.rand(num_particles * 3) -
↪    0.5).astype(np.float32)

# Execute simulations
collision_flags = simulate_collision_detection(num_objects, h_x_min,
↪    h_x_max, h_y_min, h_y_max, h_z_min, h_z_max)
updated_positions, updated_velocities =
↪    simulate_particle_system(num_particles, h_positions,
↪    h_velocities, h_masses, h_forces, dt)
print("Collision Flags: ", collision_flags)
print("Updated Positions: ", updated_positions)
print("Updated Velocities: ", updated_velocities)
```

This code defines several key functions necessary for simulating game physics:

- The PyCUDA kernel `detect_collision` checks for intersections between objects using their axis-aligned bounding boxes.

- The `update_particle_system` kernel updates the position and velocity of particles based on applied forces.

- `simulate_collision_detection` function allocates arrays, launches the collision kernel, and returns collision results.

- `simulate_particle_system` function executes the procedure for updating the states of particles over time.

The final block of code provides examples of setting up simulations with random initial conditions and performing computations using the defined CUDA kernels.

213

# Chapter 36

# Augmented Reality and CUDA

## CUDA Acceleration in Augmented Reality

In the domain of augmented reality (AR), the enhancement of processing speeds for real-time applications is paramount. CUDA, a parallel computing platform and application programming interface model created by NVIDIA, offers significant performance improvements. The complexities of AR require rapid computations to overlay digital objects onto a real-world scene effectively.

Consider a transformation operation needed for aligning virtual objects with the environment. The homogeneous transformation matrix $\mathbf{T}$ is critical for expressing the translation and rotation in 3D space:

$$\mathbf{T} = \begin{bmatrix} R_{11} & R_{12} & R_{13} & t_x \\ R_{21} & R_{22} & R_{23} & t_y \\ R_{31} & R_{32} & R_{33} & t_z \\ 0 & 0 & 0 & 1 \end{bmatrix}$$

where $R_{ij}$ components comprise the rotation matrix, and $(t_x, t_y, t_z)$ defines the translation vector. CUDA's parallel threads can manage multiple transformations simultaneously, thereby improving execution efficiency.

# Real-time Image Processing and Overlays

The integration of dynamic overlays on AR displays mandates real-time image processing. A fundamental task is edge detection, often realized through convolution operations with kernels such as the Sobel operator $K$:

$$K_x = \begin{bmatrix} -1 & 0 & 1 \\ -2 & 0 & 2 \\ -1 & 0 & 1 \end{bmatrix},$$

$$K_y = \begin{bmatrix} -1 & -2 & -1 \\ 0 & 0 & 0 \\ 1 & 2 & 1 \end{bmatrix}$$

The gradient magnitude $G$ at each pixel $(x, y)$ can be computed as:

$$G(x, y) = \sqrt{(I * K_x)^2 + (I * K_y)^2}$$

where $*$ denotes the convolution operation. CUDA enables concurrent computation across pixel grids, accelerating the derivation of $G(x, y)$ for large scale images.

# Model-View-Projection Transformations

Augmented reality relies heavily on model-view-projection (MVP) matrices for rendering graphics on cameras or displays. The vertex shader stage performs these projections, which combine transformation matrices from model coordinates to clip space:

$$\mathbf{MVP} = \mathbf{P} \cdot \mathbf{V} \cdot \mathbf{M}$$

$\mathbf{M}$ = Model matrix, transformation to world space

$\mathbf{V}$ = View matrix, transformation to camera space

$\mathbf{P}$ = Projection matrix, maps to screen space

The `glsl`-based shaders compute each vertex transformation, and CUDA can further expedite these operations when processing a vast number of vertices.

# Optimization Techniques for AR

Numerous optimization strategies can be applied to AR computations using CUDA. Techniques such as loop unrolling and memory coalescing can ensure maximum throughput and minimal latency. The latency $L$ for memory access can be minimized by ensuring data locality, reducing access time $t_{\text{access}}$:

$$L = \alpha \cdot t_{\text{access}} + \beta \cdot t_{\text{compute}}$$

where $\alpha$ and $\beta$ are coefficients representing memory access and compute operation distributions, respectively.

---

**Input:** Input images $\{I_k\}$, Transformation Matrices $\{\mathbf{T}_k\}$
**Output:** Augmented Image Set $\{\tilde{I}_k\}$
**for** *each image* $I_k$ **do**
  Load image into CUDA memory;
  Apply transformation:  $\mathbf{T}_k \cdot I_k$;
  Perform edge detection and augment;
  Store result in  $\tilde{I}_k$;

---

The above algorithm outlines real-time AR processing. CUDA allows for simultaneous image handling and computation, significantly reducing latency in AR systems. Efficient kernel execution is critical in maintaining the illusion of reality in augmented environments.

# Python Code Snippet

Below is a Python code snippet that encompasses the core computational elements of augmented reality using CUDA, focusing on transformation operations, edge detection with convolution, and optimization strategies for AR systems.

```python
import numpy as np
import pycuda.driver as cuda
import pycuda.autoinit
from pycuda.compiler import SourceModule

# Define CUDA kernel for transformation operations
transformation_kernel = """
__global__ void transform(float *input, float *output, float *T, int
↪   num_points) {
    int idx = threadIdx.x + blockIdx.x * blockDim.x;
```

```
        if (idx < num_points) {
            float x = input[3*idx];
            float y = input[3*idx + 1];
            float z = input[3*idx + 2];
            output[3*idx] = T[0] * x + T[1] * y + T[2] * z + T[3];
            output[3*idx + 1] = T[4] * x + T[5] * y + T[6] * z + T[7];
            output[3*idx + 2] = T[8] * x + T[9] * y + T[10] * z + T[11];
        }
    }
    """

    # Define CUDA kernel for Sobel edge detection
    sobel_kernel = """
    __global__ void sobel(float *input, float *output, int width, int
    ↪  height) {
        int x = threadIdx.x + blockIdx.x * blockDim.x;
        int y = threadIdx.y + blockIdx.y * blockDim.y;
        int idx = y * width + x;
        if (x > 0 && x < width-1 && y > 0 && y < height-1) {
            float Gx = -input[idx-width-1] - 2*input[idx-1] -
            ↪  input[idx+width-1]
                        + input[idx-width+1] + 2*input[idx+1] +
                        ↪  input[idx+width+1];
            float Gy = -input[idx-width-1] - 2*input[idx-width] -
            ↪  input[idx-width+1]
                        + input[idx+width-1] + 2*input[idx+width] +
                        ↪  input[idx+width+1];
            output[idx] = sqrtf(Gx * Gx + Gy * Gy);
        }
    }
    """

    # Initialize CUDA module
    mod = SourceModule(transformation_kernel + sobel_kernel)

    # Make transformations kernel ready
    transform = mod.get_function("transform")

    # Create dummy data for transformation
    num_points = 1024
    h_input = np.random.rand(num_points * 3).astype(np.float32)
    h_output = np.zeros_like(h_input)
    h_T = np.array([1, 0, 0, 1, 0, 1, 0, 1, 0, 0, 1, 1],
    ↪  dtype=np.float32)

    # Allocate device memory
    d_input = cuda.mem_alloc(h_input.size * h_input.dtype.itemsize)
    d_output = cuda.mem_alloc(h_output.size * h_output.dtype.itemsize)
    d_T = cuda.mem_alloc(h_T.size * h_T.dtype.itemsize)

    # Copy data to device
    cuda.memcpy_htod(d_input, h_input)
    cuda.memcpy_htod(d_T, h_T)
```

```
# Launch transformation kernel
block_size = 256
grid_size = (num_points + block_size - 1) // block_size
transform(d_input, d_output, d_T, np.int32(num_points),
↪   block=(block_size,1,1), grid=(grid_size,1))

# Fetch the result from GPU memory
cuda.memcpy_dtoh(h_output, d_output)
print("Transformed Output:", h_output)

# Simulation of main processing loop
def apply_transformations_and_sobel(input_data, T, width, height):
    '''
    Apply transformations and Sobel edge detection on AR image data.
    :param input_data: Image data.
    :param T: Transformation matrix.
    :param width: Image width.
    :param height: Image height.
    :return: Processed image data.
    '''
    d_input_image = cuda.mem_alloc(input_data.size *
    ↪   input_data.dtype.itemsize)
    d_output_image = cuda.mem_alloc(input_data.size *
    ↪   input_data.dtype.itemsize)
    cuda.memcpy_htod(d_input_image, input_data)

    # Launch Sobel kernel
    block_size_2d = (16, 16)
    grid_size_2d = ((width + block_size_2d[0] - 1) //
    ↪   block_size_2d[0], (height + block_size_2d[1] - 1) //
    ↪   block_size_2d[1])
    sobel = mod.get_function("sobel")
    sobel(d_input_image, d_output_image, np.int32(width),
    ↪   np.int32(height), block=block_size_2d, grid=grid_size_2d)

    # Get the result
    h_edge_output = np.zeros_like(input_data)
    cuda.memcpy_dtoh(h_edge_output, d_output_image)

    return h_edge_output

# Example of image processing
width, height = 512, 512
h_image = np.random.rand(width * height).astype(np.float32)
processed_image = apply_transformations_and_sobel(h_image, h_T,
↪   width, height)
print("Processed Image:", processed_image)
```

This code defines several functions necessary for implementing important computational operations using CUDA in augmented reality:

- `transform` CUDA kernel applies a 3D transformation matrix to vectors, useful for aligning virtual objects in AR scenes.

- `sobel` CUDA kernel performs Sobel edge detection for image processing, essential in identifying object boundaries and overlays.

- `apply_transformations_and_sobel` function handles the application of both transformations and Sobel filtering to an image dataset.

The final block of code demonstrates the use of these kernels with dummy data, showing how data is processed and transformed using CUDA's parallel computing capabilities.

# Chapter 37

# CUDA and Cryptography

## Parallelizing Cryptographic Algorithms

The augmentation of cryptographic computational throughput via CUDA is achieved through the parallelization of symmetric and asymmetric algorithms. Symmetric encryption algorithms such as AES (Advanced Encryption Standard) can utilize CUDA to offload the intensive computation of multiple rounds of encryption and decryption.

The AES encryption process consists of several transformations applied sequentially to the data block. Let $\mathbf{S}$ represent the initial state matrix and $\mathbf{K}$ denote the round key matrix. The encryption process is represented as:

$$\mathbf{S} \leftarrow \text{SubBytes}(\mathbf{S})$$

$$\mathbf{S} \leftarrow \text{ShiftRows}(\mathbf{S})$$

$$\mathbf{S} \leftarrow \text{MixColumns}(\mathbf{S})$$

$$\mathbf{S} \leftarrow \mathbf{S} \oplus \mathbf{K}$$

CUDA's parallel threads allow each transformation to be executed on separate elements, expediting the overall encryption cycle.

# Optimizing RSA with CUDA

The RSA algorithm, a quintessential asymmetric cryptographic technique, relies heavily on modular exponentiation. Acceleration is achieved by parallelizing the ModExp operation, defined as computing $c \equiv m^e \mod n$, where $(e, n)$ is the public key.

The modular exponentiation using the square-and-multiply method can be expressed in pseudocode as follows:

---

**Input:** $m$, $e$, $n$
**Output:** $c = m^e \mod n$
$c \leftarrow 1$;
$x \leftarrow m \mod n$;
**while** $e > 0$ **do**
   **if** $e \mod 2 = 1$ **then**
      $\lfloor \; c \leftarrow (c \cdot x) \mod n$;
   $x \leftarrow (x \cdot x) \mod n$;
   $e \leftarrow e // 2$;
**return** $c$

---

This inherently sequential process can be partitioned and cued for parallel execution on CUDA, taking advantage of its multiple cores by distributing the multiplication and squaring operations across different threads.

# CUDA-Enabled Hashing for Security

Cryptographic hash functions, such as SHA-256, are essential for data integrity and authenticity verification. The primary focus within CUDA is optimizing the computation of the hash's compression function, which involves bitwise operations and modular additions iterated over a message schedule.

For SHA-256, let $\mathbf{H}$ be the hash values and $\mathbf{W}$ be the message schedule. The compression function updates $\mathbf{H}$ as follows:

$$T_1 = h + \text{sigma}_1(e) + \text{ch}(e, f, g) + K_i + W_i$$
$$T_2 = \text{sigma}_0(a) + \text{maj}(a, b, c)$$
$$h \leftarrow g, \quad g \leftarrow f, \quad f \leftarrow e, \quad e \leftarrow d + T_1$$
$$d \leftarrow c, \quad c \leftarrow b, \quad b \leftarrow a, \quad a \leftarrow T_1 + T_2$$

Each hashing iteration benefits from CUDA's ability to parallelize the execution of compression across multiple data chunks.

# Improving Throughput via Memory Coalescing

To enhance cryptographic computations, attention must be given to the memory access patterns. Memory coalescing is a strategy employed in CUDA to ensure optimal throughput by aligning memory accesses of threads within a warp.

Consider a warp trying to access elements with spacing stride. Memory coalescing is ideally achieved if stride = 1. The latency $\lambda$ can, thus, be minimized to:

$$\lambda = \alpha \cdot t_{\text{uncoalesced}} + \beta \cdot t_{\text{coalesced}}$$

where $\alpha$ and $\beta$ are coefficients representing the proportion of uncoalesced and coalesced memory accesses, respectively.

Of key importance is structuring the memory layout of cryptographic data blocks to adhere to CUDA's memory coalescing guidelines, thereby minimizing the time per cryptographic computation cycle.

# Python Code Snippet

Below is a Python code snippet implementing the core computational elements of cryptographic algorithms using PyCUDA to optimize cryptographic functions such as AES, RSA, and SHA-256, including parallel execution strategies and handling of CUDA memory.

```python
import pycuda.autoinit
import pycuda.driver as cuda
from pycuda.compiler import SourceModule
import numpy as np

# AES encryption kernel
aes_kernel_code = """
__global__ void aes_encrypt(unsigned char *state, unsigned char
    *roundKey) {
    int idx = threadIdx.x;
    // Assume each thread handles one byte of AES state - simplified
    state[idx] = state[idx] ^ roundKey[idx]; // XOR with round key
}
"""

def aes_encrypt_cuda(state, key):
```

```python
    state_gpu = cuda.mem_alloc(state.nbytes)
    key_gpu = cuda.mem_alloc(key.nbytes)

    cuda.memcpy_htod(state_gpu, state)
    cuda.memcpy_htod(key_gpu, key)

    mod = SourceModule(aes_kernel_code)
    func = mod.get_function("aes_encrypt")
    func(state_gpu, key_gpu, block=(16, 1, 1))

    result = np.empty_like(state)
    cuda.memcpy_dtoh(result, state_gpu)
    return result

# RSA modular exponentiation using square-and-multiply
def rsa_mod_exp(base, exp, mod):
    result = np.uint64(1)
    base = base % mod
    while exp > 0:
        if exp % 2 == 1:
            result = (result * base) % mod
        exp = exp >> 1
        base = (base * base) % mod
    return result

# SHA-256 compression function kernel
sha256_kernel_code = """
__global__ void sha256_compress(unsigned int *H, unsigned int *W) {
    int idx = threadIdx.x;
    // Simplified compression step - assumption for parallel
    ↪    execution
    unsigned int T1 = H[7] + W[idx];
    H[7] = H[6];
    H[6] = H[5];
    H[5] = H[4];
    H[4] = H[3] + T1;
    H[3] = H[2];
    H[2] = H[1];
    H[1] = H[0];
    H[0] = T1;
}
"""

def sha256_compress_cuda(H, W):
    H_gpu = cuda.mem_alloc(H.nbytes)
    W_gpu = cuda.mem_alloc(W.nbytes)

    cuda.memcpy_htod(H_gpu, H)
    cuda.memcpy_htod(W_gpu, W)

    mod = SourceModule(sha256_kernel_code)
    func = mod.get_function("sha256_compress")
    func(H_gpu, W_gpu, block=(8, 1, 1))
```

223

```
    result_H = np.empty_like(H)
    cuda.memcpy_dtoh(result_H, H_gpu)
    return result_H

# Memory coalescing optimization kernel
memory_coalescing_kernel = """
__global__ void memory_coalescing(float *data) {
    int idx = threadIdx.x;
    // Access data with concurrent thread indexing to achieve
    ↪  coalescing
    data[idx] *= 2.0f; // Simple operation for demonstration
}
"""

def optimize_memory_coalescing(data):
    data_gpu = cuda.mem_alloc(data.nbytes)
    cuda.memcpy_htod(data_gpu, data)

    mod = SourceModule(memory_coalescing_kernel)
    func = mod.get_function("memory_coalescing")
    func(data_gpu, block=(32, 1, 1)) # Assuming warp size as 32 for
    ↪  coalescing

    result = np.empty_like(data)
    cuda.memcpy_dtoh(result, data_gpu)
    return result

# Usage example
state = np.random.randint(0, 256, size=(16,), dtype=np.uint8)
key = np.random.randint(0, 256, size=(16,), dtype=np.uint8)
aes_result = aes_encrypt_cuda(state, key)
print("AES Encrypted State:", aes_result)

base = np.uint64(2)
exp = np.uint64(10)
mod = np.uint64(17)
rsa_result = rsa_mod_exp(base, exp, mod)
print("RSA Mod Exp Result:", rsa_result)

H = np.random.randint(0, 256, size=(8,), dtype=np.uint32)
W = np.random.randint(0, 256, size=(8,), dtype=np.uint32)
sha256_result = sha256_compress_cuda(H, W)
print("SHA-256 Compressed H:", sha256_result)

data = np.linspace(0, 32, num=32, dtype=np.float32)
coalesced_result = optimize_memory_coalescing(data)
print("Coalesced Memory Result:", coalesced_result)
```

The code above defines several key functions leveraging the power of PyCUDA:

- `aes_encrypt_cuda` function demonstrates parallelization of AES encryption, focusing on the use of CUDA for XOR operations with the round key.

- `rsa_mod_exp` implements the RSA modular exponentiation using the square-and-multiply method executed serially in Python.

- `sha256_compress_cuda` leverages CUDA to parallelize the SHA-256 compression operation.

- `optimize_memory_coalescing` shows optimization techniques for memory access patterns using CUDA, ensuring coalesced memory transactions.

The provided functions and example usage illustrate the practical application of CUDA in cryptographic algorithms, showcasing how computational throughput and efficiency can be enhanced using parallel programming techniques.

# Chapter 38

# Natural Language Processing

## Parsing with CUDA

Parsing is a critical component in Natural Language Processing (NLP) that focuses on determining the grammatical structure of a sentence. In typical dependency parsing, the goal is to identify relationships, or dependencies, between "head" words and their dependents. Let $S = (w_1, w_2, \ldots, w_n)$ be a sequence of words. The parsing output could be defined as a set of dependency relations represented as ordered pairs $(h, d)$, where $h$ is the head and $d$ is the dependent, subject to the constraint that each word $w_i$ (except the root of the sentence) has exactly one head.

CUDA-based parsing capitalizes on the parallel processing of potential dependency edges, accelerating the computation. The arc-eager parsing algorithm can be expressed with transitions, e.g., SHIFT, REDUCE, which can be decomposed and executed in parallel across the sentence tokens with CUDA. The computation of dependency scores, $\text{score}(w_i, w_j)$, may employ neural network models whose computations are distributed across the GPU cores:

$$\text{score}(w_i, w_j) = \mathbf{u}^\top \tanh(\mathbf{W}_1 \mathbf{h}_i + \mathbf{W}_2 \mathbf{h}_j + \mathbf{b})$$

where $\mathbf{W}_1, \mathbf{W}_2$ are weight matrices, $\mathbf{h}_i, \mathbf{h}_j$ are vector representations of words, and $\mathbf{u}, \mathbf{b}$ are vectors.

# Tokenization Algorithms

The tokenization process involves segmenting a string of text into constituent parts, known as tokens. These tokens can include words, phrases, symbols, or other meaningful elements. CUDA accelerates tokenization by enabling concurrent processing of substrings. Given an input string $T$ of length $n$, a tokenization algorithm partitions $T$ into $k$ tokens $(t_1, t_2, \ldots, t_k)$.

Consider Grammatical Tokenization, which assigns each token $t_i$ attributes such as start and end positions (indices) and type. CUDA allows parallel scanning of the input string for delimiters or patterns:

---

**Input:** String $T$
**Output:** Tokens $t_1, t_2, \ldots, t_k$
**foreach** *character $c_i$ in $T$* **in parallel do**
    **if** $c_i$ *is a delimiter* **then**
        Mark position $i$ as a boundary;

Partition $T$ using identified boundaries;
**return** *List of tokens $t_1, t_2, \ldots, t_k$*

---

This parallel formulation reduces the linear scan complexity dramatically in practice.

# Sentiment Analysis with CUDA

Sentiment analysis is concerned with identifying and classifying opinions in text as positive, negative, or neutral. Formally, for a corpus $\mathcal{C}$, sentiment analysis assigns a label $l \in \{-1, 0, 1\}$ to each document $d \in \mathcal{C}$. CUDA expedites sentiment classification via parallel evaluation of feature vectors and sentiment prediction. Consider a feature vector $\mathbf{x} = (x_1, x_2, \ldots, x_m)$ extracted from a document. The sentiment is often inferred through logistic regression, where:

$$P(y = 1 \mid \mathbf{x}) = \frac{1}{1 + e^{-\mathbf{w}^\top \mathbf{x}}}$$

where $\mathbf{w}$ is the weight vector. CUDA allows parallelization of the logistic function evaluation over multiple documents.

Implementations of Recurrent Neural Networks (RNNs) for sentiment analysis are naturally amenable to CUDA's architecture, leveraging matrix operations for each time-step update efficiently across GPU threads:

$$\mathbf{h}_t = \sigma(\mathbf{W}_h\mathbf{x}_t + \mathbf{U}_h\mathbf{h}_{t-1} + \mathbf{b}_h)$$

where $\mathbf{W}_h, \mathbf{U}_h$ are weight matrices, and $\sigma$ denotes the activation function, often a hyperbolic tangent. Through CUDA, processing of the RNN's sequential steps is parallelized across documents and sentence tokens, thus enhancing throughput.

# Python Code Snippet

Below is a Python code snippet that encompasses the core computational elements for parsing, tokenization, and sentiment analysis using CUDA. This implementation leverages PyCUDA for GPU acceleration, detailing the GPU kernels and execution flow for these NLP tasks.

```python
import numpy as np
import pycuda.autoinit
import pycuda.driver as cuda
from pycuda.compiler import SourceModule

# Define CUDA kernel for dependency score calculation
kernel_code = """
  __global__ void dependency_scores(
      float *h, float *d, float *W1, float *W2, float *U, float *b,
      ↪ float *scores, int n) {
      int idx = blockIdx.x * blockDim.x + threadIdx.x;
      if (idx < n){
          float h_score = 0;
          for (int i = 0; i < n; i++) {
              h_score += W1[i] * h[i];
          }
          float d_score = 0;
          for (int j = 0; j < n; j++) {
              d_score += W2[j] * d[j];
          }
          scores[idx] = U[idx] * tanh(h_score + d_score + b[idx]);
      }
  }
"""

mod = SourceModule(kernel_code)
dependency_scores = mod.get_function("dependency_scores")

# Example Inputs for Dependency Parsing
n = 10  # Number of words/features
```

```python
h = np.random.rand(n).astype(np.float32)
d = np.random.rand(n).astype(np.float32)
W1 = np.random.rand(n).astype(np.float32)
W2 = np.random.rand(n).astype(np.float32)
U = np.random.rand(n).astype(np.float32)
b = np.random.rand(n).astype(np.float32)
scores = np.zeros(n).astype(np.float32)

# Allocate GPU memory and transfer data
h_gpu = cuda.mem_alloc(h.nbytes)
d_gpu = cuda.mem_alloc(d.nbytes)
W1_gpu = cuda.mem_alloc(W1.nbytes)
W2_gpu = cuda.mem_alloc(W2.nbytes)
U_gpu = cuda.mem_alloc(U.nbytes)
b_gpu = cuda.mem_alloc(b.nbytes)
scores_gpu = cuda.mem_alloc(scores.nbytes)

cuda.memcpy_htod(h_gpu, h)
cuda.memcpy_htod(d_gpu, d)
cuda.memcpy_htod(W1_gpu, W1)
cuda.memcpy_htod(W2_gpu, W2)
cuda.memcpy_htod(U_gpu, U)
cuda.memcpy_htod(b_gpu, b)
cuda.memcpy_htod(scores_gpu, scores)

# Launch the CUDA kernel
block_size = 256
grid_size = (n + block_size - 1) // block_size
dependency_scores(h_gpu, d_gpu, W1_gpu, W2_gpu, U_gpu, b_gpu,
↪   scores_gpu, np.int32(n),
                  block=(block_size, 1, 1), grid=(grid_size, 1))

# Fetch the results from GPU
cuda.memcpy_dtoh(scores, scores_gpu)

print("Dependency Scores:", scores)

# Tokenization Algorithm using CUDA
kernel_tokenization = """
  __global__ void tokenize(char *input, int *delimiters, int
↪   *token_indices, int length) {
      int idx = blockIdx.x * blockDim.x + threadIdx.x;
      if (idx < length) {
          if (input[idx] == ' ' || input[idx] == ',' || input[idx]
↪   == '.') {
              delimiters[idx] = 1;
          } else {
              delimiters[idx] = 0;
          }
          __syncthreads();
          if (idx > 0 && delimiters[idx] && !delimiters[idx - 1]) {
              token_indices[idx] = 1;
          } else {
```

```
                token_indices[idx] = 0;
            }
        }
    }
"""


mod_tokenization = SourceModule(kernel_tokenization)
tokenize = mod_tokenization.get_function("tokenize")

# Example text
text = "This is a sample sentence to tokenize.".encode('utf-8')
length = len(text)
delimiters = np.zeros(length).astype(np.int32)
token_indices = np.zeros(length).astype(np.int32)

# Allocate GPU memory
text_gpu = cuda.mem_alloc(len(text))
delimiters_gpu = cuda.mem_alloc(delimiters.nbytes)
token_indices_gpu = cuda.mem_alloc(token_indices.nbytes)

cuda.memcpy_htod(text_gpu, text)
cuda.memcpy_htod(delimiters_gpu, delimiters)
cuda.memcpy_htod(token_indices_gpu, token_indices)

# Launch the tokenization kernel
tokenize(text_gpu, delimiters_gpu, token_indices_gpu,
↪   np.int32(length),
        block=(block_size, 1, 1), grid=((length + block_size - 1)
        ↪   // block_size, 1))

# Retrieve results
cuda.memcpy_dtoh(delimiters, delimiters_gpu)
cuda.memcpy_dtoh(token_indices, token_indices_gpu)

print("Delimiters:", delimiters)
print("Token Indices:", token_indices)

# Sentiment Analysis Using CUDA
kernel_sentiment_analysis = """
  __global__ void evaluate_sentiment(float *features, float
  ↪   *weights, float *sentiments, int num_features) {
      int idx = blockIdx.x * blockDim.x + threadIdx.x;
      if (idx < num_features) {
          sentiments[idx] = 1.0 / (1.0 + exp(-weights[idx] *
          ↪   features[idx]));
      }
  }
"""


mod_sentiment = SourceModule(kernel_sentiment_analysis)
evaluate_sentiment =
↪   mod_sentiment.get_function("evaluate_sentiment")
```

```
# Example data
num_features = 100
features = np.random.rand(num_features).astype(np.float32)
weights = np.random.rand(num_features).astype(np.float32)
sentiments = np.zeros(num_features).astype(np.float32)

# Allocate memory on GPU
features_gpu = cuda.mem_alloc(features.nbytes)
weights_gpu = cuda.mem_alloc(weights.nbytes)
sentiments_gpu = cuda.mem_alloc(sentiments.nbytes)

cuda.memcpy_htod(features_gpu, features)
cuda.memcpy_htod(weights_gpu, weights)
cuda.memcpy_htod(sentiments_gpu, sentiments)

# Execute sentiment analysis kernel
evaluate_sentiment(features_gpu, weights_gpu, sentiments_gpu,
↪   np.int32(num_features),
                   block=(block_size, 1, 1), grid=((num_features +
                   ↪   block_size - 1) // block_size, 1))

# Retrieve sentiment results
cuda.memcpy_dtoh(sentiments, sentiments_gpu)

print("Sentiment Probabilities:", sentiments)
```

This Python script implements the core computational tasks
discussed for Natural Language Processing using CUDA:

- `dependency_scores`: Computes dependency scores in parallel for given words using neural network representations on a
  GPU.

- `tokenize`: Implements tokenization by identifying delimiters
  in parallel and marking token boundaries on a GPU.

- `evaluate_sentiment`: Calculates sentiment probabilities using logistic regression for feature vectors in parallel on a GPU.

The use of PyCUDA enables these computations to leverage
the massive parallelism of GPUs, drastically improving efficiency
and performance over CPU-based implementations.

# Chapter 39

# Planetary and Space Simulations

## Modeling Planetary Orbits

Simulations of planetary orbits are fundamental to many fields, including astrophysics and aerospace engineering. Utilizing CUDA technology allows for the parallel computation of planetary trajectories by implementing numerical methods on the GPU.

Let $N$ be the number of celestial bodies, each body $i$ is characterized by a state vector $\mathbf{r}_i(t), \mathbf{v}_i(t)$, representing its position and velocity at time $t$. Newton's law of universal gravitation governs the force $\mathbf{F}_{ij}$ between bodies $i$ and $j$:

$$\mathbf{F}_{ij} = G\frac{m_i m_j(\mathbf{r}_j - \mathbf{r}_i)}{\|\mathbf{r}_j - \mathbf{r}_i\|^3}$$

where $G$ is the gravitational constant, and $m_i, m_j$ are the masses of the respective celestial bodies. The acceleration $\mathbf{a}_i$ experienced by body $i$ is given by:

$$\mathbf{a}_i = \sum_{j \neq i} \frac{\mathbf{F}_{ij}}{m_i}$$

Numerical integration methods like the Verlet or Runge-Kutta are employed to update the bodies' positions and velocities. In the case of the Velocity Verlet algorithm:

$$\mathbf{r}_i(t + \Delta t) = \mathbf{r}_i(t) + \mathbf{v}_i(t)\Delta t + \frac{1}{2}\mathbf{a}_i(t)(\Delta t)^2$$

$$\mathbf{v}_i(t + \Delta t) = \mathbf{v}_i(t) + \frac{1}{2}(\mathbf{a}_i(t) + \mathbf{a}_i(t + \Delta t))\Delta t$$

CUDA enables simultaneous computations of these equations for all bodies, significantly improving simulation time, and allowing higher-fidelity models for larger systems.

## Astrodynamics and CUDA

Utilizing CUDA for parallel processing in astrodynamics involves advancing spacecraft trajectory computations and orbital analysis. Each trajectory calculation requires solving systems of ordinary differential equations, where the acceleration $\mathbf{a}$ of a spacecraft is influenced by multiple celestial bodies, expressed as:

$$\mathbf{a} = \sum_{i=1}^{N} G \frac{m_i(\mathbf{r}_i - \mathbf{r})}{\|\mathbf{r}_i - \mathbf{r}\|^3} + \mathbf{a}_{\text{non-grav}}$$

where $\mathbf{a}_{\text{non-grav}}$ accounts for perturbative forces such as solar radiation pressure. The numerical integration employed must be efficient to handle varying step sizes determined by the CUDA parallel framework.

---
**Algorithm 1:** Parallel Update of Celestial States

---
**Input:** Initial states $\mathbf{r}(0), \mathbf{v}(0)$ for $N$ bodies
**Output:** Updated states $\mathbf{r}(t), \mathbf{v}(t)$ for $N$ bodies
**foreach** *body i* **in parallel** do
    Compute current acceleration $\mathbf{a}_i$;
    Update position and velocity using numerical method;
    **if** *end of timestep* **then**
        Synchronize results;

---

## Simulating Space Physics

Beyond orbital dynamics, CUDA accelerates simulations of space physics phenomena. Electromagnetic field simulations, for example, apply Maxwell's equations in a discretized form using finite difference time domain (FDTD) methods.

In space plasma environments, charged particles' motion can be modeled by the Lorentz force equation:

$$\mathbf{F} = q(\mathbf{E} + \mathbf{v} \times \mathbf{B})$$

where $q$ is the charge, $\mathbf{E}$ is the electric field, and $\mathbf{B}$ is the magnetic field. The parallel processing capability of CUDA empowers researchers to simulate enormous grids representing space environments, solving for field values at each grid point using:

$$\mathbf{E}(t + \Delta t) = \mathbf{E}(t) + \frac{\Delta t}{\varepsilon} \nabla \times \mathbf{H}(t)$$

$$\mathbf{H}(t + \Delta t) = \mathbf{H}(t) - \frac{\Delta t}{\mu} \nabla \times \mathbf{E}(t + \Delta t)$$

These global updates occur simultaneously across the spatial grid, producing near-instantaneous simulation results that bring insights into space weather phenomena, magnetospheric science, and spacecraft design consideration.

# Python Code Snippet

Below is a Python code snippet that demonstrates simulation of celestial mechanics, astrodynamics, and space physics using PyCUDA, allowing for parallel execution of updates and calculations on GPU.

```python
import pycuda.autoinit
import pycuda.driver as cuda
from pycuda.compiler import SourceModule
import numpy as np

N = 5  # Number of celestial bodies
G_CONST = 6.67430e-11  # Gravitational constant

positions = np.random.rand(N, 3).astype(np.float32)
velocities = np.random.rand(N, 3).astype(np.float32)
masses = np.random.rand(N).astype(np.float32)

# Allocate GPU memory for positions, velocities, and forces
positions_gpu = cuda.mem_alloc(positions.nbytes)
velocities_gpu = cuda.mem_alloc(velocities.nbytes)
masses_gpu = cuda.mem_alloc(masses.nbytes)
acceleration_gpu = cuda.mem_alloc(positions.nbytes)

# Transfer data to GPU
cuda.memcpy_htod(positions_gpu, positions)
cuda.memcpy_htod(velocities_gpu, velocities)
```

234

```python
cuda.memcpy_htod(masses_gpu, masses)

# CUDA kernel for updating positions and velocities using Velocity
↪   Verlet method
kernel_code = """
__global__ void update_celestial_bodies(float3 *positions, float3
↪   *velocities, float *masses, float3 *acceleration, float delta_t,
↪   int N) {
    int idx = blockIdx.x * blockDim.x + threadIdx.x;
    if (idx >= N) return;

    float3 pos = positions[idx];
    float3 vel = velocities[idx];
    float m_i = masses[idx];

    // Calculate gravitational acceleration
    float3 acc = make_float3(0.0f, 0.0f, 0.0f);

    for (int j = 0; j < N; ++j) {
        if (j != idx) {
            float3 r_j = positions[j];
            float m_j = masses[j];
            float3 r_ij = r_j - pos;
            float dist_sqr = r_ij.x * r_ij.x + r_ij.y * r_ij.y +
            ↪   r_ij.z * r_ij.z + 1e-10;
            float inv_dist_cubed = rsqrtf(dist_sqr * dist_sqr *
            ↪   dist_sqr);
            acc += (G_CONST * m_j * inv_dist_cubed) * r_ij;
        }
    }
    acceleration[idx] = acc;

    // Update position and velocity
    pos += vel * delta_t + 0.5f * acc * (delta_t * delta_t);
    vel += acc * delta_t;

    positions[idx] = pos;
    velocities[idx] = vel;
}
"""

mod = SourceModule(kernel_code)
update_func = mod.get_function("update_celestial_bodies")

# Helper function
def simulate_celestial_bodies(delta_t):
    update_func(
        positions_gpu, velocities_gpu, masses_gpu, acceleration_gpu,
        np.float32(delta_t), np.int32(N),
        block=(N, 1, 1), grid=(1, 1)
    )

# Example call to the simulation function
```

```
simulate_celestial_bodies(0.01)

# Transfer results back to host
cuda.memcpy_dtoh(positions, positions_gpu)
cuda.memcpy_dtoh(velocities, velocities_gpu)

print("Updated Positions:", positions)
print("Updated Velocities:", velocities)
```

This code outlines the utilization of CUDA via PyCUDA for simulating gravitational dynamics among celestial bodies:

- `positions`, `velocities`, and `masses` store the state vectors and characteristics of each celestial body.

- The kernel `update_celestial_bodies` embodies the core logic for computing gravitational forces and updating state vectors across all bodies in parallel.

- GPU memory is managed using PyCUDA's functionality to allocate and transfer data to and from the GPU device.

- The simulation includes parallel calculations of gravitational interactions among bodies, applying Newton's laws using a discretized numerical integration technique.

- The final block executes the kernel to perform a single update step, printing updated positions and velocities.

This parallel approach significantly boosts computational efficiency, enabling sophisticated simulations of complex astrophysical models.

# Chapter 40

# Monte Carlo Simulations

## Principles of Monte Carlo Methods

Monte Carlo methods are a class of computational algorithms that rely on repeated random sampling to obtain numerical results. The primary use of these methods is to solve problems that may be deterministic in principle but are logistically infeasible by direct computation. These methods find applications across various domains, especially in statistical physics and quantitative finance.

Let $f(\mathbf{x})$ be a function defined on a domain $\mathbb{D}$, for which an integral or expected value must be evaluated. The Monte Carlo estimate of an integral is:

$$\int_{\mathbb{D}} f(\mathbf{x}) \, d\mathbf{x} \approx \frac{1}{N} \sum_{i=1}^{N} f(\mathbf{x}_i)$$

where $\mathbf{x}_i$ are sample points drawn from the probability distribution over $\mathbb{D}$.

The accuracy of a Monte Carlo simulation improves with the increase of sample size $N$, as governed by the Central Limit Theorem. The estimate follows a normal distribution whose variance diminishes as:

$$\sigma^2 = \frac{\mathrm{Var}(f)}{N}$$

# Monte Carlo in Statistical Physics

In statistical physics, Monte Carlo methods are employed to simulate systems with potentially infinite degrees of freedom at thermal equilibrium. Typical applications include evaluation of partition functions or simulating lattice models.

Consider a system described by a Hamiltonian, $H(\mathbf{x})$, where the state probabilities follow the Boltzmann distribution:

$$P(\mathbf{x}) = \frac{e^{-\beta H(\mathbf{x})}}{Z}$$

with $Z = \int e^{-\beta H(\mathbf{x})}\, d\mathbf{x}$ being the partition function and $\beta = \frac{1}{k_B T}$ is the inverse temperature.

Monte Carlo methods, particularly the Metropolis-Hastings algorithm, are instrumental in sampling from $P(\mathbf{x})$. In this context, the acceptance probability $A(\mathbf{x} \to \mathbf{x}')$ is given by:

$$A(\mathbf{x} \to \mathbf{x}') = \min\left(1, \frac{P(\mathbf{x}')}{P(\mathbf{x})}\right)$$

# Monte Carlo in Financial Modeling

In quantitative finance, Monte Carlo methods are ubiquitously applied for option pricing and risk management. The simulation process involves stochastic differential equations (SDEs) characteristic of financial models, such as:

$$dS_t = \mu S_t\, dt + \sigma S_t\, dW_t$$

where $S_t$ is the asset price at time $t$, $\mu$ is the drift coefficient, $\sigma$ the volatility, and $W_t$ a Wiener process.

The European call option price can be estimated using the expected payoff in a risk-neutral framework:

$$C_0 = e^{-rT}\mathbb{E}[\max(S_T - K, 0)]$$

Monte Carlo methods simulate the paths of $S_t$ to generate the distribution needed for the expectation.

---
**Algorithm 2:** Monte Carlo Option Pricing
---
**Input:** Initial asset price $S_0$, strike price $K$, interest rate
$r$, volatility $\sigma$, time to maturity $T$, number of
paths $M$

**Output:** Estimated option price

**foreach** *path m* **in parallel do**

> Simulate path $S_t$ using discretized Euler-Maruyama
> method;
>
> Compute path payoff $\max(S_T - K, 0)$;

**return** *mean of discounted payoffs*
---

# Implementation on GPUs

The acceleration of Monte Carlo simulations on GPUs leverages their parallel architecture to evaluate multiple sample paths concurrently. For a physical or financial system represented on NVIDIA's CUDA platform, the update of each path is managed by independent threads, which allows massive parallelization.

The implementation of the Euler-Maruyama method for SDEs in CUDA is as follows:

$$S_{t+\Delta t} = S_t + \mu S_t \Delta t + \sigma S_t \sqrt{\Delta t}\, \mathtt{randn}() \qquad (40.1)$$

Here, $\mathtt{randn}()$ denotes a pseudorandom number generator producing standard normal variates.

---
**Algorithm 3:** GPU-Accelerated Monte Carlo Simulation
---
**Input:** Parameters and initial conditions

**foreach** *thread t* **do**

> Initialize $S_t$;
>
> **foreach** *time step* $\Delta t$ **do**
>
> > Update asset price $S_{t+\Delta t}$;
>
> Store final payoff;

Synchronize threads to compute the average payoff and
calculate the present value;
---

The exploitation of GPU capabilities results in significant computational speedups, rendering real-time simulations feasible and practical, thus enhancing the efficacy of Monte Carlo methods across various computationally intensive applications.

# Python Code Snippet

Below is a Python code snippet that encompasses the core computational elements of Monte Carlo simulations for both statistical physics applications and financial modeling, focusing particularly on GPU acceleration using PyCUDA.

```python
import pycuda.autoinit
import pycuda.driver as drv
import numpy as np
from pycuda.compiler import SourceModule

# CUDA kernel for Monte Carlo simulation of SDE
mod = SourceModule("""
__global__ void simulate_paths(float *s_out, float s_0, float mu,
    float sigma, float dt, int steps, int paths)
{
    int idx = blockIdx.x * blockDim.x + threadIdx.x;

    if (idx < paths) {
        float s_t = s_0;

        // Seed for the random number
        unsigned int seed = idx;

        // leverage GPU's built-in RNG
        for (int i = 0; i < steps; i++) {
            float dW = sqrtf(dt) * curand_normal(&seed);
            s_t = s_t + mu * s_t * dt + sigma * s_t * dW;
        }
        s_out[idx] = s_t;
    }
}
""", no_extern_c=True)

simulate_paths = mod.get_function("simulate_paths")

# Parameters
S_0 = 100.0          # Initial asset price
mu = 0.05            # Drift
sigma = 0.2          # Volatility
T = 1.0              # Time to maturity
N = 365              # Steps
M = 40000            # Paths
dt = T / N           # Timestep

# Prepare memory on host and device
s_out = np.zeros(M, dtype=np.float32)

# Launch the Monte Carlo simulation on GPU
block_size = 256
```

```
grid_size = (M + block_size - 1) // block_size
simulate_paths(drv.Out(s_out), np.float32(S_0), np.float32(mu),
↪ np.float32(sigma), np.float32(dt), np.int32(N), np.int32(M),
↪ block=(block_size, 1, 1), grid=(grid_size, 1))

# Calculate option price
K = 100.0               # Strike price
r = 0.01                # Interest rate
payoff_call = np.maximum(s_out - K, 0)   # European call option
↪ payoff
C_0 = np.exp(-r * T) * np.mean(payoff_call)

print("Estimated European Call Option Price: ", C_0)
```

---

This code defines the essential functionalities necessary for executing Monte Carlo simulations, particularly suited for option pricing:

- A CUDA kernel `simulate_paths` generates asset price paths in parallel leveraging the GPU's architecture, exhibiting each path's stochastic changes following the Euler-Maruyama method.

- Simulation parameters include asset initial price, drift, volatility, and the number of steps and paths.

- The code calculates the expected payoff of a European call option using the results from the simulation, demonstrating the application of Monte Carlo methods to financial models.

This implemented approach efficiently distributes the computation of Monte Carlo paths across the GPU's many core architecture, facilitating high-performance parallel simulations.

# Chapter 41

# Fluid Dynamics Simulations

## Theoretical Foundations of Fluid Dynamics

Fluid dynamics is governed by the Navier-Stokes equations, which describe how the velocity field $\mathbf{v}(\mathbf{x}, t)$ of a fluid evolves over time. The incompressible Navier-Stokes equations are given by:

$$\frac{\partial \mathbf{v}}{\partial t} + (\mathbf{v} \cdot \nabla)\mathbf{v} = -\nabla p + \nu \nabla^2 \mathbf{v} + \mathbf{f}, \qquad (41.1)$$

$$\nabla \cdot \mathbf{v} = 0, \qquad (41.2)$$

where $\nu$ is the kinematic viscosity, $p$ signifies pressure, and $\mathbf{f}$ denotes external forces applied to the fluid.

These equations encompass both convective $((\mathbf{v} \cdot \nabla)\mathbf{v})$ and diffusive $(\nu \nabla^2 \mathbf{v})$ properties of fluid flow, essential for simulating complex phenomena in aerodynamics and hydrodynamics.

## Discretization Techniques

Numerical solutions to the Navier-Stokes equations require discretization. Finite difference methods (FDM), finite volume methods (FVM), and finite element methods (FEM) are prominent discretization techniques. Using a spatial discretization scheme, the velocity and pressure fields are evaluated at discrete grid points.

For the finite difference approach, the discrete form is provided by central differencing schemes. The discrete Laplacian for velocity, essential for viscous diffusion, is given by:

$$\nabla^2 \mathbf{v} \approx \frac{\mathbf{v}_{i+1,j} - 2\mathbf{v}_{i,j} + \mathbf{v}_{i-1,j}}{\Delta x^2} + \frac{\mathbf{v}_{i,j+1} - 2\mathbf{v}_{i,j} + \mathbf{v}_{i,j-1}}{\Delta y^2}$$

The time-stepping can be implemented using an explicit forward Euler method for temporal discretization:

$$\mathbf{v}_{i,j}^{n+1} = \mathbf{v}_{i,j}^{n} + \Delta t \left( -(\mathbf{v} \cdot \nabla)\mathbf{v} + \nu\nabla^2\mathbf{v} - \nabla p + \mathbf{f} \right)$$

# Parallelization Strategy on GPU

The parallelism capabilities inherent in GPU architectures can be exploited using CUDA to handle large computational grids typical of fluid simulations. Each discrete operation, including updating velocities, pressures, and forces, can be executed in parallel threads. The pressure Poisson equation given by:

$$\nabla^2 p = \frac{1}{\Delta t}\nabla \cdot \mathbf{v}$$

is particularly intensive and well-suited for parallel computing. This is efficiently solved via iterative methods such as Jacobi or Gauss-Seidel methods within the CUDA framework.

---

**Algorithm 4:** GPU-Accelerated Fluid Dynamics Simulation

---

**Input:** Initial velocity $\mathbf{v}_0$, pressure $p_0$, grid size, simulation parameters

**foreach** *time step n* **do**

    **foreach** *thread t* **do**

        Calculate intermediate velocity field $\mathbf{v}^*$ using explicit time-stepping;

        Solve pressure Poisson equation iteratively for pressure field $p^{n+1}$;

        Correct velocity field: $\mathbf{v}^{n+1} = \mathbf{v}^* - \Delta t\nabla p^{n+1}$;

    Synchronize threads

---

# Application to Aerodynamics and Hydro-dynamics

In aerodynamics and hydrodynamics, simulating the flow around objects involves the assessment of drag and lift forces, which are calculated from surface pressure and shear stress distributions. These forces are evaluated via the integrals over the object surface $\mathcal{S}$:

$$\mathbf{F} = \int_{\mathcal{S}} \left( -p\mathbf{n} + \tau \right) \, d\mathcal{S}$$

where $\mathbf{n}$ denotes the surface normal and $\tau$ is the shear stress tensor. Effective parallelization on GPUs enables real-time computations necessary for interactive design spaces and real-time feedback, facilitating enhanced fluid dynamic analyses in complex engineering systems.

# Python Code Snippet

Below is a Python code snippet that encompasses the core computational elements for fluid dynamics simulations using CUDA, including numerical discretization, memory management, and parallel execution strategy.

```python
import pycuda.autoinit
import pycuda.driver as cuda
from pycuda.compiler import SourceModule
import numpy as np

# CUDA kernel for updating velocity field
velocity_update_kernel = """
__global__ void update_velocity(float *v_x, float *v_y, float
↪ *pressure, float *f,
                                 float dx, float dy, float dt, int
                                 ↪ nx, int ny) {
    int i = blockIdx.x * blockDim.x + threadIdx.x;
    int j = blockIdx.y * blockDim.y + threadIdx.y;

    if (i < nx && j < ny) {
        int idx = j * nx + i;

        float dvx_dt = - (v_x[idx] * (v_x[idx + 1] - v_x[idx - 1]) /
        ↪ (2 * dx))
                       - (v_y[idx] * (v_x[idx + nx] - v_x[idx - nx])
                       ↪ / (2 * dy))
```

```
                          - (pressure[idx + 1] - pressure[idx - 1]) /
                       ↪    (2 * dx)
                          + f[idx];

          float dvy_dt = - (v_x[idx] * (v_y[idx + 1] - v_y[idx - 1]) /
          ↪  (2 * dx))
                          - (v_y[idx] * (v_y[idx + nx] - v_y[idx - nx])
                          ↪   / (2 * dy))
                          - (pressure[idx + nx] - pressure[idx - nx]) /
                          ↪    (2 * dy)
                          + f[idx];

          v_x[idx] += dt * dvx_dt;
          v_y[idx] += dt * dvy_dt;
      }
  }
  """


# Initialize fluid domain parameters
nx, ny = 256, 256
dx, dy = 1.0 / nx, 1.0 / ny
dt = 0.01

v_x = np.zeros((ny, nx), dtype=np.float32)
v_y = np.zeros((ny, nx), dtype=np.float32)
pressure = np.zeros((ny, nx), dtype=np.float32)
f = np.ones((ny, nx), dtype=np.float32)

# Allocate memory on the GPU
v_x_gpu = cuda.mem_alloc(v_x.nbytes)
v_y_gpu = cuda.mem_alloc(v_y.nbytes)
pressure_gpu = cuda.mem_alloc(pressure.nbytes)
f_gpu = cuda.mem_alloc(f.nbytes)

# Transfer data to GPU
cuda.memcpy_htod(v_x_gpu, v_x)
cuda.memcpy_htod(v_y_gpu, v_y)
cuda.memcpy_htod(pressure_gpu, pressure)
cuda.memcpy_htod(f_gpu, f)

# Compile CUDA code
mod = SourceModule(velocity_update_kernel)
update_velocity = mod.get_function("update_velocity")

# Set up execution configuration
block_size = (16, 16, 1)
grid_size = (nx // block_size[0], ny // block_size[1])

# Execute GPU kernel for each time step
for time_step in range(100):
    update_velocity(v_x_gpu, v_y_gpu, pressure_gpu, f_gpu,
                    np.float32(dx), np.float32(dy), np.float32(dt),
                    np.int32(nx), np.int32(ny),
```

```
                    block=block_size, grid=grid_size)

# Copy results back to host
cuda.memcpy_dtoh(v_x, v_x_gpu)
cuda.memcpy_dtoh(v_y, v_y_gpu)

print("Velocity field updated successfully.")
```

This code snippet defines the necessary CUDA kernel and associated Python code to perform core fluid dynamics calculations:

- The `velocity_update_kernel` is a CUDA kernel that updates the velocity field within the flow domain based on the discrete Navier-Stokes equations.

- Initialization of computational parameters like grid dimensions (`nx` and `ny`), spacing (`dx` and `dy`), and time step (`dt`).

- Allocation and transfer of memory between host and device are achieved using `cuda.mem_alloc` and `cuda.memcpy_htod`.

- Execution of the kernel with the `update_velocity` function, configured for parallel execution across a specified grid and block size, representing the discretized fluid domain.

- Finally, results are transferred back to the host memory and printed to verify the update process of the velocity field.

# Chapter 42

# FRACTALS: Benoit Mandelbrot Visualization

## Mathematical Framework of Mandelbrot Sets

The Mandelbrot set is a well-known fractal defined in the complex plane, comprising complex numbers $c$ for which the sequence defined by the iteration $z_{n+1} = z_n^2 + c$ remains bounded. The initial condition is typically $z_0 = 0$. The set can be expressed as:

$$M = \{c \in \mathbb{C} : \limsup_{n \to \infty} \|z_n\| < \infty\}$$

This recursive relation is evaluated up to a maximum number of iterations, $N$, to determine whether the series diverges or remains within a bounded region. The boundary of the Mandelbrot set exhibits complicated structures leading to its fractal nature.

## Numerical Approximation and Visualization

For a given resolution, the Mandelbrot set can be visualized by evaluating the escape time algorithm. Each pixel on the screen corresponds to a complex number $c$. If the iteration of $z_{n+1} = z_n^2 + c$ does not exceed a specific threshold $\|z_n\| > R$ within $N$ iterations, the point is considered part of the Mandelbrot set. The choice of $R$ is arbitrary but typically set to 2, based on the properties of complex quadratic polynomials.

# 1  Escape Time Algorithm

Begin with the complex plane, where points correspond to pixels. Calculate the orbit of each point using:

$$z_{n+1} = z_n^2 + c, \quad \text{with } z_0 = 0$$

Escaped is the boolean condition:

$$\texttt{Escaped}(z_n, R) = \begin{cases} \texttt{True}, & \text{if } \|z_n\| > R \\ \texttt{False}, & \text{otherwise} \end{cases} \tag{42.1}$$

---

**Algorithm 5:** Escape Time Algorithm for Mandelbrot Set Visualization

---

**Data:** Resolution (`width`, `height`), max iterations `N`
**foreach** *pixel (x, y) in image* **do**
    c = map (x, y) to complex plane;
    z = 0;
    i = 0;
    **while** *i < N and not Escaped(z, R)* **do**
        z = z * z + c;
        i += 1;
    **end**
    color pixel (x, y) based on the value of i;
**end**

---

# Parallelization with CUDA for High-Performance Visualization

CUDA facilitates parallel processing of computational tasks on the GPU. Each point $c$ on the complex plane is independently evaluated for membership in the Mandelbrot set, making it an ideal candidate for parallelization.

# 1  CUDA-based Implementation

The core computation for visualizing the Mandelbrot set involves assigning a GPU thread per pixel, performing iterative complex number computations, and storing the results. The key computation translates to:

$$z_{n+1} = \texttt{fma}(z_n, z_n, c)$$

where `fma` stands for fused multiply-add operation enhancing precision. The GPU accelerates iterations by executing thousands of threads simultaneously.

# Rendering the Fractal in the Complex Plane

The final rendered image derives from the varied coloring techniques applied to the escape iteration count. Implementing dynamic coloring schemes improves visual realism and detail in fractal images. Each thread computes a color value based on the number of iterations before escaping:

$$\texttt{color} = \begin{cases} \texttt{map}(i), & \text{if } i < N \\ \texttt{black}, & \text{otherwise} \end{cases}$$

Hence, rendering the Mandelbrot set in CUDA translates complex mathematical formulations into visually tangible forms, portraying the intricacies of fractal geometries.

# Python Code Snippet

Below is a Python code snippet that implements the key elements of Mandelbrot set visualization using CUDA. The code utilizes PyCUDA to leverage GPU capabilities for rendering the fractal efficiently.

```python
import numpy as np
import matplotlib.pyplot as plt
import pycuda.autoinit
import pycuda.driver as drv
from pycuda.compiler import SourceModule

# CUDA kernel for Mandelbrot computation
mandelbrot_kernel = SourceModule("""
```

```
__global__ void mandelbrot(float *output, int width, int height,
↪   float x_min, float x_max, float y_min, float y_max, int
↪   max_iter) {
    int idx = threadIdx.x + blockIdx.x * blockDim.x;
    int idy = threadIdx.y + blockIdx.y * blockDim.y;
    int index = idy * width + idx;

    float x0 = x_min + idx * (x_max - x_min) / width;
    float y0 = y_min + idy * (y_max - y_min) / height;
    float x = 0.0;
    float y = 0.0;
    int iteration = 0;
    float xtemp;

    while (x*x + y*y <= 4.0 && iteration < max_iter) {
        xtemp = x*x - y*y + x0;
        y = 2*x*y + y0;
        x = xtemp;
        iteration++;
    }

    output[index] = iteration;
}
""")

# Parameters for the Mandelbrot set
width, height = 800, 600
x_min, x_max = -2.0, 1.0
y_min, y_max = -1.0, 1.0
max_iter = 256

# Initialize output and block/grid size
output = np.zeros((width, height), np.float32)
blockdim = (16, 16, 1)
griddim = (int(width / blockdim[0]), int(height / blockdim[1]), 1)

# Allocate device memory and copy output to it
output_gpu = drv.mem_alloc(output.nbytes)

# Get the kernel function
mandelbrot = mandelbrot_kernel.get_function("mandelbrot")

# Run the kernel
mandelbrot(output_gpu, np.int32(width), np.int32(height),
↪   np.float32(x_min), np.float32(x_max),
        np.float32(y_min), np.float32(y_max), np.int32(max_iter),
        ↪   block=blockdim, grid=griddim)

# Copy the results to host
drv.memcpy_dtoh(output, output_gpu)

# Normalize and plot the result
```

```
plt.imshow(np.log(output + 1), cmap='inferno', extent=(x_min, x_max,
↪ y_min, y_max))
plt.colorbar()
plt.title('Mandelbrot Set Visualization')
plt.xlabel('Re(c)')
plt.ylabel('Im(c)')
plt.show()
```

This code snippet breaks down the essential components for
visualizing the Mandelbrot set using CUDA:

- The `mandelbrot_kernel` defines the CUDA kernel for calculating Mandelbrot iterations.

- Input parameters such as `width`, `height`, x_min, x_max, y_min,
  y_max, and `max_iter` are set to initialize the complex plane
  and iteration limit.

- Memory management is handled by allocating GPU memory
  for the output array with `drv.mem_alloc`.

- The Mandelbrot kernel executes via `mandelbrot()` with the
  defined blocks and grid dimensions for parallel execution.

- The results are transferred from GPU to CPU using
  `drv.memcpy_dtoh` for visualization using Matplotlib.

- Finally, the Mandelbrot set is normalized and plotted using
  colormaps to highlight fractal structures.

# Chapter 43

# Using Unified Memory in CUDA

## Introduction to Unified Memory

Unified memory in CUDA represents a significant advancement in simplifying memory management between host and device. Traditional memory handling in CUDA necessitates explicit copying of data between the host and device, which can be error-prone and cumbersome. Unified memory, introduced in CUDA 6, allows for a shared memory space that is accessible by both CPU and GPU, mitigating the need for manual data transfers.

The model enables developers to allocate memory with a single `cudaMallocManaged` call. This memory is automatically accessible from both the host and device, and the CUDA runtime system manages data movement under the hood. The declaration is as follows:

$$cudaMallocManaged(ptr, size)$$

Here, `ptr` is the pointer to the memory location, and `size` specifies the number of bytes allocated. The unified approach simplifies porting applications to heterogeneous platforms, reducing the cognitive load on developers.

# Memory Consistency and Coherency

Unified memory introduces new considerations regarding consistency and coherency. The CUDA runtime system ensures that memory accesses from the CPU and GPU are coherent, employing a combination of hardware and software mechanisms to migrate and replicate memory pages as needed. The critical concept is that the consistency of the memory representation is maintained across the host and device.

The CUDA execution model must enforce synchronization through mechanisms such as `cudaDeviceSynchronize` to ensure memory contents are up-to-date post kernel execution. The use of memory fences and flushes may be required in custom implementations to guarantee coherency, formulated as:

$$cudaDeviceSynchronize()$$

Understanding the memory access patterns helps to optimize the automatic migration provided by unified memory, as it is based on page faults and demand paging techniques.

# Performance Implications

Unified memory can potentially introduce overhead due to implicit data transfers. Performance characteristics are influenced by the data placement strategy, which can be managed explicitly through prefetching and migration hints available in CUDA 8 and later. These advanced features provide more control over where data resides during computations.

The developer can guide the system using:

$$cudaMemPrefetchAsync(ptr, count, dstDevice)$$

Prefetching reduces latency associated with page faults, thereby improving performance. By understanding the logical flow of data and computation, developers can utilize these capabilities to achieve a balance between simplicity and performance.

# Algorithmic Use Case

---

**Algorithm 6:** Example showcasing Unified Memory in CUDA

---

**Data:** Size N, arrays A, and B on unified memory

cudaMallocManaged(&A, N × sizeof(float));

cudaMallocManaged(&B, N × sizeof(float));

**for** $i$ = $0$ **to** $N$ **do**

 | A[i] = i;

**end**

kernel«<blocks, threadsPerBlock»>(A, B, N);

cudaDeviceSynchronize();

---

In the above example, both arrays A and B are allocated using unified memory. The GPU kernel updates B based on A without explicit data transfers. Synchronization ensures updated results are visible to the host, exemplifying unified memory's contributions to programming efficiency in CUDA.

# Conclusion

Unified memory in CUDA serves as a pivotal evolution in GPU programming paradigms, streamlining data management between CPU and GPU. Its capabilities facilitate easier programming by abstracting manual data movement, enabling focus on computational logic and algorithmic advancements.

# Python Code Snippet

Below is a Python code snippet that demonstrates the use of unified memory in CUDA, including memory allocation, a kernel launch, and synchronization using PyCUDA.

```
import pycuda.autoinit
import pycuda.driver as cuda
import numpy as np
from pycuda.compiler import SourceModule

# Kernel code
mod = SourceModule("""
__global__ void increment(float *a, float *b, int N) {
    int idx = threadIdx.x + blockIdx.x * blockDim.x;
```

```
    if (idx < N) {
        b[idx] = a[idx] + 1.0f;
    }
}
""")
increment_kernel = mod.get_function("increment")

# Size of the array
N = 10

# Allocate unified memory
A = cuda.managed_zeros(N, dtype=np.float32,
↪   mem_flags=cuda.mem_attach_global)
B = cuda.managed_zeros(N, dtype=np.float32,
↪   mem_flags=cuda.mem_attach_global)

# Initialize array A
for i in range(N):
    A[i] = float(i)

# Define thread and block sizes
threads_per_block = 256
blocks = (N + threads_per_block - 1) // threads_per_block

# Launch kernel
increment_kernel(cuda.Out(B), cuda.InOut(A), np.int32(N),
↪   block=(threads_per_block, 1, 1), grid=(blocks, 1))

# Synchronize device
cuda.Context.synchronize()

# Output results
print("Array A:", A)
print("Array B after increment:", B)
```

---

This code performs the following steps:

- Defines a CUDA kernel `increment` that adds 1 to each element of the input array and stores the result in a second array.

- Uses PyCUDA's `managed_zeros` function to allocate unified memory for arrays `A` and `B`. This memory is accessible on both the host and device without explicit data transfers.

- Initializes array `A` with sequential values from 0 to `N-1`.

- Calculates the number of blocks and launches the CUDA kernel using PyCUDA, passing the managed arrays as parameters.

255

- Executes `cuda.Context.synchronize()` to ensure all GPU operations are complete before accessing memory on the host.

- Prints the contents of arrays `A` and `B` to verify the correct operation of the kernel and utilization of unified memory. The output demonstrates how unified memory simplifies management by handling data transfers automatically.

# Chapter 44

# Implementing Bayesian Inference Models

## Bayesian Inference Framework

Bayesian inference is fundamentally grounded in updating the probability estimate for a hypothesis as more evidence or information becomes available. Mathematically, it leverages Bayes' Theorem, which is represented as:

$$P(H|E) = \frac{P(E|H) \cdot P(H)}{P(E)} \tag{44.1}$$

where $P(H|E)$ is the posterior probability, $P(E|H)$ is the likelihood, $P(H)$ is the prior, and $P(E)$ is the marginal likelihood.

## Parallelism in Bayesian Computations

The integration of CUDA in Bayesian inference significantly expedites the estimation process by capitalizing on the inherent parallelizable nature of probability calculations. Given a large dataset and a complex model, the evaluating of likelihoods for multiple parameters can be decomposed into parallel operations.

## 1 Parallel Posterior Computation

For a Bayesian model with parameter vector $\theta$ and data $D = \{x_1, x_2, \ldots, x_n\}$, the posterior distribution can be expressed and computed as:

$$P(\theta|D) \propto P(D|\theta) \cdot P(\theta) \qquad (44.2)$$

The data likelihood $P(D|\theta)$ can be parallelized by evaluating the probability of each data point $x_i$ independently across CUDA threads:

$$P(D|\theta) = \prod_{i=1}^{n} P(x_i|\theta) \qquad (44.3)$$

where each $P(x_i|\theta)$ is calculated by each thread, enabling distributed computation and reduced execution time compared to sequential processing.

---

**Algorithm 7:** Parallel Likelihood Calculation

---
**Data:** Parameter vector $\theta$, dataset $D$
**Result:** Likelihood $P(D|\theta)$
`cudaMallocManaged(&likelihoods, n × sizeof(float));`
`parallel-compute` $\Rightarrow P(x_i|\theta)$ for each $x_i \in D$;
`cudaDeviceSynchronize();`
`aggregate` $\Rightarrow \prod_{i=1}^{n}$ `likelihoods`$[i]$;

---

# Prior Distributions and their Parallel Evaluation

Bayesian analysis often involves a prior distribution, $P(\theta)$, representing initial parameter beliefs. The choice and computation of prior can also leverage CUDA parallelism when computing mainly involves complex distributions over large parameter spaces.

$$P(\theta) = f(\theta; \alpha, \beta) \qquad (44.4)$$

For computationally intensive priors, evaluations over a grid of $\theta$ values are suited to parallel deployment, with threads assigned distinct priors:

$$\text{Evaluate } P(\theta_k) \text{ independently for } \theta_k \in \Theta \qquad (44.5)$$

A kernel function can be utilized to iteratively compute the prior for a large dimensional parameter space, parallelizing compute operations effectively.

# Posterior Distribution Sampling

The posterior distribution typically necessitates sampling methods such as Markov Chain Monte Carlo (MCMC), where samples from $P(\theta|D)$ are acquired to approximate integrals and hypothesis testing.

## 1  Implementing Parallel MCMC

Using CUDA threads to perform multiple chains or parallelize the calculations within a single chain is advantageous. Consider the Metropolis-Hastings algorithm structured for parallel execution:

---
**Algorithm 8:** Parallel Metropolis-Hastings Sampling

---
**Data:** Initial parameter $\theta_0$, dataset $D$
**Result:** Sampled posterior distribution
**for** *each chain* **do**
  Initialize `theta`;
  **for** *iteration from 1 to maxIter* **do**
    Propose `theta*` from proposal distribution;
    `Accept or reject theta* based on posterior`
    `probability`;
  Collect samples;
`cudaDeviceSynchronize()`;

---

CUDA improvements can iteratively lead to remarkable speed-up in generating diversified sample paths supporting a robust estimation of the posterior.

# Python Code Snippet

Below is a Python code snippet that implements the core computational elements of Bayesian inference, including the calculation of likelihoods, priors, posterior sampling, and parallelization using PyCUDA.

---

```python
import pycuda.autoinit
import pycuda.driver as cuda
import numpy as np
from pycuda.compiler import SourceModule

# CUDA kernel code for likelihood calculation
mod = SourceModule("""
```

```
__global__ void likelihood_kernel(float *theta, float *data, float
↪ *likelihoods, int n, int m) {
    int idx = threadIdx.x + blockIdx.x * blockDim.x;
    if (idx < n) {
        float theta_val = theta[idx % m];
        float likelihood = 1.0;
        for (int i = 0; i < n; i++) {
            float diff = data[i] - theta_val;
            likelihood *= exp(-diff * diff / 2.0) / sqrt(2.0 *
            ↪ 3.141592653589793);
        }
        likelihoods[idx] = likelihood;
    }
}
""")

# Function to compute likelihoods
def compute_likelihoods(theta, data):
    n = len(data)
    m = len(theta)
    likelihoods = np.zeros(n, dtype=np.float32)

    theta_gpu = cuda.mem_alloc(theta.nbytes)
    data_gpu = cuda.mem_alloc(data.nbytes)
    likelihoods_gpu = cuda.mem_alloc(likelihoods.nbytes)

    cuda.memcpy_htod(theta_gpu, theta)
    cuda.memcpy_htod(data_gpu, data)

    func = mod.get_function("likelihood_kernel")
    func(theta_gpu, data_gpu, likelihoods_gpu, np.int32(n),
    ↪ np.int32(m), block=(256, 1, 1), grid=(n // 256 + 1, 1))

    cuda.memcpy_dtoh(likelihoods, likelihoods_gpu)

    return likelihoods

# Example parameters and data
theta = np.array([1.0, 2.0, 3.0], dtype=np.float32)  # Example
↪ parameter vector
data = np.random.normal(0, 1, 1000).astype(np.float32)  # Simulated
↪ data

# Compute the likelihood
likelihoods = compute_likelihoods(theta, data)
print("Likelihoods:", likelihoods)

# Define prior computation (example using uniform distribution)
def compute_prior(theta):
    return np.ones_like(theta) / len(theta)

# Calculate posterior (unnormalized for demonstration)
posteriors = likelihoods * compute_prior(theta)
```

```
print("Posterior:", posteriors)

# Simplified MCMC setup (conceptual implementation for
↪  demonstration)
def metropolis_hastings(iterations, theta_init, data):
    samples = []
    theta_current = theta_init
    current_likelihood =
    ↪  compute_likelihoods(np.array([theta_current]), data)[0]

    for _ in range(iterations):
        theta_proposal = theta_current + np.random.normal(0, 0.1)
        proposed_likelihood =
        ↪  compute_likelihoods(np.array([theta_proposal]), data)[0]

        acceptance_ratio = proposed_likelihood / current_likelihood
        if np.random.rand() < acceptance_ratio:
            theta_current = theta_proposal
            current_likelihood = proposed_likelihood

        samples.append(theta_current)

    return np.array(samples)

# Run MCMC to sample posterior
mcmc_samples = metropolis_hastings(1000, 2.0, data)
print("MCMC Samples:", mcmc_samples)
```

This code defines several key functions necessary for implementing Bayesian inference using CUDA:

- `compute_likelihoods` function uses a CUDA kernel to compute the likelihood of data given parameters, parallelizing the multiplication of individual probability values.

- `compute_prior` computes the prior distribution, exemplified by a uniform prior.

- Posterior probabilities are computed as the product of likelihoods and priors, leading to an unnormalized posterior distribution.

- `metropolis_hastings` implements a basic MCMC algorithm to sample the posterior distribution, showcasing a conceptual implementation that can be expanded and optimized.

These components allow for parallel computation of Bayesian inference elements, leveraging the power of GPUs to handle large datasets and complex models.

# Chapter 45

# Fast Fourier Transform (FFT) Applications

## Mathematical Foundation of FFT

The Fourier Transform is a fundamental tool in signal processing, providing a frequency domain representation of time-domain signals. For a discrete signal $x[n]$, the Discrete Fourier Transform (DFT) is given by:

$$X[k] = \sum_{n=0}^{N-1} x[n] \cdot e^{-i2\pi kn/N}$$

where $X[k]$ is the DFT of the signal at frequency bin $k$, $x[n]$ is the time-domain signal, and $N$ is the number of samples.

The Fast Fourier Transform (FFT) is an optimized algorithm to compute the DFT efficiently, reducing complexity from $\mathcal{O}(N^2)$ to $\mathcal{O}(N \log N)$. It is expressed as a recursive decomposition:

$$X[k] = X_{\text{even}}[k] + e^{-i2\pi k/N} \cdot X_{\text{odd}}[k]$$

where $X_{\text{even}}$ and $X_{\text{odd}}$ are the DFTs of the even-indexed and odd-indexed inputs, respectively.

## CUDA-Accelerated FFT Computation

The parallel nature of the FFT algorithm makes it particularly suitable for GPU acceleration using CUDA. Each stage of the FFT involves computations that can be distributed across multiple CUDA threads, enhancing performance.

# 1 Parallel Computation Strategy

The Cooley-Tukey algorithm, a popular FFT implementation, splits a DFT of size $N$ into two interleaved DFTs of size $N/2$. This strategy is leveraged within a CUDA-kernel as follows:

---

**Algorithm 9:** CUDA FFT Kernel

---

**Data:** Complex array x, size $N$
**Result:** Transformed array X
shared_memory $\leftarrow$ load $x$;
for *stride = 1 to log2(N)* do
    index $\leftarrow$ threadIdx.x;
    phase $\leftarrow e^{-i2\pi \cdot \text{index}/N}$;
    X[index] $\leftarrow$ X[index] + X[index + stride] $\cdot$ phase;
    barrier synchronize;

---

# 2 Memory Data Layout Optimization

Efficient memory access is crucial for maximizing FFT performance on GPUs. The Radix-2 FFT algorithm utilizes shared_memory to store intermediate results, thereby minimizing global memory transactions. Reordering the input data into a bit-reversed order further optimizes the memory access pattern, aligning with the warp execution model.

# 3 Benchmarking CUDA FFT Performance

The performance of the CUDA-accelerated FFT can be empirically analyzed by comparing computation time against CPU-based FFT implementations. Metrics such as throughput and speedup are evaluated over varying signal lengths, highlighting substantial improvements primarily in datasets with sizes that are powers of two, compatible with Radix-2 algorithms.

# Application in Signal Processing

FFT plays a pivotal role in various signal processing applications, ranging from spectral analysis to convolution and filtering. CUDA acceleration greatly enhances real-time processing capabilities, which are critical in fields such as telecommunications, medical imaging, and audio processing.

# 1 Spectral Analysis

In spectral analysis, FFTs decompose signals into constituent frequencies, enabling analysis of signal characteristics. The CUDA-accelerated FFT facilitates rapid transformations, crucial for real-time spectrum monitoring applications, where delays are intolerable.

# 2 Convolution and Filtering

Convolution operations in the frequency domain offer computational advantages due to the convolution theorem:

$$y[n] = x[n] * h[n] \quad \Rightarrow \quad Y[k] = X[k] \cdot H[k]$$

where $Y[k]$, $X[k]$, and $H[k]$ are the Fourier transforms of the output, input, and impulse response, respectively. CUDA facilitates efficient FFT-based convolution, particularly when the signal and filter lengths are substantial.

# Cross-Industry Analytical Applications

The efficacy of CUDA-accelerated FFT extends beyond traditional signal processing into fields requiring rapid data transformation and analysis, such as finance, seismic imaging, and scientific simulations, driving advancements in data analytics and predictive modeling through efficient computational frameworks.

# Python Code Snippet

Below is a Python code snippet that demonstrates how to perform Fast Fourier Transform (FFT) using PyCUDA for accelerated computation, highlighting key concepts such as complex number handling, thread synchronization, and memory management.

```
import pycuda.autoinit
import pycuda.gpuarray as gpuarray
import numpy as np
```

```
import scipy.fftpack as fft
from pycuda.elementwise import ElementwiseKernel
import pycuda.driver as cuda

# Initialize input data
N = 1024
x = np.random.rand(N).astype(np.complex64)

# Transfer data to the GPU
x_gpu = gpuarray.to_gpu(x)

# Kernel for FFT using Cooley-Tukey algorithm
fft_kernel = ElementwiseKernel(
    "pycuda::complex<float>* x, pycuda::complex<float>* X, int N",
    """
    int index = i;
    int stride = 1;
    while (stride < N) {
        int partner = index ^ stride;   // XOR to find the butterfly
        ↪  partner
        if (partner > index) {
            pycuda::complex<float> t = exp(-I *
            ↪  3.14159265358979323846f * stride / N) * x[partner];
            x[partner] = x[index] - t;
            x[index] += t;
        }
        stride *= 2;
        __syncthreads();
    }
    X[index] = x[index];
    """,
    "fft_kernel")

# Output array
X_gpu = gpuarray.empty_like(x_gpu)

# Execute the FFT kernel
fft_kernel(x_gpu, X_gpu, N)

# Retrieve results from the GPU
X = X_gpu.get()

# Verify against CPU computation
X_cpu = fft.fft(x)
print("GPU FFT matches CPU FFT:", np.allclose(X, X_cpu, atol=1e-5))
```

---

This code defines key functions for implementing CUDA-accelerated Fast Fourier Transform (FFT) with PyCUDA:

- The data is initialized and transferred to the GPU using `gpuarray.to_gpu`.

- The `fft_kernel` function encapsulates the FFT computation, facilitating distributed workloads across CUDA threads for parallel execution.

- Complex number operations, synchronization with `__syncthreads()`, and data transfer between GPU and CPU memory are effectively managed for performance.

- Validation against CPU results is performed using `scipy.fftpack.fft` to ensure accuracy of the GPU computation.

The final code block illustrates the method's capability to deliver efficient GPU-based FFT calculations, confirmed by comparing results obtained from a standard CPU library.

# Chapter 46

# CUDA for Video Encoding and Decoding

## Mathematical Background of Video Encoding

Video encoding is the process of converting video data into a digitally compressed format. The fundamental mathematical concept revolves around the discrete cosine transform (DCT), which represents a signal in terms of cosine functions oscillating at different frequencies. The DCT for a signal $f[x, y]$ can be formulated as:

$$F[u,v] = \sum_{x=0}^{N-1} \sum_{y=0}^{M-1} f[x,y] \cdot \cos\left(\frac{\pi(2x+1)u}{2N}\right) \cdot \cos\left(\frac{\pi(2y+1)v}{2M}\right)$$

where $F[u, v]$ is the DCT coefficient, $N$ and $M$ denote the dimensions of the image block, and $u, v$ are frequency variables.

CUDA can optimize the computation of the DCT by exploiting the parallel nature of the cosine operations and simultaneous data manipulation across multiple processing cores.

# CUDA-Accelerated Video Processing Framework

Employing CUDA for video encoding and decoding involves parallelizing several tasks that can run concurrently across multiple threads. The following sections describe key areas in CUDA-accelerated video processing.

## 1 Parallel DCT Implementation

The DCT can be parallelized using CUDA by dividing the video frame into smaller blocks, which are then processed individually by separate threads within a block. A common algorithm applied is:

---

**Data:** Frame $f$ of size $N \times M$
**Result:** DCT coefficients $F$
blockDim $\leftarrow (16, 16)$;
gridDim $\leftarrow (N/16, M/16)$;
**foreach** *block in gridDim* **do**
    sharedMemory $\leftarrow$ load block data;
    **foreach** *thread in blockDim* **do**
        DCT computation;
        store result;
    barrier synchronize;

---

Each thread calculates part of the DCT for a sub-block of the frame, resulting in a marked improvement in performance compared to sequential execution.

## 2 Entropy Coding with CUDA

The power of entropy coding lies in its ability to compress data by representing frequently occurring symbols with fewer bits. The Huffman coding algorithm commonly used in video encoding can be adapted for CUDA:

$$E_i = - \sum_{j=0}^{n} p(j) \cdot \log_2(p(j))$$

where $E_i$ denotes the entropy, and $p(j)$ the probability of each symbol. CUDA parallelizes the calculation of symbol frequencies and the construction of the Huffman tree.

---
**Algorithm 10:** Parallel Huffman Coding
---
**Data:** Symbol set $s$
**Result:** Encoded data $e$
calculate histogram using CUDA;
generate Huffman tree using parallel reduction;
assign codes based on tree;
encode data with generated codes;
---

# Decoding Optimization with GPU Resources

CUDA enables significant performance gains in video decoding by leveraging its thousands of cores. The parallel processing capabilities are particularly effective in the context of:

## 1 Inverse DCT

The inverse DCT (IDCT) is necessary to reconstruct image blocks from compressed data. The mathematical operation for a block is given by:

$$f[x, y] = \frac{1}{4} \sum_{u=0}^{N-1} \sum_{v=0}^{M-1} \alpha(u)\alpha(v)F[u, v] \cos\left(\frac{\pi(2x + 1)u}{2N}\right) \cos\left(\frac{\pi(2y + 1)v}{2M}\right)$$

where $\alpha(u), \alpha(v)$ are scaling factors. Parallel processing applications in CUDA follow the logic established for DCT but in reverse:

parallelize over blocks and threads compute IDCT for each sub-block aggregate results into the full frame

## 2 Motion Compensation

CUDA's ability to process vectors efficiently enhances the video decoding pipeline through optimized motion compensation, where the displacements of pixel blocks are calculated and adjusted. The prediction error reduction is computed as:

$$P[x, y] = f[x, y] - \hat{f}[x - dx, y - dy]$$

where $dx$ and $dy$ represent motion vectors. CUDA threads independently compute these vectors for various blocks, ensuring rapid updates and minimum lag.

269

# CUDA Libraries for Video Processing

Several CUDA libraries facilitate efficient GPU utilization for video tasks. These include:

## 1 NVIDIA Video Codec SDK

The Video Codec SDK provides APIs for hardware-accelerated video decoding. Its integration with CUDA allows direct manipulation of data without intermediate copying, optimizing the throughput:

    cudaMemcpyAsync nvEncodeAPI Function Integration

## 2 cuBLAS and cuFFT

CUDA libraries such as cuBLAS and cuFFT are instrumental for matrix operations and FFT computations. They enable researchers and professionals to directly apply advanced mathematical transformations within their video encoding and decoding workflows.

# Python Code Snippet

Below is a Python code snippet that demonstrates the implementation of core algorithms and mathematical computations for CUDA-accelerated video processing, particularly focusing on DCT and Huffman coding, leveraging the PyCUDA library for GPU acceleration.

```python
import pycuda.autoinit
import pycuda.driver as cuda
import numpy as np
from pycuda.compiler import SourceModule

# Define CUDA kernel for DCT computation
dct_kernel = SourceModule("""
__global__ void dct(float *d_f, float *d_F, int N, int M) {
    int x = blockIdx.x * blockDim.x + threadIdx.x;
    int y = blockIdx.y * blockDim.y + threadIdx.y;

    if (x < N && y < M) {
        float cu = x == 0 ? sqrt(1.0 / N) : sqrt(2.0 / N);
        float cv = y == 0 ? sqrt(1.0 / M) : sqrt(2.0 / M);

        float sum = 0.0;
```

```
            for (int i = 0; i < N; ++i) {
                for (int j = 0; j < M; ++j) {
                    float dct = d_f[i * M + j] *
                                cos((2.0 * i + 1.0) * x * 3.14159 / (2.0
                                ↪     * N)) *
                                cos((2.0 * j + 1.0) * y * 3.14159 / (2.0
                                ↪     * M));
                    sum += dct;
                }
            }
            d_F[x * M + y] = cu * cv * sum;
        }
    }
    """)


    def perform_dct(h_f, N, M):
        h_F = np.zeros_like(h_f).astype(np.float32)
        d_f = cuda.mem_alloc(h_f.nbytes)
        d_F = cuda.mem_alloc(h_F.nbytes)

        cuda.memcpy_htod(d_f, h_f)
        cuda.memcpy_htod(d_F, h_F)

        block_size = (16, 16, 1)
        grid_size = ((N + 15) // 16, (M + 15) // 16, 1)

        dct_func = dct_kernel.get_function("dct")
        dct_func(d_f, d_F, np.int32(N), np.int32(M), block=block_size,
        ↪    grid=grid_size)

        cuda.memcpy_dtoh(h_F, d_F)
        return h_F

    # Define CUDA kernel for Huffman coding (simplified version)
    huffman_kernel = SourceModule("""
    __global__ void huffman(int *d_freq, int *d_encoded, int n) {
        // Simple parallel histogram calculation
        int tid = blockIdx.x * blockDim.x + threadIdx.x;
        if (tid < n) {
            atomicAdd(&d_freq[tid], 1);
        }
    }
    """)


    def huffman_encode(h_data, n):
        h_freq = np.zeros(n, dtype=np.int32)
        d_data = cuda.mem_alloc(h_data.nbytes)
        d_freq = cuda.mem_alloc(h_freq.nbytes)

        cuda.memcpy_htod(d_data, h_data)
        cuda.memcpy_htod(d_freq, h_freq)

        block_size = (256, 1, 1)
```

```
grid_size = ((n + 255) // 256, 1, 1)

huffman_func = huffman_kernel.get_function("huffman")
huffman_func(d_data, d_freq, np.int32(n), block=block_size,
↪  grid=grid_size)

cuda.memcpy_dtoh(h_freq, d_freq)
return h_freq

# Sample data
h_f = np.random.rand(16, 16).astype(np.float32)
N, M = h_f.shape
h_data = np.random.randint(0, 100, size=N * M).astype(np.int32)

# Perform DCT using CUDA
dct_result = perform_dct(h_f.flatten(), N, M)

# Encode data using Huffman coding
huffman_result = huffman_encode(h_data, 100)

print("DCT Result:", dct_result)
print("Huffman Frequency:", huffman_result)
```

The code snippet provided showcases crucial CUDA operations essential for efficient video processing tasks:

- **perform_dct** function leverages CUDA for discrete cosine transform, breaking down image data into frequency components through parallel execution.

- **huffman_encode** encapsulates a basic framework for parallelizing the calculation of symbol frequencies, a key step in Huffman coding.

Sample data and kernel configurations are demonstrated, illustrating how parallel computation can be executed on a GPU using PyCUDA.

# Chapter 47

# Medical Imaging and CUDA

## Accelerating MRI Simulations

The acceleration of Magnetic Resonance Imaging (MRI) simulations using CUDA exploits the inherent parallel structure of MRI reconstruction algorithms. Central to MRI imaging is the Fourier transform, used to convert raw data from the frequency domain to the spatial domain. The inverse discrete Fourier transform (IDFT) plays a pivotal role and can be expressed as:

$$f[n] = \frac{1}{N} \sum_{k=0}^{N-1} F[k] e^{i2\pi kn/N}$$

where $f[n]$ denotes the reconstructed image, $F[k]$ is the frequency domain data, and $N$ is the number of data points. CUDA facilitates the parallel computation of these transforms across the GPU's cores, yielding significant speed gains.

The CUDA-based optimization of IDFT for MRI simulations involves dividing the dataset into smaller partitions, each processed by a warp or block of threads. The performance improvement hinges on minimizing memory latency through coalesced memory access patterns and efficient utilization of shared memory.

# CT Scan Computation Enhancement

Computed Tomography (CT) scans rely heavily on algorithms such as filtered back projection for image reconstruction. In this context, the Radon transform and its inverse are of primary importance. The continuous inverse Radon transform can be defined as:

$$f(x, y) = \int_0^\pi g(\theta, x \cos \theta + y \sin \theta) \, d\theta$$

where $g(\theta, s)$ represents the projection of the scanned object at angle $\theta$ and position $s$. CUDA enhances CT scan simulations by parallelizing the calculation of projections and contributions to each image pixel.

---

**Data:** Projection data $g$
**Result:** Reconstructed image $f$
Initialize shared memory
**foreach** *projection angle* $\theta$ **do**
  **foreach** *image pixel* $(x, y)$ **do**
    Compute contribution using CUDA threads;
    Accumulate result to shared memory;

Aggregate results for full image reconstruction;

---

The parallel nature of CUDA allows the computation of projections from all angles simultaneously, reducing total computation time considerably.

# Advanced Image Reconstruction Algorithms

Reconstruction of medical images often involves solving complex linear systems that are computationally intensive. The application of iterative methods such as Conjugate Gradient (CG) tailored for CUDA accelerates convergence by handling matrix-vector products in bulk:

$$\mathbf{A}\mathbf{x} = \mathbf{b}$$

where $\mathbf{A}$ is the system matrix, $\mathbf{x}$ is the image vector, and $\mathbf{b}$ is the data vector derived from the scanner. CUDA executes large-scale parallel operations on matrix entries and vector components, dramatically enhancing throughput and allowing for real-time imaging capabilities.

Employing libraries like `cuBLAS` facilitates matrix operations, making these large-scale multiplications feasible within clinical time constraints. Enhanced performance metrics directly correlate with efficient GPU memory operations and parallel kernel executions.

# CUDA-Optimized Algorithms for Image Enhancement

CUDA's potential is further leveraged in algorithms designed for noise reduction, edge detection, and image segmentation within medical imaging processes. One common technique is Gaussian filtering, whose kernel application to each pixel is defined as:

$$G(x, y) = \frac{1}{2\pi\sigma^2} e^{-\frac{x^2+y^2}{2\sigma^2}}$$

For medical images, CUDA facilitates the convolution of the image matrix with the Gaussian kernel in parallel, resulting in significant gains in processing speed. Advanced operations are conducted using `cuFFT` for frequency domain transformations, further expediting the denoising processes.

Furthermore, segmentation algorithms benefit from CUDA by decomposing the computations required to label or classify each pixel into several threads, leveraging the power of GPUs to concurrently resolve segmentation maps.

---

**Data:** Image matrix
**Result:** Segmented image
```
Load image block into shared memory
```
**foreach** *pixel in image* **do**
  | Compute segment label using parallel kernel;
```
Output segmented image result;
```

---

The efficiency increase permits the application of sophisticated machine-learning models and classification algorithms, critical for diagnostic imaging and further enhancing the diagnostic accuracy.

# Python Code Snippet

Below is a Python code snippet that implements the core algorithms and formulas covered in the chapter, including IDFT acceleration, CT scan computations, image reconstruction using the

Conjugate Gradient method, and application of CUDA-optimized algorithms for image enhancement.

```python
import pycuda.driver as cuda
import pycuda.autoinit
from pycuda.compiler import SourceModule
import numpy as np

# CUDA kernel code for IDFT
mod_idft = SourceModule("""
__global__ void idft(float *F_real, float *F_imag, float *f_real,
↪ float *f_imag, int N) {
    int n = threadIdx.x + blockIdx.x * blockDim.x;
    float sum_real = 0.0f;
    float sum_imag = 0.0f;
    for (int k = 0; k < N; ++k) {
        float angle = 2.0 * 3.14159265358979 * k * n / N;
        sum_real += F_real[k] * cos(angle) + F_imag[k] * sin(angle);
        sum_imag += F_imag[k] * cos(angle) - F_real[k] * sin(angle);
    }
    f_real[n] = sum_real / N;
    f_imag[n] = sum_imag / N;
}
""")

# Function for IDFT execution
def idft_cuda(F):
    N = len(F)
    F_real = F.real.astype(np.float32)
    F_imag = F.imag.astype(np.float32)
    f_real = np.zeros_like(F_real)
    f_imag = np.zeros_like(F_imag)

    F_real_gpu = cuda.mem_alloc(F_real.nbytes)
    F_imag_gpu = cuda.mem_alloc(F_imag.nbytes)
    f_real_gpu = cuda.mem_alloc(f_real.nbytes)
    f_imag_gpu = cuda.mem_alloc(f_imag.nbytes)

    cuda.memcpy_htod(F_real_gpu, F_real)
    cuda.memcpy_htod(F_imag_gpu, F_imag)

    block_size = 256
    grid_size = (N + block_size - 1) // block_size

    idft = mod_idft.get_function("idft")
    idft(F_real_gpu, F_imag_gpu, f_real_gpu, f_imag_gpu,
    ↪ np.int32(N), block=(block_size, 1, 1), grid=(grid_size, 1))

    cuda.memcpy_dtoh(f_real, f_real_gpu)
    cuda.memcpy_dtoh(f_imag, f_imag_gpu)

    return f_real + 1j * f_imag
```

```python
# Example data
F_example = np.fft.fft(np.array([1, 2, 3, 4], dtype=np.complex64))

# Execute IDFT using CUDA
f_result = idft_cuda(F_example)
print('IDFT result:', f_result)

# CUDA kernel for Gaussian filtering
mod_gaussian_filter = SourceModule("""
__global__ void gaussian_filter(float *image, float *filtered, int
↪ width, int height, float *kernel, int k_dim) {
    int x = threadIdx.x + blockIdx.x * blockDim.x;
    int y = threadIdx.y + blockIdx.y * blockDim.y;

    if (x >= width || y >= height) return;

    float result = 0.0f;
    int half_k = k_dim / 2;

    for (int i = -half_k; i <= half_k; i++) {
        for (int j = -half_k; j <= half_k; j++) {
            int x_ = min(max(x + i, 0), width - 1);
            int y_ = min(max(y + j, 0), height - 1);
            result += image[y_ * width + x_] * kernel[(j + half_k) *
            ↪ k_dim + (i + half_k)];
        }
    }
    filtered[y * width + x] = result;
}
""")

# Function to perform Gaussian filtering
def gaussian_filter_cuda(image, kernel):
    image = image.astype(np.float32)
    filtered = np.zeros_like(image)

    width, height = image.shape
    k_dim = kernel.shape[0]

    image_gpu = cuda.mem_alloc(image.nbytes)
    filtered_gpu = cuda.mem_alloc(filtered.nbytes)
    kernel_gpu = cuda.mem_alloc(kernel.nbytes)

    cuda.memcpy_htod(image_gpu, image)
    cuda.memcpy_htod(kernel_gpu, kernel)

    block_size = (16, 16)
    grid_size = (int(np.ceil(width / block_size[0])),
    ↪ int(np.ceil(height / block_size[1])))

    filter = mod_gaussian_filter.get_function("gaussian_filter")
```

```
filter(image_gpu, filtered_gpu, np.int32(width),
↪   np.int32(height), kernel_gpu, np.int32(k_dim),
        block=block_size, grid=grid_size)

cuda.memcpy_dtoh(filtered, filtered_gpu)
return filtered

# Example image and Gaussian kernel
image_example = np.random.random((512, 512)).astype(np.float32)
kernel_example = np.array([[1/16, 1/8, 1/16], [1/8, 1/4, 1/8],
↪   [1/16, 1/8, 1/16]], dtype=np.float32)

# Execute Gaussian filtering using CUDA
filtered_result = gaussian_filter_cuda(image_example,
↪   kernel_example)
print('Filtered result:', filtered_result)
```

This code defines several key CUDA implementations:

- The `idft_cuda` function performs the Inverse Discrete Fourier Transform on GPU, utilizing CUDA parallelism for efficiency.

- The `gaussian_filter_cuda` function applies a Gaussian filter to an image using PyCUDA, showcasing a common image enhancement approach.

- CUDA kernels are defined within the `SourceModule`, leveraging GPU efficiency for computationally heavy operations.

- Example arrays are transformed and processed, highlighting key CUDA applications in MRI simulations and image processing tasks.

# Chapter 48

# Non-linear Optimization Problems

## Gradient Descent Methods

Gradient descent is a fundamental approach in solving non-linear optimization problems, particularly in machine learning and computational mathematics. Consider the optimization problem:

$$\min_{\mathbf{x} \in \mathbb{R}^n} f(\mathbf{x})$$

where $f : \mathbb{R}^n \to \mathbb{R}$ is a differentiable function. The iterative update rule for gradient descent is expressed as:

$$\mathbf{x}_{k+1} = \mathbf{x}_k - \alpha_k \nabla f(\mathbf{x}_k)$$

with $\alpha_k$ representing the step size. The computation of the gradient $\nabla f(\mathbf{x}_k)$ is inherently parallelizable, thereby allowing CUDA to accelerate these computations through the concurrent execution of partial derivative evaluations.

## CUDA Optimization for Gradient Calculations

CUDA's architecture facilitates the massive parallel computation required for efficient gradient evaluations. Each element in the gradient vector can be computed independently as:

$$\frac{\partial f}{\partial x_i} = \lim_{\epsilon \to 0} \frac{f(x_1, \ldots, x_i + \epsilon, \ldots, x_n) - f(x_1, \ldots, x_i, \ldots, x_n)}{\epsilon}$$

Employing the CUDA framework allows multiple threads to simultaneously evaluate these derivatives. This parallelism is typically implemented using `cuBLAS` for linear algebra operations and synchronization mechanisms to manage dependencies.

---

**Data:** Initial point $\mathbf{x}_0$, Learning rate $\alpha$, Maximum iterations

**Result:** Optimized point $\mathbf{x}^*$

Initialize $\mathbf{x} = \mathbf{x}_0$

**while** *stopping criterion not met* **do**

    Compute gradients $\nabla f(\mathbf{x})$ using CUDA threads;

    Update $\mathbf{x} \leftarrow \mathbf{x} - \alpha \nabla f(\mathbf{x})$;

**return x**

---

Optimal memory access patterns and coalescing are achieved via shared memory usage, significantly reducing computation time.

# Adaptive Learning Rates

In more sophisticated optimization algorithms, adaptive learning rates can be utilized to improve convergence properties. A common technique is the momentum method, modifying the update equation to:

$$\mathbf{v}_{k+1} = \beta \mathbf{v}_k + \alpha \nabla f(\mathbf{x}_k)$$

$$\mathbf{x}_{k+1} = \mathbf{x}_k - \mathbf{v}_{k+1}$$

where $\beta$ is a damping factor. These updates leverage the parallel reduce operations in CUDA to efficiently compute the velocity vector $\mathbf{v}$.

# Non-linear Conjugate Gradient

The non-linear conjugate gradient method improves upon gradient descent by using conjugacy to accelerate convergence. The update rule involves a linear combination of the current gradient and the previous update direction:

$$\mathbf{x}_{k+1} = \mathbf{x}_k + \alpha_k \mathbf{p}_k$$

$$\mathbf{p}_{k+1} = -\nabla f(\mathbf{x}_{k+1}) + \beta_k \mathbf{p}_k$$

$$\beta_k = \frac{\|\nabla f(\mathbf{x}_{k+1})\|^2}{\|\nabla f(\mathbf{x}_k)\|^2}$$

Each stage of the algorithm requires intensive vector operations, which are efficiently handled using CUDA's parallel processing capabilities. This method involves a sequence of matrix-vector products and vector updates, adequately supported by the cuBLAS library to expedite computation.

## Solving L-BFGS with CUDA

The Limited-memory Broyden–Fletcher–Goldfarb–Shanno (L-BFGS) method is particularly suited for problems with a large number of variables due to its limited memory requirement. Its iteration relies on:

$$\mathbf{s}_k = \mathbf{x}_{k+1} - \mathbf{x}_k$$

$$\mathbf{y}_k = \nabla f(\mathbf{x}_{k+1}) - \nabla f(\mathbf{x}_k)$$

The Hessian or its approximation is not explicitly required, but efficient buffer management and vector operations are crucial. CUDA's memory hierarchy supports such algorithms by providing rapid access and update of the necessary historical gradient information.

The implementation of such algorithms within CUDA requires careful coordination and efficient memory allocation strategies, ensuring the reduction of computational overhead through effective use of device memory and shared operations.

## Python Code Snippet

Below is a Python code snippet that encompasses the core computational elements for solving non-linear optimization problems using CUDA. The snippet includes gradient descent and adaptive gradient updates with the PyCUDA library for GPU acceleration.

```python
import pycuda.autoinit
import pycuda.gpuarray as gpuarray
import numpy as np
import pycuda.driver as cuda
from pycuda.compiler import SourceModule

mod = SourceModule("""
__global__ void compute_gradient(float *x, float *grad, int n) {
    int idx = blockIdx.x * blockDim.x + threadIdx.x;
    if (idx < n) {
        grad[idx] = 2 * x[idx]; // Example: derivative of f(x) = x^2
    }
}

__global__ void update_position(float *x, float *grad, float alpha,
↪    int n) {
    int idx = blockIdx.x * blockDim.x + threadIdx.x;
    if (idx < n) {
        x[idx] -= alpha * grad[idx];
    }
}
""")

compute_gradient = mod.get_function("compute_gradient")
update_position = mod.get_function("update_position")

def gradient_descent(x_host, alpha, iterations, block_size=256):
    n = x_host.size
    x_gpu = gpuarray.to_gpu(x_host.astype(np.float32))
    grad_gpu = gpuarray.empty(n, np.float32)
    grid_size = (n + block_size - 1) // block_size

    for _ in range(iterations):
        compute_gradient(x_gpu, grad_gpu, np.int32(n),
        ↪    block=(block_size, 1, 1), grid=(grid_size, 1))
        update_position(x_gpu, grad_gpu, np.float32(alpha),
        ↪    np.int32(n), block=(block_size, 1, 1), grid=(grid_size,
        ↪    1))

    return x_gpu.get()

# Initial data
x_initial = np.random.rand(1024).astype(np.float32)

# Hyperparameters
learning_rate = 0.01
max_iterations = 1000

# Execute gradient descent
optimized_x = gradient_descent(x_initial, learning_rate,
↪    max_iterations)
```

```
print("Optimized x:", optimized_x)
```

This code defines and executes functions to compute gradients and update positions using a simple gradient descent algorithm accelerated by CUDA:

- `compute_gradient` is a CUDA kernel that calculates gradients in parallel.

- `update_position` is another CUDA kernel that updates each position in space using the computed gradient.

- `gradient_descent` integrates both kernels, hosting the data transfer between CPU and GPU and executing the iterative optimization routine.

In this implementation, the derivative used is specific to a simple quadratic function $f(x) = x^2$ for illustration purposes. The code transfers a NumPy array to the GPU memory space, applies the iterative gradient descent updates, and retrieves the optimized values back to the CPU.

# Chapter 49

# Spatial Data Analysis

## Mathematical Foundations of Spatial Data

Spatial data analysis involves operations that manage and explore spatial characteristics and relationships in datasets. Mathematically, spatial data can be represented as a set of points, lines, and polygons in an $n$-dimensional space, embedded in a field $\mathbb{R}^n$. Formally, a point can be denoted as $\mathbf{p}_i = (x_1, x_2, \ldots, x_n) \in \mathbb{R}^n$.

The distance metric is essential in spatial analysis, typically defined using the Euclidean distance:

$$d(\mathbf{p}_i, \mathbf{p}_j) = \sqrt{\sum_{k=1}^{n}(x_{i,k} - x_{j,k})^2}$$

To effectively manage and analyze large volumes of spatial data, a variety of data structures such as quad-trees or $k$-d trees are employed. The essential operation of nearest neighbor search can be computed by identifying points $\mathbf{p}_j$ such that:

$$\min_{\mathbf{p}_j \in P} d(\mathbf{p}_i, \mathbf{p}_j)$$

## Parallelizing Spatial Computations with CUDA

CUDA provides a robust platform for parallelizing operations in spatial data analysis. The capability to simultaneously evaluate

284

distances or generate spatial transformations enhances computational efficiency. Consider the problem of computing pairwise distances among a set of points, which can be expressed as:

$$D = [d(\mathbf{p}_i, \mathbf{p}_j)]_{i,j=1}^{m}$$

With CUDA, individual elements of the distance matrix $D$ can be calculated in parallel, distributing the workload across the available GPU threads. CUDA's `cuBLAS` and `cuDNN` libraries offer optimized routines for linear algebra operations, useful in calculating pairwise distances through batch processing.

---

**Data:** Set of points $P = \{\mathbf{p}_1, \mathbf{p}_2, \ldots, \mathbf{p}_n\}$
**Result:** Pairwise distance matrix $D$
Initialize distance matrix $D = 0$
**for** *each point* $\mathbf{p}_i \in P$ **do**
    Launch CUDA threads for parallel distance computation;
    **for** *each point* $\mathbf{p}_j \in P$ **do**
        Compute $d(\mathbf{p}_i, \mathbf{p}_j)$ using Euclidean metric;
        Update $D_{i,j} \leftarrow d(\mathbf{p}_i, \mathbf{p}_j)$;
    Synchronize threads
**return** *Distance matrix* $D$

---

The use of CUDA ensures that spatial queries such as range searches are executed swiftly, facilitating large-scale spatial analysis that is infeasible with serial computation.

# Spatial Interpolation and Regression

Spatial interpolation techniques, such as kriging or inverse distance weighting, are employed to predict and fill in missing spatial data based on known measurements. Formally, the prediction of a point $\mathbf{p}$ is given by:

$$Z(\mathbf{p}) = \sum_{i=1}^{N} \lambda_i Z(\mathbf{p}_i)$$

where $\lambda_i$ are weights obtained from a semivariogram model or an inverse distance algorithm.

The parallel computation method with CUDA for estimating these weights involves assessing the influence of surrounding data points on any given prediction point, processed concurrently across GPU threads to expedite time-consuming operations.

# Using Spatial Data Structures with CUDA

Spatial indexing systems such as $k$-d trees or R-trees expedite querying and retrieval operations in spatial datasets. In CUDA, the construction and traversal of these structures leverage GPU threads. For a $k$-d tree, the process involves:

- Recursively partitioning space: Split data at median along axis $k$

- Iteratively constructing subtrees in parallel

Given a query point $\mathbf{q}$, a CUDA implementation would handle the search for the nearest or range queries in an efficient, parallel manner by distributing the workload across nodes of the tree structure.

The traversal can be summarized as:

Traverse($Node$) :

    if $Node.isLeaf()$ then

      Process leaf node points

    else

      Traverse left and right children nodes concurrently

Incorporating CUDA accelerates the resolution of high-dimensional spatial queries and aids in the analysis of complex geographical datasets by optimizing data parallelism and memory accesses through coalescing and shared memory usage.

# Python Code Snippet

Below is a Python code snippet that involves parallelizing spatial computations such as pairwise distance computation and nearest neighbor search using PyCUDA. The code also includes the construction of a simple $k$-d tree.

```
import pycuda.autoinit  # Automatically manage GPU contexts
import pycuda.driver as cuda
```

```python
import numpy as np
from pycuda.compiler import SourceModule
from scipy.spatial import KDTree

# Define the CUDA kernel for computing pairwise distances
distance_kernel = """
__global__ void compute_distances(float *points, float *distances,
↪   int num_points, int dimensions) {
    int idx = threadIdx.x + blockIdx.x * blockDim.x;
    if (idx < num_points * num_points) {
        int i = idx / num_points;
        int j = idx % num_points;
        float dist = 0.0;
        for (int k = 0; k < dimensions; k++) {
            float diff = points[i * dimensions + k] - points[j *
            ↪   dimensions + k];
            dist += diff * diff;
        }
        distances[idx] = sqrt(dist);
    }
}
"""

# Compile the kernel
mod = SourceModule(distance_kernel)
compute_distances = mod.get_function("compute_distances")

# Generate random spatial data for demonstration
num_points = 10
dimensions = 3
points = np.random.rand(num_points, dimensions).astype(np.float32)

# Allocate memory and transfer data
points_gpu = cuda.mem_alloc(points.nbytes)
cuda.memcpy_htod(points_gpu, points)

# Prepare the matrix to store distances
distances = np.empty((num_points, num_points), dtype=np.float32)
distances_gpu = cuda.mem_alloc(distances.nbytes)

# Define the block and grid sizes
block_size = 256
grid_size = (num_points * num_points + block_size - 1) // block_size

# Launch the kernel
compute_distances(points_gpu, distances_gpu, np.int32(num_points),
↪   np.int32(dimensions), block=(block_size, 1, 1), grid=(grid_size,
↪   1))

# Fetch computed distances from the GPU
cuda.memcpy_dtoh(distances, distances_gpu)

# Example KDTree usage for nearest neighbor search
```

287

```
tree = KDTree(points)
query_point = np.random.rand(1, dimensions)
dist_nn, index = tree.query(query_point)

print("Pairwise Distances:\n", distances)
print(f"Nearest Neighbor to {query_point} is at index {index} with
↪    distance {dist_nn}")
```

This code handles several key elements of spatial data analysis with CUDA:

- The `compute_distances` kernel computes pairwise Euclidean distances between points in a highly parallelized manner by using CUDA threads.

- Initialization of GPU memory and data transfer is handled using `pycuda.driver` functions, showing efficient management of GPU resources.

- A demonstration of nearest neighbor search is conducted using `scipy.spatial.KDTree`, illustrating how structures can facilitate spatial queries.

- The grid and block sizes for the CUDA kernel define how work is distributed to GPU threads, emphasizing efficient resource use in CUDA programming.

- Finally, the results, including the computed distance matrix and nearest neighbor results, demonstrate applying GPU computation results.

# Chapter 50

# Genomics and CUDA

## Modeling Genomic Sequences

Genomic sequences are represented by strings composed of a finite set of nucleotides, typically denoted by the alphabet $\Sigma = \{A, C, G, T\}$. The analysis of such sequences often requires transforming this string data into quantitative models suitable for computational operations. An essential operation is string matching, where given a pattern $P = p_1 p_2 \ldots p_m$ of length $m$ and a text $T = t_1 t_2 \ldots t_n$ of length $n$, the task is to determine all positions $j$ such that $t_{j+1} t_{j+2} \ldots t_{j+m} = p_1 p_2 \ldots p_m$.

The computational challenge primarily arises due to the large size of genomic datasets, necessitating efficient algorithms and architectures for processing. This is where CUDA (Compute Unified Device Architecture) offers parallel processing capabilities that can significantly enhance the execution speed of such algorithms.

## Parallel Sequence Alignment

Sequence alignment is a critical method in genomics that involves comparing sequences to identify regions of similarity. This task is computationally intensive and typically employs dynamic programming techniques, such as Needleman-Wunsch or Smith-Waterman algorithms, which align two sequences optimally. The alignment score $S(i, j)$ can be defined recursively:

$$S(i,j) = \max \begin{cases} S(i-1, j-1) + \text{score}(x_i, y_j), \\ S(i-1, j) + \text{gap\_penalty}, \\ S(i, j-1) + \text{gap\_penalty} \end{cases}$$

CUDA can parallelize these operations by allocating independent cells of the alignment matrix to separate threads, significantly accelerating computation times. Each thread computes a single cell score by reading from its neighboring cells, enabling large-scale parallel execution.

# Efficient Genome Assembly Algorithms

Genome assembly reassembles short DNA sequences into full chromosomes. A common approach involves constructing a de Bruijn graph where each node represents a $k$-mer, and edges suggest potential adjacency based on overlaps. Mapping reads into this graph involves substantial parallel graph traversal and can be efficiently accelerated using CUDA by delegating different reads and $k$-mer matches to multiple threads.

$$G = (V, E), \text{ where each } v \in V \text{ represents a } k\text{-mer}$$

Constructing and traversing such a graph involves the utilization of shared memory for adjacency lists and parallel reductions to aggregate path findings across the graph.

# GPU-Accelerated Phylogenetic Analysis

Phylogenetic analysis infers the evolutionary relationships among various species. This analysis utilizes tree structures and matrix operations to compute distance matrices based on genetic sequence similarities, commonly through a substitution model such as Jukes-Cantor:

$$d_{i,j} = -\frac{3}{4} \ln \left( 1 - \frac{4}{3} p_{i,j} \right)$$

where $p_{i,j}$ represents the proportion of differing sites. Implementing this algorithm on a CUDA platform benefits from parallel processing of each matrix computation across GPU threads, enabling rapid evaluation over large sets of genetic data.

# CUDA-enabled Genomic Data Storage and Retrieval

With the exponential growth of genomic datasets, efficient data storage, and retrieval systems have become indispensable. Utilizing GPU memory for high-throughput operations expedites retrieval processes, often relying on parallel hashing and indexing techniques to map genomic data swiftly. Structures akin to bloom filters can be employed in CUDA to perform fast membership queries:

$$\text{Bloom Filter: } B(x) = \bigwedge_k h_k(x)$$

where $h_k$ are hash functions computed in parallel, ensuring rapid determination of sequence presence within large genomic databases.

# Python Code Snippet

Below is a Python code snippet that illustrates the core computational strategies for genomic data analysis using CUDA, including sequence alignment and phylogenetic analysis via GPU acceleration.

```python
import numpy as np
import pycuda.autoinit
import pycuda.driver as cuda
from pycuda.compiler import SourceModule

# GPU Kernel for Parallel Sequence Alignment (e.g., Smith-Waterman
↪    Algorithm)
kernel_code = """
```

```
__global__ void sequence_alignment_kernel(int *d_matrix, char
↪  *d_seq1, char *d_seq2,
                                            int n, int m, int
                                            ↪  gap_penalty) {
    int idx = blockIdx.x * blockDim.x + threadIdx.x;
    if (idx < n * m) {
        int i = idx / m;
        int j = idx % m;
        if (i > 0 && j > 0) {
            int match = (d_seq1[i-1] == d_seq2[j-1]) ? 2 : -1;
            int diag = d_matrix[(i-1) * m + (j-1)] + match;
            int up = d_matrix[(i-1) * m + j] + gap_penalty;
            int left = d_matrix[i * m + (j-1)] + gap_penalty;
            d_matrix[i * m + j] = max(0, max(diag, max(up, left)));
        }
    }
}
"""


def run_sequence_alignment(seq1, seq2, gap_penalty=-2):
    n = len(seq1) + 1
    m = len(seq2) + 1
    alignment_matrix = np.zeros((n, m), dtype=np.int32)

    # Allocate GPU memory
    d_seq1 = cuda.to_device(np.array(list(seq1.encode()),
    ↪  dtype=np.char))
    d_seq2 = cuda.to_device(np.array(list(seq2.encode()),
    ↪  dtype=np.char))
    d_matrix = cuda.to_device(alignment_matrix)

    # Compile kernel
    mod = SourceModule(kernel_code)
    sequence_alignment =
    ↪  mod.get_function("sequence_alignment_kernel")

    # Launch kernel on the GPU
    block_size = 256
    grid_size = (n * m + block_size - 1) // block_size
    sequence_alignment(d_matrix, d_seq1, d_seq2, np.int32(n),
    ↪  np.int32(m), np.int32(gap_penalty),
                    block=(block_size, 1, 1), grid=(grid_size,
                    ↪  1))

    # Copy result back to host
    alignment_matrix = cuda.from_device(d_matrix,
    ↪  alignment_matrix.shape, alignment_matrix.dtype)
    return alignment_matrix

# Example Sequences
seq1 = "ACGT"
seq2 = "CGT"
alignment_matrix_result = run_sequence_alignment(seq1, seq2)
```

```
print("Alignment Matrix:")
print(alignment_matrix_result)

# GPU-Accelerated Phylogenetic Analysis for Distance Calculation
# Example sequences in binary format
sequences = ["ACGT", "CGTT", "AGGT"]
differing_sites = [1, 2, 3]
d_matrix = np.zeros((len(sequences), len(sequences)),
↪   dtype=np.float32)

# Distance calculation kernel
distance_kernel_code = """
__global__ void distance_matrix_kernel(float *d_matrix, int
↪   *diff_sites, int num_seq) {
    int idx = blockIdx.x * blockDim.x + threadIdx.x;
    if (idx < num_seq * num_seq) {
        int i = idx / num_seq;
        int j = idx % num_seq;
        if (i < j) {
            float p_ij = float(diff_sites[i * num_seq + j]) /
            ↪   float(strlen(seq[i]));
            d_matrix[i * num_seq + j] = -0.75f * log(1.0f -
            ↪   (4.0f/3.0f) * p_ij);
            d_matrix[j * num_seq + i] = d_matrix[i * num_seq + j];
            ↪   // Symmetric matrix
        }
    }
}
"""

def calculate_phylogenetic_distances(diff_sites, num_seq):
    d_matrix = np.zeros((num_seq, num_seq), dtype=np.float32)

    # Compile and get CUDA function
    mod = SourceModule(distance_kernel_code)
    distance_matrix_kernel =
    ↪   mod.get_function("distance_matrix_kernel")

    # Allocate device memory
    d_diff_sites = cuda.to_device(np.array(diff_sites,
    ↪   dtype=np.int32))
    d_d_matrix = cuda.to_device(d_matrix)

    # Launch kernel
    block_size = 256
    grid_size = (num_seq * num_seq + block_size - 1) // block_size
    distance_matrix_kernel(d_d_matrix, d_diff_sites,
    ↪   np.int32(num_seq),
                            block=(block_size, 1, 1),
                            ↪   grid=(grid_size, 1))

    # Retrieve result
```

```
d_matrix = cuda.from_device(d_d_matrix, d_matrix.shape,
↪ d_matrix.dtype)
return d_matrix

# Example differing sites between sequences
diff_sites = [0, 2, 1, 2, 0, 1, 1, 1, 0] # Example on a 3x3 matrix
↪ for 3 sequences
phylogenetic_distances =
↪ calculate_phylogenetic_distances(diff_sites, len(sequences))
print("Phylogenetic Distance Matrix:")
print(phylogenetic_distances)
```

This Python code includes several key components useful for CUDA-accelerated genomic data processing:

- The `sequence_alignment_kernel` function implements parallel sequence alignment using a dynamic programming approach, accelerated by CUDA.

- The `run_sequence_alignment` function manages the execution and data handling for sequence alignment on the GPU.

- The `distance_matrix_kernel` function computes phylogenetic distances between sequences using a substitution model, optimized with CUDA parallel threads.

- The `calculate_phylogenetic_distances` function sets up and retrieves results from the CUDA kernel to analyze evolutionary relationships between sequences.

These snippets highlight how CUDA can efficiently manage complex and data-intensive genomic algorithm implementations by leveraging parallel GPU resources.

# Chapter 51

# High-Frequency Trading Algorithms

## Introduction to High-Frequency Trading

High-Frequency Trading (HFT) encompasses automated trading strategies that execute a large number of orders within short time frames, capitalizing on minuscule price discrepancies and market inefficiencies. The essence of HFT is the deployment of sophisticated algorithms and high-performance computing resources that necessitate minimal latency and maximal throughput to gain a competitive advantage in financial markets.

Utilizing CUDA (Compute Unified Device Architecture) offers significant potential in optimizing the computational intensity of HFT systems, effectively enhancing both the speed and efficiency of algorithmic strategies.

## Algorithmic Trading Models

At the core of HFT strategies are algorithmic trading models, which often rely upon statistical arbitrage, market making, and liquidity detection. These models evaluate market conditions and execute trades based on calculated probabilities and stochastic processes.

The stochastic differential equation used in modeling price dynamics can be represented as follows:

$$dS_t = \mu S_t dt + \sigma S_t dW_t \tag{51.1}$$

Here, $S_t$ denotes the asset price at time $t$, $\mu$ is the drift coefficient, $\sigma$ represents the volatility, and $dW_t$ is a Wiener process.

# 1  Risk Management with HFT

Risk assessment in HFT strategies is often handled by analyzing VaR (Value at Risk) and ES (Expected Shortfall), which quantify potential losses over a specified time frame. The formulas for these are expressed as:

$$\text{VaR} = \inf\{\alpha \in \mathbb{R} : P(L > \alpha) \le \beta\} \tag{51.2}$$

$$\text{ES} = \mathbb{E}[L \mid L > \text{VaR}] \tag{51.3}$$

where $L$ represents potential losses and $\beta$ is the confidence level.

# Parallel Computing for Algorithm Optimization

The high computational demand of HFT necessitates parallel computing approaches to slash processing time and increase strategy efficacy. The deployment of CUDA-enabled GPUs facilitates the parallelization of core algorithmic components such as order placement, risk calculators, and statistical analysis engines.

# 1  GPU-Accelerated Order Matching

Order matching in an exchange can be formulated as a matchmaking function leveraging priority queues and is expressed algorithmically as:

---

**Data:** Put Order $o_n$ in Queue
**Result:** Order $o_n$ matched or queued
**foreach** *incoming order $o_n$* **do**
    **if** MatchOrder($o_n$) **then**
        Execute trade and remove matched order;
    **else**
        InsertQueue($o_n$);

---

# CUDA Enhancement in Latency Reduction

Minimizing latency is paramount in HFT, as even microsecond delays can lead to loss of trading opportunities. CUDA optimizations enable data parallelism techniques that distribute computational tasks across GPUs, ensuring rapid execution of market orders and aligned decision-making processes.

$$T_{\text{latency}} = T_{\text{network}} + T_{\text{processing}} \tag{51.4}$$

Here, $T_{\text{latency}}$ represents total latency, decomposed into network delay $T_{\text{network}}$ and processing delay $T_{\text{processing}}$, both of which can be minimized using CUDA's real-time computational abilities.

# Algorithmic Optimization Strategies

Efficient exploitation of CUDA architecture can be achieved by configuring kernel functions to perform high-frequency simulations of trading scenarios and price impact models.

For instance, the calculation of delta hedging strategies would involve continuously monitoring the option's delta $\Delta$ and dynamically adjusting a portfolio:

$$\Delta = \frac{\partial C}{\partial S} \tag{51.5}$$

where $C$ denotes the option price and $S$ the underlying asset price.

## 1  Statistical Analysis and Pattern Recognition

An integral part of HFT includes statistical analysis and pattern recognition in time-series data, often employing mathematical models like the Kalman filter:

$$\begin{aligned} x_{k+1} &= Ax_k + Bu_k + w_k \\ z_k &= Hx_k + v_k \end{aligned} \tag{51.6}$$

Here, $x_k$ is the state vector, $z_k$ is the observation, $A$ and $H$ are matrices representing the system dynamics, $w_k$ and $v_k$ are process and observation noises respectively. CUDA can expedite these computations across multiple securities to identify arbitrage opportunities.

This exploration illustrates the deployment of advanced mathematical algorithms augmented by CUDA's parallel processing capabilities, enhancing High-Frequency Trading strategies in modern financial markets.

# Python Code Snippet

Below is a Python code snippet that encompasses the core computational elements of High-Frequency Trading strategies leveraging CUDA for enhanced computational efficiency and algorithmic execution performance.

```python
import pycuda.driver as cuda
import pycuda.autoinit
import numpy as np
from pycuda.compiler import SourceModule

# Function to calculate asset price dynamics using stochastic
↪   differential equation
mod = SourceModule("""
__global__ void price_dynamics(float *S, float mu, float sigma,
↪   float *dW, int N)
{
    int idx = threadIdx.x + blockIdx.x * blockDim.x;
    if (idx < N) {
        S[idx] = S[idx] * exp((mu - 0.5 * sigma * sigma) + sigma *
        ↪   dW[idx]);
    }
}
""")

# Initialize parameters
N = 1000000
S_t = np.full(N, 100, dtype=np.float32)
mu = 0.05
sigma = 0.2
dW_t = np.random.randn(N).astype(np.float32)

# Allocate memory on GPU and launch kernel
S_gpu = cuda.mem_alloc(S_t.nbytes)
dW_gpu = cuda.mem_alloc(dW_t.nbytes)
cuda.memcpy_htod(S_gpu, S_t)
cuda.memcpy_htod(dW_gpu, dW_t)

price_dynamics = mod.get_function("price_dynamics")
price_dynamics(S_gpu, np.float32(mu), np.float32(sigma), dW_gpu,
↪   np.int32(N), block=(256,1,1), grid=(N//256,1))
```

```python
# Retrieve results from GPU
cuda.memcpy_dtoh(S_t, S_gpu)

# Function to calculate Value at Risk and Expected Shortfall
def calculate_risk_metrics(L, beta=0.95):
    L_sorted = np.sort(L)
    VaR_index = int((1 - beta) * len(L_sorted))
    VaR = L_sorted[VaR_index]
    ES = np.mean(L_sorted[VaR_index:])
    return VaR, ES

# Example data for loss distribution
losses = np.random.normal(loc=10, scale=5, size=1000000)

# Calculate VaR and ES
VaR, ES = calculate_risk_metrics(losses)

print("Value at Risk (VaR):", VaR)
print("Expected Shortfall (ES):", ES)
```

This code defines several key functions necessary for the implementation and optimization of High-Frequency Trading strategies using NVIDIA's CUDA platform:

- The CUDA kernel in `price_dynamics` simulates asset price dynamics based on a stochastic differential equation model.

- `calculate_risk_metrics` calculates the Value at Risk (VaR) and Expected Shortfall (ES) for a given loss distribution, providing essential risk management insights.

The CUDA programming allows for the efficient parallel processing of large datasets, drastically reducing the computational time needed for high-frequency trading simulations and risk assessments. The final block of code demonstrates the application of these elements to real-world data scenarios.

# Chapter 52

# Games AI Optimization

## Introduction to Games AI Computation

Artificial Intelligence (AI) within games encompasses various strategies aimed at enhancing player experiences through the development of responsive and challenging virtual opponents. The integration of AI within games necessitates substantial computational resources due to the complexity and real-time demands of these algorithms. CUDA (Compute Unified Device Architecture) provides a powerful framework to accelerate AI computations, resulting in faster and more intelligent game responses.

## AI Pathfinding Algorithms

Central to game AI optimization is the efficient computation of pathfinding algorithms, often implemented using graph-based methods such as A* or Dijkstra's algorithm. These algorithms are essential for navigating virtual environments and require substantial computational power to perform efficiently in dynamic scenarios.

The A* algorithm is formalized by the evaluation of nodes using:

$$f(n) = g(n) + h(n) \tag{52.1}$$

Here, $f(n)$ represents the estimated total cost of the cheapest solution path going through node $n$, $g(n)$ denotes the cost from the start node to $n$, and $h(n)$ is the heuristic cost estimate from $n$ to the goal.

# 1   Acceleration with CUDA

Leveraging CUDA, the parallelization of node evaluations in pathfinding can be achieved by distributing nodes across threads on the GPU, allowing simultaneous computation of costs, as expressed mathematically by parallel execution:

$$\texttt{node\_cost}[i] = g(i) + h(i), \quad \forall i \in \texttt{active\_nodes} \tag{52.2}$$

This parallelism drastically reduces computation times compared to traditional CPU implementations by exploiting the massive parallel processing capabilities of modern GPUs.

# Game AI Behavior Trees

In the realm of game AI, behavior trees offer a structured mechanism to model decision-making processes. These trees are utilized to dictate logic for game agents, allowing for diverse and emergent behavior patterns.

A behavior tree can be expressed recursively as nodes with the structure:

$$T(n) = \begin{cases} C_n & \text{if } n \text{ is a leaf} \\ B(n) & \text{otherwise} \end{cases} \tag{52.3}$$

where $C_n$ denotes a condition at leaf node $n$, and $B(n)$ represents a sub-tree or composite behavior encapsulating decisions and actions.

# 1   Parallel Execution with CUDA

Given the hierarchical nature of behavior trees, their traversal and execution can be parallelized by assigning sub-trees to separate CUDA threads, facilitating efficient and simultaneous execution:

```
Data: Behavior Tree T with root r
Function Traverse(node):
    if node is leaf then
        | Execute action;
    else
        | foreach child in node.children in parallel do
        |     | Traverse(child);

Traverse(r)
```

This method allows for the rapid processing of AI behaviors, enhancing the responsiveness and complexity of in-game entities.

# Neural Network-Based AI Strategies

Deep learning techniques have been increasingly incorporated into game AI to facilitate learning-based strategies that adapt to player actions. Neural networks enable the modeling of complex AI behaviors through numerous interconnected neurons, each processing a specific aspect of decision-making.

A feedforward neural network can be compactly represented by the set of equations:

$$a^{(l+1)} = \sigma \left( W^{(l)} a^{(l)} + b^{(l)} \right) \tag{52.4}$$

where $a^{(l)}$ represents the activations of layer $l$, $W^{(l)}$ and $b^{(l)}$ are the weights and biases connecting layers $l$ and $l+1$, and $\sigma$ is the activation function, often chosen to be non-linear such as the ReLU or logistic function.

## 1   CUDA-based Neural Network Acceleration

Neural network training and inference tasks are particularly well-suited for parallel execution on GPUs due to their inherently data-parallel nature. CUDA leverages this by executing matrix-vector operations, present in the computation of neural layers, simultaneously across many processing units:

$$z^{(l)} = W^{(l)} a^{(l-1)} + b^{(l)}, \quad \forall l \in \texttt{layers} \tag{52.5}$$

The increased throughput afforded by CUDA thus significantly accelerates neural network computations, leading to more adaptive and intelligent AI systems within games.

# Python Code Snippet

Below is a Python code snippet that encompasses the core computational elements related to AI optimization in gaming, focusing on pathfinding, behavior trees, and neural network-based strategies using CUDA for acceleration.

```python
import numpy as np
import pycuda.autoinit
import pycuda.driver as cuda
from pycuda.compiler import SourceModule

# Define A* evaluation function for GPU
mod = SourceModule("""
__global__ void a_star_eval(float *g_costs, float *h_costs, float
↪ *f_costs, int num_nodes) {
    int idx = blockIdx.x * blockDim.x + threadIdx.x;
    if (idx < num_nodes) {
        f_costs[idx] = g_costs[idx] + h_costs[idx];
    }
}
""")

a_star_eval = mod.get_function("a_star_eval")

def pathfinding_cuda(g_costs, h_costs):
    num_nodes = len(g_costs)
    f_costs = np.zeros_like(g_costs)

    # Allocate memory on GPU
    g_costs_gpu = cuda.mem_alloc(g_costs.nbytes)
    h_costs_gpu = cuda.mem_alloc(h_costs.nbytes)
    f_costs_gpu = cuda.mem_alloc(f_costs.nbytes)

    # Transfer data to GPU
    cuda.memcpy_htod(g_costs_gpu, g_costs)
    cuda.memcpy_htod(h_costs_gpu, h_costs)

    # Execute the kernel
    a_star_eval(g_costs_gpu, h_costs_gpu, f_costs_gpu,
    ↪ np.int32(num_nodes), block=(256,1,1), grid=(int((num_nodes +
    ↪ 255) // 256),1))

    # Transfer the result back to CPU
    cuda.memcpy_dtoh(f_costs, f_costs_gpu)

    # Free memory on GPU
    g_costs_gpu.free()
    h_costs_gpu.free()
    f_costs_gpu.free()
```

```python
    return f_costs

# Define behavior tree execution function
def traverse_behavior_tree(tree):
    result = []
    for node in tree:
        if 'action' in node:
            result.append(node['action'])
        elif 'children' in node:
            result.extend(traverse_behavior_tree(node['children']))
    return result

# Define neural network forward pass
mod_nn = SourceModule("""
__global__ void nn_forward(float *W, float *a_prev, float *b, float
↪  *a_curr, int input_size, int output_size) {
    int idx = blockIdx.x * blockDim.x + threadIdx.x;
    if (idx < output_size) {
        float z = b[idx];
        for (int j = 0; j < input_size; j++) {
            z += W[idx * input_size + j] * a_prev[j];
        }
        a_curr[idx] = 1 / (1 + exp(-z));  // Sigmoid activation
    }
}
""")

nn_forward = mod_nn.get_function("nn_forward")

def neural_network_forward(W, a_prev, b):
    input_size = a_prev.shape[0]
    output_size = b.shape[0]

    a_curr = np.zeros((output_size,), dtype=np.float32)

    # Allocate memory on GPU
    W_gpu = cuda.mem_alloc(W.nbytes)
    a_prev_gpu = cuda.mem_alloc(a_prev.nbytes)
    b_gpu = cuda.mem_alloc(b.nbytes)
    a_curr_gpu = cuda.mem_alloc(a_curr.nbytes)

    # Transfer data to GPU
    cuda.memcpy_htod(W_gpu, W)
    cuda.memcpy_htod(a_prev_gpu, a_prev)
    cuda.memcpy_htod(b_gpu, b)

    # Execute the kernel
    nn_forward(W_gpu, a_prev_gpu, b_gpu, a_curr_gpu,
    ↪  np.int32(input_size), np.int32(output_size),
    ↪  block=(256,1,1), grid=(int((output_size + 255) // 256),1))

    # Transfer the result back to CPU
    cuda.memcpy_dtoh(a_curr, a_curr_gpu)
```

```
# Free memory on GPU
W_gpu.free()
a_prev_gpu.free()
b_gpu.free()
a_curr_gpu.free()

return a_curr

# Sample data for demonstration
g_costs = np.array([1, 2, 3, 4], dtype=np.float32)
h_costs = np.array([4, 3, 2, 1], dtype=np.float32)
f_costs = pathfinding_cuda(g_costs, h_costs)
print("F costs from A*:", f_costs)

behavior_tree = [{'action': 'move_to'}, {'children': [{'action':
    'pickup'}, {'action': 'drop'}]}]
traversed_actions = traverse_behavior_tree(behavior_tree)
print("Behavior tree actions:", traversed_actions)

W = np.random.rand(3, 4).astype(np.float32)   # Random weight
    initialization
a_prev = np.random.rand(4).astype(np.float32)   # Random input layer
    activation
b = np.random.rand(3).astype(np.float32)   # Random biases
a_curr = neural_network_forward(W, a_prev, b)
print("Neural network output:", a_curr)
```

This code defines several key functions necessary for optimizing game AI computations with CUDA:

- `pathfinding_cuda` utilizes CUDA to accelerate the evaluation of pathfinding algorithms such as A*, significantly reducing computation time by parallelizing node cost calculations across the GPU.

- `traverse_behavior_tree` outlines a method for traversing a behavior tree, simulating AI decision-making, enabling developers to reason about complex agent behaviors efficiently.

- `neural_network_forward` leverages CUDA to perform fast forward passes through neural network layers, capitalizing on GPU parallelism to speed up AI strategies employing machine learning.

The final block of code demonstrates the application of these functions using sample data, highlighting the computational enhancements achieved through GPU acceleration.

# Chapter 53

# Weather Forecasting Models

## Introduction to Weather Forecasting

Weather forecasting involves the prediction of atmospheric conditions at a specific location and time. Accurate predictions are critical for agriculture, shipping, aviation, and public safety. Modern forecasting models use mathematical models to simulate the atmosphere's future state, utilizing large datasets from observations and previous forecasts.

## Mathematical Foundations of Predictive Models

Central to weather forecasting models are the partial differential equations (PDEs) that govern atmospheric dynamics. These equations include the Navier-Stokes equations, which describe fluid motion:

$$\frac{\partial \mathbf{v}}{\partial t} + (\mathbf{v} \cdot \nabla)\mathbf{v} = -\frac{1}{\rho}\nabla p + \nu \nabla^2 \mathbf{v} + \mathbf{f} \qquad (53.1)$$

where $\mathbf{v}$ represents the velocity field, $\rho$ is the density, $p$ the pressure, $\nu$ the kinematic viscosity, and $\mathbf{f}$ external forces such as gravity and Coriolis effect.

The thermodynamic state is described by the thermodynamic energy equation:

$$\frac{\partial T}{\partial t} + (\mathbf{v} \cdot \nabla)T = Q + \frac{R}{\rho c_p}\nabla^2 T \qquad (53.2)$$

where $T$ denotes temperature, $Q$ is the heat added per unit mass, $R$ is the ideal gas constant, and $c_p$ the specific heat at constant pressure.

# Numerical Methods for Weather Simulation

Solving the aforementioned PDEs requires discretization techniques, such as finite difference or finite volume methods, which approximate derivatives by discrete differences. The discretization of a PDE can be exemplified as:

$$\frac{\partial u}{\partial x} \approx \frac{u_{i+1} - u_i}{\Delta x} \qquad (53.3)$$

## 1   Time-stepping Schemes

The temporal evolution in weather models can be captured using explicit or implicit time-stepping methods. An example is the Euler forward method for updating temperature:

$$T^{n+1} = T^n + \Delta t \left(-(\mathbf{v} \cdot \nabla)T^n + Q^n\right) \qquad (53.4)$$

where superscripts $n$ and $n+1$ indicate discrete time steps.

# CUDA Acceleration for Weather Models

The massive computational demands of weather models require efficient parallel implementations. CUDA (Compute Unified Device Architecture) enables the parallel execution of numerical methods on GPUs, significantly enhancing computational throughput.

## 1   Parallelizing the Navier-Stokes Solver

Consider a CUDA kernel for the time integration of velocity fields derived from Navier-Stokes. The update for velocity can be parallelized by distributing grid points across threads:

---

**Data:** Velocity field v, pressure p, density rho, viscosity nu
**Function** Integrate($v$, $p$, $rho$, $nu$):
   **foreach** *grid point* **in parallel** do
      v[i] = v[i] +
      $\Delta t \times \left(-\frac{1}{\text{rho[i]}} \times \nabla\text{p[i]} + \nu\nabla^2\text{v[i]} + \text{f}\right)$;

---

This structure capitalizes on the concurrent execution capabilities of GPUs.

# Handling Large Datasets

Weather prediction involves vast datasets from satellite imagery and sensors. Efficient handling and processing of these datasets necessitate CUDA-based parallel I/O operations. The data is often stored in multidimensional arrays, with CUDA kernels performing operations like interpolation or data assimilation:

$$T_{i,j}^{new} = \alpha \cdot T_{i,j}^{obs} + (1 - \alpha) \cdot T_{i,j}^{model} \tag{53.5}$$

where $T_{i,j}^{new}$ is the updated temperature, $T_{i,j}^{obs}$ the observed temperature, $T_{i,j}^{model}$ the model's prior estimate, and $\alpha$ a weighting factor.

## 1   Data Interpolation Technique

Interpolating observed data over a grid can be accelerated using CUDA. The interpolation process involves evaluating grid point values using surrounding data points in a parallel manner:

---

**Data:** Observed data obs_data, grid grid
**Function** InterpolateData(*obs_data, grid*):
   **foreach** *grid point* **in parallel** do
      grid[i] = $\Phi$(obs_data) ;       // Interpolate

---

This process is essential for integrating disparate data sources into the forecasting model.

# Evaluation of Model Accuracy

Error metrics such as Root Mean Square Error (RMSE) are crucial to evaluating model accuracy:

$$\text{RMSE} = \sqrt{\frac{1}{N} \sum_{i=1}^{N} (P_i - O_i)^2} \qquad (53.6)$$

Here, $P_i$ is the predicted value, $O_i$ the observed value, and $N$ the number of observations. RMSE computations benefit from CUDA's ability to perform large-scale arithmetic operations efficiently across numerous data points.

## Python Code Snippet

Below is a Python code snippet that provides implementations for solving differential equations using CUDA for weather forecasting models, including aspects like Navier-Stokes equations, velocity field updates, and data interpolation.

```python
import numpy as np
import pycuda.autoinit
import pycuda.driver as cuda
from pycuda.compiler import SourceModule

# Define the Navier-Stokes update kernel
mod = SourceModule("""
__global__ void velocity_update(float *v, float *p, float *rho,
↪   float *nu, float *f, int N, float dt) {
    int i = blockIdx.x * blockDim.x + threadIdx.x;
    if (i < N) {
        // Perform a simple explicit time-stepping for velocity
        ↪   update
        v[i] += dt * ( - 1.0/rho[i] * (p[i+1] - p[i]) + nu[i] *
        ↪   (v[i-1] - 2 * v[i] + v[i+1]) + f[i] );
    }
}
""")

# Parameters initialization for demonstration purposes
N = 1024   # Number of grid points
dt = 0.01 # Time step size

v = np.zeros(N, dtype=np.float32)
p = np.zeros(N, dtype=np.float32)
rho = np.ones(N, dtype=np.float32)
nu = np.ones(N, dtype=np.float32) * 0.1
f = np.zeros(N, dtype=np.float32)

# Allocate device memory
v_gpu = cuda.mem_alloc(v.nbytes)
```

```python
p_gpu = cuda.mem_alloc(p.nbytes)
rho_gpu = cuda.mem_alloc(rho.nbytes)
nu_gpu = cuda.mem_alloc(nu.nbytes)
f_gpu = cuda.mem_alloc(f.nbytes)

# Transfer data to the GPU
cuda.memcpy_htod(v_gpu, v)
cuda.memcpy_htod(p_gpu, p)
cuda.memcpy_htod(rho_gpu, rho)
cuda.memcpy_htod(nu_gpu, nu)
cuda.memcpy_htod(f_gpu, f)

# Get the kernel function
velocity_update = mod.get_function("velocity_update")

# Launch kernel
block_size = 256
num_blocks = (N + block_size - 1) // block_size
velocity_update(v_gpu, p_gpu, rho_gpu, nu_gpu, f_gpu, np.int32(N),
↪ np.float32(dt), block=(block_size, 1, 1), grid=(num_blocks, 1))

# Retrieve results from the GPU
cuda.memcpy_dtoh(v, v_gpu)

print("Updated velocity field:", v)

# Simple data interpolation kernel for handling large datasets
mod_interp = SourceModule("""
__global__ void interpolate(float *obs_data, float *grid, int N) {
    int i = blockIdx.x * blockDim.x + threadIdx.x;
    if (i < N) {
        // Simple linear interpolation placeholder
        grid[i] = (obs_data[i] + obs_data[i+1]) / 2.0;
    }
}
""")

obs_data = np.random.rand(N + 1).astype(np.float32)   # Observed data
↪ with an extra point for safe access
grid = np.zeros(N, dtype=np.float32)

obs_data_gpu = cuda.mem_alloc(obs_data.nbytes)
grid_gpu = cuda.mem_alloc(grid.nbytes)

cuda.memcpy_htod(obs_data_gpu, obs_data)

interpolate = mod_interp.get_function("interpolate")
interpolate(obs_data_gpu, grid_gpu, np.int32(N), block=(block_size,
↪ 1, 1), grid=(num_blocks, 1))

cuda.memcpy_dtoh(grid, grid_gpu)
```

```
print("Interpolated grid data:", grid)
```

This code defines several key CUDA kernels and functions necessary for weather forecasting models:

- The kernel for `velocity_update` computes the updated velocity field from the Navier-Stokes equations leveraging variables like pressure and density.

- `interpolate` performs data interpolation on observed datasets to fit them onto a computational grid, essential for data assimilation.

- Setup includes device memory allocation and memory transfers using PyCUDA to and from the GPU for efficient computation.

The final block of code demonstrates the implementation of numerical methods in a parallelized fashion, managing grid data and updating velocities in a CUDA-enabled environment.

# Chapter 54

# Boolean Satisfiability Problems (SAT)

## Boolean Satisfiability Problems

Boolean Satisfiability Problem (SAT) is the task of determining if there exists an assignment of boolean variables that satisfies a given boolean formula. A boolean formula is expressed in conjunctive normal form (CNF), which is a conjunction of clauses, where each clause is a disjunction of literals. Formally, let $\phi$ be a boolean formula represented as:

$$\phi = \bigwedge_{i=1}^{m} \bigvee_{j=1}^{k_i} l_{i,j}$$

where $l_{i,j}$ are literals, each being a variable $x_i$ or its negation $\neg x_i$.

## SAT in Cryptography and Hardware Verification

In cryptographic applications, SAT solvers are employed for checking the equivalence of boolean circuits and cryptographic protocol verification. SAT is crucial in verifying hardware designs where the goal is to determine the satisfiability of constraints representing circuit conditions or properties.

# CUDA Implementation for SAT Solving

Graphics Processing Units (GPUs) offer substantial parallelism that can be leveraged to solve SAT problems more efficiently. CUDA (Compute Unified Device Architecture) provides the framework necessary to implement SAT solvers on GPUs.

## 1 Parallel Clause Evaluation

The parallelization of clause evaluation can significantly speed up the SAT-solving process. Each clause can be evaluated independently across different threads:

$$C_i(v) = \bigvee_{j=1}^{k_i} (l_{i,j} \oplus \neg v_j) \tag{54.1}$$

where $C_i(v)$ is the evaluation of clause $i$ with variable assignment $v$.

---

**Data:** Clauses clauses, variables vars
**Function** EvaluateClauses(*clauses, vars*):
    **foreach** *clause in clauses* **in parallel** do
        result[clause] = False;
        **foreach** *literal in clause* do
            **if** *literal == vars[literal.index]* **then**
                result[clause] = True;
                break;

---

## 2 Conflict-Driven Clause Learning (CDCL)

A sophisticated strategy is Conflict-Driven Clause Learning (CDCL), enhancing DPLL (Davis-Putnam-Logemann-Loveland) algorithms by learning from conflicts to prune search space. Consider a CNF formula $F$, when a conflict arises at decision level $d$, a clause $C$ is learned. $C$ contains the negations of the assignments causing the conflict:

$$C = \bigvee \neg D_i \quad \text{where } D_i \text{ are decision literals at level } d$$

For efficient implementation, decision clauses can be evaluated and stored using CUDA:

```
Data: Current assignment assignment, conflict clause
      conflict_clause
Function LearnClause(assignment, conflict_clause):
    new_clause = empty array;
    foreach literal in conflict_clause do
        if literal not satisfied by assignment then
            new_clause.append(negate(literal));
    clauses.append(new_clause);
```

# 3  Parallel Backjumping and Heuristics

The ability to jump back multiple levels in the decision tree at once enables rapid convergence. Backjumping can be managed by dynamically tracking implications across solution paths:

$$d = \max\{\text{level of } l \mid l \in \text{conflict clause}\} \qquad (54.2)$$

Additionally, applying heuristics like VSIDS (Variable State Independent Decaying Sum) for dynamic variable ordering optimizes step decisions.

# 4  Handling Large Instances with CUDA

Leveraging CUDA's memory model allows the efficient handling of vast quantities of variables and clauses. This involves partitioning the CNF formulas and employing shared memory for frequently accessed literals. The load balancing between CUDA threads and blocks is crucial to ensure the coefficients of performance:

$$\text{Load}_b = \frac{\lambda(b)}{|b|} \quad \text{where } \lambda(b) \text{ is the workload of block } b \qquad (54.3)$$

The SAT solver's performance on CUDA hinges on minimizing divergence within warps and optimizing global memory access patterns for the evaluation of candidate solutions across the search space.

# Python Code Snippet

Below is a Python code snippet that implements the SAT-solving mechanism on CUDA using PyCUDA for evaluating clauses, conflict clause learning, and managing backjumping with heuristics.

```python
import pycuda.autoinit
import pycuda.driver as cuda
from pycuda.compiler import SourceModule
import numpy as np

# Define the CUDA kernel
mod = SourceModule("""
__global__ void evaluate_clauses(int *clauses, int *vars, bool
↪    *result, int num_vars, int num_clauses) {
    int idx = blockIdx.x * blockDim.x + threadIdx.x;
    if (idx < num_clauses) {
        result[idx] = false;
        for (int i = 0; i < num_vars; ++i) {
            int literal = clauses[idx * num_vars + i];
            if (literal == vars[i]) {
                result[idx] = true;
                break;
            }
        }
    }
}

__global__ void learn_clause(int *conflict_clause, int *assignment,
↪    int *new_clause, int num_literals) {
    int idx = threadIdx.x;
    if (idx < num_literals) {
        if (assignment[idx] != conflict_clause[idx]) {
            new_clause[idx] = conflict_clause[idx];
        }
    }
}
""")

# Function to evaluate clauses using CUDA
def evaluate_clauses(clauses, vars):
    num_clauses, num_vars = clauses.shape
    result = np.zeros(num_clauses, dtype=np.bool)
    clauses_gpu = cuda.mem_alloc(clauses.nbytes)
    vars_gpu = cuda.mem_alloc(vars.nbytes)
    result_gpu = cuda.mem_alloc(result.nbytes)

    cuda.memcpy_htod(clauses_gpu, clauses)
    cuda.memcpy_htod(vars_gpu, vars)

    func = mod.get_function("evaluate_clauses")
    func(clauses_gpu, vars_gpu, result_gpu, np.int32(num_vars),
↪    np.int32(num_clauses), block=(256,1,1),
↪    grid=(num_clauses//256+1,1))

    cuda.memcpy_dtoh(result, result_gpu)
```

315

```
    return result

# Function to learn new conflict-driven clauses
def learn_clause(conflict_clause, assignment):
    num_literals = len(conflict_clause)
    new_clause = np.zeros_like(conflict_clause)

    conflict_clause_gpu = cuda.mem_alloc(conflict_clause.nbytes)
    assignment_gpu = cuda.mem_alloc(assignment.nbytes)
    new_clause_gpu = cuda.mem_alloc(new_clause.nbytes)

    cuda.memcpy_htod(conflict_clause_gpu, conflict_clause)
    cuda.memcpy_htod(assignment_gpu, assignment)

    func_learn = mod.get_function("learn_clause")
    func_learn(conflict_clause_gpu, assignment_gpu, new_clause_gpu,
    ↪   np.int32(num_literals), block=(256,1,1))

    cuda.memcpy_dtoh(new_clause, new_clause_gpu)
    return new_clause

# Example variables and clauses
vars = np.array([True, False, True, False], dtype=np.int32)
clauses = np.array([[1, 0, 1, 0], [0, 1, 0, 1], [1, 1, 0, 0]],
↪   dtype=np.int32)

# Execute evaluation
result = evaluate_clauses(clauses, vars)
print("Clause Evaluation Results:", result)

# Example conflict clause and assignment for conflict-driven
↪   learning
conflict_clause = np.array([1, 0, 0, 1], dtype=np.int32)
assignment = np.array([1, 0, 1, 0], dtype=np.int32)

# Learn from conflict
new_clause = learn_clause(conflict_clause, assignment)
print("Learned Clause from Conflict:", new_clause)
```

This Python code uses PyCUDA to implement key SAT-solving techniques:

- `evaluate_clauses` function evaluates clauses in parallel to determine SAT problem satisfiability.

- `learn_clause` demonstrates conflict-driven clause learning using GPU capabilities, which is essential for efficient SAT solving.

- The example includes initialization of clause and variable ar-

316

rays and performs both evaluation and conflict-driven learning.

- This implementation showcases the data transfer to and from GPU memory and utilizes PyCUDA to perform parallel operations, leveraging CUDA's strengths.

The code enables broad SAT problem-solving tasks to be offloaded to GPU, greatly improving computational speed and efficiency over traditional CPU-based methods.

# Chapter 55

# CUDA and Robotics

## Pathfinding Algorithms

Pathfinding is a fundamental aspect of robotics, involving the computation of optimal paths from a starting point to a target point while navigating a grid or network of nodes. The classic algorithm used in conjunction with CUDA for this task is the A* (A-star) algorithm, which can be optimized to exploit the parallel processing capabilities of GPUs.

The A* algorithm employs a heuristic function $h(n)$, defined as an estimate of the cost from node $n$ to the goal. The total cost function $f(n)$ is given by:

$$f(n) = g(n) + h(n)$$

where $g(n)$ is the exact cost from the start node to node $n$.

To parallelize this on CUDA, one can divide the grid into blocks, with each thread responsible for exploring potential paths from a given node. The update function for the neighbors $N(n)$ of a node $n$ can be delineated as:

$$g(n') = \min(g(n') + c(n, n'), g(n) + h(n)) \tag{55.1}$$

where $c(n, n')$ is the cost of moving from node $n$ to node $n'$.

**Data:** Graph nodes nodes, heuristic values heuristics,
start startNode, goal goalNode

**Function** AStarCUDA(*nodes, heuristics, startNode, goalNode*)**:**

Initialize priority queue openSet with startNode;

**while** *openSet is not empty* **do**

current = Extract node with lowest $f(n)$ from openSet;

**if** *current == goalNode* **then**
return *ReconstructPath(current)*

Remove current from openSet;

**foreach** *neighbor n' of current* **in parallel** **do**

tentative_gScore = gScore[current] + Distance(current, n');

**if** *tentative_gScore < gScore[n']* **then**

cameFrom[n'] = current;
gScore[n'] = tentative_gScore;
fScore[n'] = gScore[n'] + heuristics[n'];

**if** *n' not in openSet* **then**
Add n' to openSet;

return *failure*

# Vision Processing

Vision processing tasks, crucial for robotic systems, involve complex operations such as image recognition, feature extraction, and object tracking. GPUs provide an advantage in handling these operations concurrently across image pixels or data batches. The convolution operation, a staple in vision processing, can be expressed as follows for a discrete signal:

$$(y * w)[i] = \sum_j y[i - j] \cdot w[j]$$

Utilizing the parallel architecture of CUDA, these computations can be conducted in parallel, enhancing efficiency. For instance, image filtering can be parallelized by assigning different portions of the image to distinct blocks and threads.

# Sensor Data Analysis

Modern robotics relies heavily on sensor data to perceive and interact with the environment. The data collected from various sensors can be extensive and require real-time processing to provide meaningful insights. Consider the dataset $S$, capturing sensor readings over time. The analysis of this dataset often involves applying transformations and aggregations across time windows.

An operation such as computing a moving average over a window size $k$ can be articulated as:

$$\overline{x}_i = \frac{1}{k} \sum_{j=0}^{k-1} x_{i-j}$$

When implemented with CUDA, this operation can take advantage of shared memory to minimize access times and improve computation speed. Each block of threads can process separate windows of the data, facilitating real-time analysis.

By strategically deploying these techniques across a fleet of robotic agents, one can significantly enhance their autonomous functionalities and decision-making capabilities, leveraging the computational prowess of CUDA-enabled devices.

# Python Code Snippet

Below is a Python code snippet encompassing the core computational elements of the algorithms and data processing described in the chapter, leveraging the PyCUDA library to implement pathfinding with the A* algorithm, vision processing through convolution, and sensor data analysis with moving averages.

```
import pycuda.autoinit
import pycuda.driver as cuda
from pycuda.compiler import SourceModule
import numpy as np

# A* algorithm implementation in CUDA
mod_astar = SourceModule("""
__global__ void astar(float *gScore, int *cameFrom, float
↪    *heuristics, bool *openSet,
                       int *neighbors, float *costs, int num_nodes,
                          ↪  int start, int goal) {
    int idx = threadIdx.x + blockIdx.x * blockDim.x;
```

```
    if (idx >= num_nodes || !openSet[idx]) return;

    float tentative_gScore = gScore[idx] + costs[idx];
    if (tentative_gScore < gScore[neighbors[idx * num_nodes + idx]])
    ↪ {
        gScore[neighbors[idx * num_nodes + idx]] = tentative_gScore;
        cameFrom[neighbors[idx * num_nodes + idx]] = idx;
    }
}
""")

def run_astar(grid_size, start, goal, costs):
    num_nodes = grid_size * grid_size
    gScore = np.full(num_nodes, float('inf'), dtype=np.float32)
    gScore[start] = 0
    cameFrom = np.full(num_nodes, -1, dtype=np.int32)
    heuristics = np.random.rand(num_nodes).astype(np.float32)  #
    ↪ Placeholder
    openSet = np.full(num_nodes, False, dtype=np.bool)
    openSet[start] = True
    neighbors = np.arange(num_nodes * num_nodes).astype(np.int32)  #
    ↪ Placeholder

    func = mod_astar.get_function("astar")
    func(cuda.InOut(gScore), cuda.InOut(cameFrom),
    ↪ cuda.In(heuristics), cuda.InOut(openSet),
        cuda.In(neighbors), cuda.In(costs), np.int32(num_nodes),
        ↪ np.int32(start), np.int32(goal),
        block=(256, 1, 1), grid=(num_nodes//256+1, 1))

    return cameFrom

# Convolution for Vision Processing
mod_convolution = SourceModule("""
__global__ void convolution(float *signal, float *filter, float
↪ *output, int signal_size, int filter_size) {
    int idx = threadIdx.x + blockIdx.x * blockDim.x;
    if (idx >= signal_size) return;

    float result = 0.0;
    for (int j = 0; j < filter_size; ++j) {
        if (idx - j >= 0) {
            result += signal[idx - j] * filter[j];
        }
    }
    output[idx] = result;
}
""")

def run_convolution(signal, filter):
    signal_size = len(signal)
    filter_size = len(filter)
```

```python
    output = np.zeros_like(signal, dtype=np.float32)

    func = mod_convolution.get_function("convolution")
    func(cuda.In(signal), cuda.In(filter), cuda.Out(output),
    ↪   np.int32(signal_size), np.int32(filter_size),
        block=(256, 1, 1), grid=(signal_size//256+1, 1))

    return output

# Moving average for Sensor Data Analysis
mod_moving_average = SourceModule("""
__global__ void moving_average(float *sensor_data, float
↪   *moving_avg, int data_size, int window_size) {
    int idx = threadIdx.x + blockIdx.x * blockDim.x;

    if (idx >= data_size) return;

    float sum = 0.0;
    for (int j = 0; j < window_size; ++j) {
        if (idx - j >= 0) {
            sum += sensor_data[idx - j];
        }
    }
    moving_avg[idx] = sum / window_size;
}
""")

def run_moving_average(data, window_size):
    data_size = len(data)
    moving_avg = np.zeros_like(data, dtype=np.float32)

    func = mod_moving_average.get_function("moving_average")
    func(cuda.In(data), cuda.Out(moving_avg), np.int32(data_size),
    ↪   np.int32(window_size),
        block=(256, 1, 1), grid=(data_size//256+1, 1))

    return moving_avg

# Example data
grid_costs = np.random.rand(100).astype(np.float32)
signal = np.random.rand(1024).astype(np.float32)
filter = np.random.rand(10).astype(np.float32)
sensor_data = np.random.rand(1024).astype(np.float32)

came_from_result = run_astar(10, 0, 99, grid_costs)
convolution_result = run_convolution(signal, filter)
moving_avg_result = run_moving_average(sensor_data, 5)

print("Came From:", came_from_result)
print("Convolution Output:", convolution_result)
print("Moving Average Result:", moving_avg_result)
```

This code implements several key CUDA computations for robotics applications:

- The CUDA kernel for `astar` function handles the A* pathfinding algorithm, assigning computation of tentative scores in parallel.

- The `convolution` kernel enables parallel calculations of filtering tasks for vision processing, demonstrating efficiency in GPU computations.

- The `moving_average` kernel computes window-based averaging of sensor data, optimizing for real-time processing needs.

The Python functions serve as interfaces to these kernels, demonstrating their application in sample problems, reflecting how parallel computation enhances speed and efficiency.

# Chapter 56

# Social Network Analysis

## Introduction to Social Network Analytics

Social network analysis (SNA) involves the exploration and modeling of relationships among entities such as individuals, organizations, or systems. The relationships are represented primarily as graphs $G = (V, E)$, where $V$ denotes the set of vertices (nodes) and $E$ the set of edges connecting these vertices. The large scale and complexity of social networks, necessitating substantial computational power, can benefit from the parallel capabilities of CUDA.

## Graph Representation and Storage

Graph data structures are critical for efficient manipulation and computation. For a social network graph $G$, let $A$ be its adjacency matrix, where:

$$A_{ij} = \begin{cases} 1, & \text{if there is an edge from node } i \text{ to node } j \\ 0, & \text{otherwise} \end{cases}$$

Alternately, an adjacency list representation may be employed to optimize storage and accesses for sparse graphs, often encountered in expansive social network datasets.

# Centrality Measures

Centrality metrics quantify the significance or influence of a node within a network. Common metrics include degree, closeness, and betweenness centrality. The degree centrality $C_D(v)$ of a node $v$ is given by:

$$C_D(v) = \deg(v) = \sum_{i=1}^{n} A_{vi}$$

Closeness centrality, measuring the reciprocal of the average shortest path length from a node to all others, is defined as:

$$C_C(v) = \frac{1}{\sum_{u \neq v} d(u, v)}$$

Betweenness centrality, representing the number of shortest paths passing through a node, is articulated by:

$$C_B(v) = \sum_{s \neq v \neq t} \frac{\sigma_{st}(v)}{\sigma_{st}}$$

where $\sigma_{st}(v)$ is the count of shortest paths from $s$ to $t$ passing through $v$.

# Implementation of Parallel Algorithms

CUDA's capabilities enable the acceleration of centrality calculations and graph traversal methods, crucial for large datasets. The parallel algorithms can distribute calculations among numerous threads, each responsible for processing different nodes or edges. For calculating degree centrality in parallel, one can implement:

---

**Data:** Adjacency list `adjList`, number of nodes `numNodes`
**Function** `DegreeCentrality`(*adjList, numNodes*):
  **Result:** Array `degree` containing degree centrality for each node
  Initialize `degree` array with zeros;
  **foreach** *node v in parallel* **do**
    `degree[v] = length(adjList[v]);`
  **return** *degree*

---

# Community Detection Algorithms

Community detection involves identifying clusters of nodes within a network that are more densely connected internally. A popular method is the Louvain algorithm, which optimizes modularity $Q$, defined for a partition $P$ of the graph as:

$$Q = \frac{1}{2m} \sum_{i,j} \left[ A_{ij} - \frac{k_i k_j}{2m} \right] \delta(c_i, c_j)$$

where $k_i$ is the degree of node $i$, $m$ is the total number of edges, and $\delta(c_i, c_j)$ is 1 if nodes $i$ and $j$ belong to the same community, 0 otherwise.

# Information Diffusion and Influence Maximization

Information diffusion models study how information propagates across a network. The Independent Cascade Model and Linear Threshold Model are widely utilized frameworks. In the Independent Cascade Model, each node activated at time $t$ attempts to activate each inactive neighbor $v$ with a probability $p$:

$$P(u \text{ activates } v) = 1 - (1-p)^{N(u)}$$

where $N(u)$ is the set of active neighbors of $v$.

Influence maximization seeks to identify a set of initial nodes $S$ with maximum potential to spread information across the network. The optimal set maximizes the expected total influence $\sigma(S)$.

# Conclusion

The utilization of CUDA for social network analysis facilitates the processing of vast datasets typical within this domain, fostering deeper insights through advanced computational techniques. By leveraging GPU acceleration for graph analytics, the computational overhead associated with such large-scale analysis is significantly reduced.

# Python Code Snippet

Below is a Python code snippet demonstrating the use of PyCUDA to handle social network analysis tasks including graph representation, centrality measure calculations, and basic parallel algorithms.

```python
import pycuda.autoinit
import pycuda.driver as cuda
import numpy as np
from pycuda.compiler import SourceModule

# Generate some example data
num_nodes = 100
adjacency_list_example = np.random.randint(0, 2, size=(num_nodes,
↪   num_nodes)).astype(np.float32)

# Kernel source code
kernel_code = """
__global__ void degree_centrality(float *adj_list, float *degree,
↪   int num_nodes) {
    int idx = blockIdx.x * blockDim.x + threadIdx.x;
    if (idx < num_nodes) {
        float count = 0;
        for (int i = 0; i < num_nodes; ++i) {
            count += adj_list[idx * num_nodes + i];
        }
        degree[idx] = count;
    }
}

__global__ void closeness_centrality(float *adj_list, float
↪   *closeness, int num_nodes) {
    int idx = blockIdx.x * blockDim.x + threadIdx.x;
    if (idx < num_nodes) {
        float sum_distances = 0;
        for (int i = 0; i < num_nodes; ++i) {
            if (i != idx) {
                float distance = adj_list[idx * num_nodes + i]; //
↪               Simplified distance
                sum_distances += distance > 0 ? 1 / distance : 0;
            }
        }
        closeness[idx] = num_nodes / sum_distances;
    }
}
"""

# Compile the kernel code
mod = SourceModule(kernel_code)
degree_centrality = mod.get_function("degree_centrality")
closeness_centrality = mod.get_function("closeness_centrality")
```

```
# Allocate memory on the device
adj_list_gpu = cuda.mem_alloc(adjacency_list_example.nbytes)
degree_gpu = cuda.mem_alloc(adjacency_list_example.shape[0] *
↪   np.float32().nbytes)
closeness_gpu = cuda.mem_alloc(adjacency_list_example.shape[0] *
↪   np.float32().nbytes)

# Transfer data to the device
cuda.memcpy_htod(adj_list_gpu, adjacency_list_example)

# Define grid and block
block_size = 256
grid_size = (num_nodes + block_size - 1) // block_size

# Call the kernels
degree_centrality(adj_list_gpu, degree_gpu, np.int32(num_nodes),
↪   block=(block_size, 1, 1), grid=(grid_size, 1))
closeness_centrality(adj_list_gpu, closeness_gpu,
↪   np.int32(num_nodes), block=(block_size, 1, 1), grid=(grid_size,
↪   1))

# Retrieve results
degree_result = np.empty_like(adjacency_list_example[:, 0])
closeness_result = np.empty_like(adjacency_list_example[:, 0])
cuda.memcpy_dtoh(degree_result, degree_gpu)
cuda.memcpy_dtoh(closeness_result, closeness_gpu)

# Output
print("Degree Centrality:", degree_result)
print("Closeness Centrality:", closeness_result)
```

---

This code snippet defines necessary CUDA kernels and sets up an example case to compute key centrality metrics using PyCUDA:

- The 'degree_centrality' kernel calculates the degree centrality for each node based on its adjacency list.

- The 'closeness_centrality' kernel calculates an approximate closeness centrality using simplified distance measures.

- Both metrics are computed in parallel for all nodes, taking advantage of CUDA's thread execution model.

- The example demonstrates memory allocation, data transfer between host and device, kernel execution, and retrieval of results, crucial steps in leveraging GPU acceleration for social network analysis tasks.

This Python code offers a foundation for extending to more complex tasks and optimizations within the field of social network analysis using GPU resources.

# Chapter 57

# Audio Processing Applications

## Introduction to Audio Processing with CUDA

Audio processing encompasses a wide range of applications, including filtering, enhancement, and real-time effects deployment. The computational demands for these tasks increase as audio complexity and quality improve. CUDA's parallel processing capabilities significantly bolster the efficiency of audio processing pipelines by enabling simultaneous handling of audio samples.

## Audio Filtering Techniques

Audio filtering forms the bedrock of signal processing, employed for noise suppression, feature extraction, and quality enhancement. A fundamental filter, the finite impulse response (FIR) filter, is characterized by its impulse response $h[n]$, implemented as:

$$y[n] = \sum_{k=0}^{N-1} h[k] \cdot x[n-k]$$

where $x[n]$ is the input signal, $y[n]$ is the filtered signal, and $N$ is the filter length. Parallel computation of the convolution operation inherent in FIR filtering is facilitated by CUDA, encompassing the distribution of workloads for each output sample across multiple threads.

# Signal Enhancement Algorithms

Signal enhancement involves the amplification of desired signal components while attenuating noise. The Wiener filter, optimal in the least-squares sense, serves to restore signals distorted by additive noise. It is delineated by the transfer function $H(\omega)$:

$$H(\omega) = \frac{S_{xy}(\omega)}{S_{xx}(\omega)}$$

where $S_{xy}(\omega)$ is the cross-spectral density of the input and desired signals, and $S_{xx}(\omega)$ is the power spectral density of the input signal. CUDA accelerates the inversion and multiplication operations in the frequency domain required for Wiener filter operation.

# Real-time Audio Effects Implementation

Real-time audio effects impose strict performance constraints, necessitating rapid processing to minimize latency. Effects such as reverb, echo, and modulation are typically realized via a combination of time and frequency domain manipulations. The reverberation effect, often expressed as a recursive filter, is given by:

$$y[n] = g \cdot y[n - d] + x[n]$$

where $g$ is the feedback gain, $d$ is the delay time, and $y[n]$ is the output. Utilizing CUDA, each thread computes a distinct segment of the audio frame, efficiently applying recursive algorithms across the dataset.

# Algorithm for Parallel FIR Filtering

---

**Data:** Input signal x, filter coefficients h, filter length N,
           output signal y, signal length L

**Function** FIRFilter($x$, $h$, $N$, $y$, $L$):

     **Result:** Filtered signal y

     **for** *each sample n in parallel* **do**

         y[n] = 0;

         **for** $k = 0$ to $N - 1$ **do**

             **if** $n \geq k$ **then**

                 | y[n] += h[k] $\cdot$x[$n - k$]

     **return** $y$

---

The above pseudocode elucidates the parallel execution of the FIR filter utilizing CUDA, whereby each audio sample $n$ is filtered independently.

# Python Code Snippet

Below is a Python code snippet that encompasses the core computational elements for parallel FIR filtering, signal enhancement using Wiener filtering, and real-time audio effects implementation using CUDA for audio processing.

```python
import pycuda.autoinit
import pycuda.driver as cuda
import numpy as np
from pycuda.compiler import SourceModule

# FIR filter kernel implementation
FIR_KERNEL = """
__global__ void fir_filter(float *y, float *x, float *h, int N, int
    L) {
    int n = blockDim.x * blockIdx.x + threadIdx.x;
    if (n < L) {
        float acc = 0;
        for (int k = 0; k < N; ++k) {
            if (n >= k)
                acc += h[k] * x[n - k];
        }
        y[n] = acc;
    }
}
"""
```

```python
# Initialize filter parameters
h = np.array([0.2, 0.3, 0.4], dtype=np.float32)
x = np.random.rand(1024).astype(np.float32)
N = len(h)
L = len(x)
y = np.zeros_like(x)

# Compile the kernel
mod = SourceModule(FIR_KERNEL)
fir_filter = mod.get_function("fir_filter")

# Allocate device memory and transfer data
x_gpu = cuda.mem_alloc(x.nbytes)
y_gpu = cuda.mem_alloc(y.nbytes)
h_gpu = cuda.mem_alloc(h.nbytes)

cuda.memcpy_htod(x_gpu, x)
cuda.memcpy_htod(h_gpu, h)

# Launch kernel
block_size = 256
grid_size = (L + block_size - 1) // block_size
fir_filter(y_gpu, x_gpu, h_gpu, np.int32(N), np.int32(L),
↪  block=(block_size, 1, 1), grid=(grid_size, 1))

# Copy result back to host
cuda.memcpy_dtoh(y, y_gpu)

# Define Wiener filter function
def wiener_filter(Sxy, Sxx, freq):
    H = Sxy / Sxx
    return H[freq]

# Define real-time audio effect (reverb) function
def apply_reverb(y, g, d):
    for n in range(d, len(y)):
        y[n] = g * y[n - d] + y[n]
    return y

# Signal enhancement using the Wiener filter
Sxy = np.random.rand(100).astype(np.float32)
Sxx = np.random.rand(100).astype(np.float32)
freq = np.random.randint(0, 100)
enhanced_signal = wiener_filter(Sxy, Sxx, freq)

# Apply reverb effect
g = 0.7
d = 5
y_after_reverb = apply_reverb(np.copy(y), g, d)

print("FIR Filtered signal:", y)
print("Enhanced Signal:", enhanced_signal)
```

```
print("Reverb Applied Signal:", y_after_reverb)
```

This code defines several key functions necessary for implementing audio processing techniques using CUDA:

- `fir_filter` is a CUDA kernel function that implements parallel FIR filtering through the convolution of input signals with filter coefficients.

- `wiener_filter` calculates the Wiener filter output for enhancing noisy audio signals.

- `apply_reverb` simulates the application of a reverb effect on an audio signal, demonstrating a basic recursive filter operation.

The final block of code shows example outputs for each key function, demonstrating their usage in audio processing tasks.

# Chapter 58

# Astrophysics Simulations

## Stellar Formation Modeling

Astrophysical simulations of stellar formation involve complex fluid dynamics and thermodynamics. These simulations are typically governed by the Navier-Stokes equations coupled with gravitational interactions. In CUDA, these equations can be expressed and solved in parallel, providing a significant performance advantage due to the massive number of particles involved.

The continuum model for fluid flow in stellar atmospheres can be encapsulated in the equation:

$$\frac{\partial \mathbf{v}}{\partial t} + (\mathbf{v} \cdot \nabla)\mathbf{v} = -\frac{1}{\rho}\nabla P + \mathbf{g} + \nu \Delta \mathbf{v}$$

where $\mathbf{v}$ denotes the velocity field, $\rho$ the density, $P$ the pressure, $\mathbf{g}$ the gravitational force, and $\nu$ the kinematic viscosity. CUDA enables the decomposition of the simulation domain, distributing calculations of these partial differential equations across thousands of threads.

## Black Hole Dynamics Simulation

The simulation of black hole dynamics encompasses solving Einstein's field equations, expressed succinctly in geometric units as:

$$G_{\mu\nu} + \Lambda g_{\mu\nu} = \frac{8\pi G}{c^4} T_{\mu\nu}$$

where $G_{\mu\nu}$ is the Einstein tensor, $\Lambda$ the cosmological constant, $g_{\mu\nu}$ the metric tensor, $G$ Newton's gravitational constant, $c$ the speed of light, and $T_{\mu\nu}$ the stress-energy tensor. These equations are typically non-linear, and CUDA's parallelism allows for computationally intensive tasks such as tensor computations to be performed efficiently.

The numerical relativity techniques utilized here often employ a discretized spacetime mesh, with CUDA performing updates to the metric at each grid point using finite difference methods.

# Particle-Based Astrophysical Models

Astrophysical phenomena are also modeled using particle-based simulations, where the system is represented by a large number of discrete particles. CUDA excels at handling these simulations due to its nature of parallel computation. The gravitational interactions between particles can be calculated using the Barnes-Hut algorithm, which reduces the complexity to $O(N \log N)$.

The acceleration $\mathbf{a}_i$ of a particle $i$ due to gravitational interactions is given by:

$$\mathbf{a}_i = -G \sum_{j \neq i} \frac{m_j (\mathbf{r}_i - \mathbf{r}_j)}{\|\mathbf{r}_i - \mathbf{r}_j\|^3}$$

where $G$ is the gravitational constant, $m_j$ the mass of particle $j$, and $\mathbf{r}_i$ and $\mathbf{r}_j$ are the positions of particles $i$ and $j$, respectively. CUDA facilitates the implementation of the summation over particles by distributing computation tasks among multiple threads.

# Algorithm for Gravitational Interactions

---

**Data:** Particle positions r and masses m
**Result:** Computed accelerations a
**Function** ComputeAccelerations($r$, $m$, $a$):

> **for** *each particle i in parallel* **do**
>> a[i] = 0;
>> **for** *each particle j ≠ i* **do**
>>> r_diff = r[i] - r[j];
>>> distance =
>>> $\|$r_diff$\|$ a$[i]+ = -G \cdot$ m$[j] \cdot \frac{\text{r\_diff}}{\text{distance}^3}$

> **return** a

---

This algorithm demonstrates the parallel calculation of gravitational accelerations using CUDA, with initialization and execution phases that align complex computations over the distributed architecture.

# Conclusion

Astrophysical simulations using CUDA provide significant performance benefits in simulating complex phenomena such as star formation and black hole dynamics. Through efficient handling of massive parallelism, CUDA enables detailed and large-scale simulations otherwise computationally prohibitive.

# Python Code Snippet

Below is a Python code snippet that implements core computational elements for astrophysical simulations, focusing on solving fluid dynamics equations and gravitational interactions using PyCUDA.

---

```python
import numpy as np
import pycuda.autoinit
import pycuda.driver as cuda
from pycuda.compiler import SourceModule

# Device function in CUDA to compute velocity, assuming a simplified
↪ simulation
mod = SourceModule("""
```

```
__global__ void compute_velocity(float *v, float *rho, float *P,
↪   float *g, float *nu, int N) {
    int idx = threadIdx.x + blockDim.x * blockIdx.x;
    if (idx < N) {
        float dv_dt = -(1.0 / rho[idx]) * (P[idx]) + g[idx] +
        ↪   nu[idx];
        v[idx] += dv_dt;
    }
}
""")

def stellar_formation_simulation():
    # Sample parameters for the simulation
    N = 1024   # Number of particles
    v = np.zeros(N, dtype=np.float32)
    rho = np.ones(N, dtype=np.float32) * 1.0
    P = np.random.rand(N).astype(np.float32)
    g = np.random.rand(N).astype(np.float32)
    nu = np.random.rand(N).astype(np.float32)

    # Allocate space for arrays on the device
    v_gpu = cuda.mem_alloc(v.nbytes)
    rho_gpu = cuda.mem_alloc(rho.nbytes)
    P_gpu = cuda.mem_alloc(P.nbytes)
    g_gpu = cuda.mem_alloc(g.nbytes)
    nu_gpu = cuda.mem_alloc(nu.nbytes)

    # Copy data to GPU
    cuda.memcpy_htod(v_gpu, v)
    cuda.memcpy_htod(rho_gpu, rho)
    cuda.memcpy_htod(P_gpu, P)
    cuda.memcpy_htod(g_gpu, g)
    cuda.memcpy_htod(nu_gpu, nu)

    # Launch CUDA kernel
    compute_velocity = mod.get_function("compute_velocity")
    block_size = 256
    blocks = (N + block_size - 1) // block_size
    compute_velocity(v_gpu, rho_gpu, P_gpu, g_gpu, nu_gpu,
    ↪   np.int32(N), block=(block_size, 1, 1), grid=(blocks, 1))

    # Copy result back to host
    cuda.memcpy_dtoh(v, v_gpu)
    return v

def gravitational_interaction_simulation():
    # Barnes-Hut algorithm implementation
    particles = 1024
    positions = np.random.rand(particles, 3).astype(np.float32)
    masses = np.random.rand(particles).astype(np.float32)
    accelerations = np.zeros_like(positions)

    positions_gpu = cuda.mem_alloc(positions.nbytes)
```

```
    masses_gpu = cuda.mem_alloc(masses.nbytes)
    accelerations_gpu = cuda.mem_alloc(accelerations.nbytes)

    cuda.memcpy_htod(positions_gpu, positions)
    cuda.memcpy_htod(masses_gpu, masses)

    mod = SourceModule("""
    __global__ void compute_acceleration(float *positions, float
    ↪  *masses, float *accelerations, int particles) {
        int idx = threadIdx.x + blockIdx.x * blockDim.x;
        if (idx < particles) {
            float3 pos_i = make_float3(positions[3*idx],
            ↪  positions[3*idx + 1], positions[3*idx + 2]);
            float3 acc = make_float3(0.0, 0.0, 0.0);
            for (int j = 0; j < particles; ++j) {
                if (j != idx) {
                    float3 pos_j = make_float3(positions[3*j],
                    ↪  positions[3*j + 1], positions[3*j + 2]);
                    float3 r = pos_j - pos_i;
                    float dist_sqr = dot(r, r);
                    float inv_dist3 = rsqrt(dist_sqr * dist_sqr *
                    ↪  dist_sqr);
                    acc += (r * masses[j]) * inv_dist3;
                }
            }
            accelerations[3*idx] = acc.x;
            accelerations[3*idx + 1] = acc.y;
            accelerations[3*idx + 2] = acc.z;
        }
    }
    """)

    compute_acceleration = mod.get_function("compute_acceleration")
    block_size = 256
    blocks = (particles + block_size - 1) // block_size
    compute_acceleration(positions_gpu, masses_gpu,
    ↪  accelerations_gpu, np.int32(particles), block=(block_size,
    ↪  1, 1), grid=(blocks, 1))

    cuda.memcpy_dtoh(accelerations, accelerations_gpu)
    return accelerations

# Run simulations
velocities = stellar_formation_simulation()
accelerations = gravitational_interaction_simulation()

print("Stellar Formation Velocities:")
print(velocities)

print("Gravitational Interactions Accelerations:")
print(accelerations)
```

This Python code covers the following functions crucial for astrophysical simulations:

- `stellar_formation_simulation` simulates fluid dynamics equations in stellar formation, showcasing how CUDA can compute the velocity field based on pressure, gravity, and viscosity.

- `gravitational_interaction_simulation` implements a parallelized version of the Barnes-Hut algorithm to calculate gravitational accelerations of particles, demonstrating how complex interactions can be managed effectively across thousands of threads.

These functions leverage the pyCUDA library to perform computations necessary for astrophysical models, illustrating the power of GPU-accelerated computing.

# Chapter 59

# Electromagnetic Simulations

## Maxwell's Equations and CUDA Implementation

Maxwell's equations form the foundation of electromagnetic theory, governing the behavior of electric and magnetic fields. These can be compactly expressed in differential form as:

$$\nabla \cdot \mathbf{E} = \frac{\rho}{\varepsilon_0},$$

$$\nabla \cdot \mathbf{B} = 0,$$

$$\nabla \times \mathbf{E} = -\frac{\partial \mathbf{B}}{\partial t},$$

$$\nabla \times \mathbf{B} = \mu_0 \mathbf{J} + \mu_0 \varepsilon_0 \frac{\partial \mathbf{E}}{\partial t},$$

where $\mathbf{E}$ and $\mathbf{B}$ represent the electric and magnetic fields, $\rho$ is the charge density, $\varepsilon_0$ is the permittivity of free space, $\mu_0$ is the permeability of free space, and $\mathbf{J}$ is the current density. CUDA enables the efficient computation of these equations by parallelizing the spatial domain and utilizing boundary conditions that are seamlessly integrated into the simulation kernel.

# Discretization Scheme

The Finite-Difference Time-Domain (FDTD) method discretizes both the spatial and temporal derivatives in Maxwell's equations. The central-difference approximation yields:

$$\frac{\mathbf{E}^{n+1} - \mathbf{E}^n}{\Delta t} \approx -\nabla \times \mathbf{B}^{n+1/2},$$

$$\frac{\mathbf{B}^{n+1/2} - \mathbf{B}^{n-1/2}}{\Delta t} \approx -\nabla \times \mathbf{E}^n,$$

where $\Delta t$ represents the time step size, and superscripts denote the discrete time levels. CUDA's parallel architecture allows computation of these updates simultaneously across numerous spatial grid points.

# Algorithm for FDTD Simulation

---

**Data:** Electric field array E and magnetic field array B
**Result:** Updated electromagnetic fields E and B
**Function** UpdateFields(*E, B, parameters*):
    **for** *each grid point* $i, j, k$ *in parallel* **do**
        E_new[i, j, k] = E[i, j, k] +
        $\Delta t \times (\nabla \times \mathbf{B}[i,j,k])$ B_new[$i,j,k$] =
        B[$i,j,k$] $- \Delta t \times (\nabla \times \mathbf{E}[i,j,k])$
    **return** E_new, B_new

---

The algorithm updates the electric and magnetic fields within a 3D grid framework, exploiting CUDA's capacity for high parallelization in processing three-dimensional arrays of data. Each thread computes the updates of $\mathbf{E}$ and $\mathbf{B}$ at different lattice points concurrently.

# Applications to Communication Technologies

The enhanced computational capabilities provided by CUDA allow for the rapid simulation of electromagnetic wave propagation in various media, fundamental for the design of advanced communication systems. The solution of Maxwell's equations with CUDA accelerates the assessment of wave interactions with complex structures and material properties.

The interaction of electromagnetic waves with conducting surfaces, which is essential in antenna design, can be approximated by:

$$\mathbf{J}_s = \sigma \mathbf{E}_t,$$

where $\mathbf{J}_s$ represents the surface current density, $\sigma$ is the surface conductivity, and $\mathbf{E}_t$ is the tangential component of the electric field. By leveraging the CUDA parallelization framework, these calculations can be efficiently incorporated into electromagnetic compatibility evaluations and optimizations for high-frequency communication hardware.

The rapid advancements and increases in data transmission speeds have concomitantly driven the need for sophisticated simulation environments, and CUDA-based electromagnetic simulations represent a critical tool in addressing the computational demands posed by such developments.

# Python Code Snippet

Below is a Python code snippet that provides the implementation of Maxwell's equations for electromagnetic simulations using the Finite-Difference Time-Domain (FDTD) method on a CUDA platform, where CUDA's parallelism significantly boosts computational efficiency for 3D grid updates of electric $\mathbf{E}$ and magnetic $\mathbf{B}$ fields.

```python
import numpy as np
import pycuda.autoinit
from pycuda import gpuarray
from pycuda.compiler import SourceModule

# CUDA kernel for updating electromagnetic fields
FDTD_UPDATE_KERNEL = """
__global__ void update_fields(float *E, float *B, float *E_new,
↪    float *B_new,
                              int nx, int ny, int nz, float dt) {
    int i = blockDim.x * blockIdx.x + threadIdx.x;
    int j = blockDim.y * blockIdx.y + threadIdx.y;
    int k = blockDim.z * blockIdx.z + threadIdx.z;

    if (i < nx && j < ny && k < nz) {
        int idx = i + j * nx + k * nx * ny;
```

```
        // Example update rule using central differences
        float curl_B = (B[idx + 1] - B[idx]) - (B[idx + nx] -
        ↪   B[idx]);
        float curl_E = (E[idx + 1] - E[idx]) - (E[idx + nx] -
        ↪   E[idx]);

        E_new[idx] = E[idx] + dt * curl_B;
        B_new[idx] = B[idx] - dt * curl_E;
    }
}
"""

def main():
    nx, ny, nz = 100, 100, 100
    dt = 0.01
    E = np.random.rand(nx, ny, nz).astype(np.float32)
    B = np.random.rand(nx, ny, nz).astype(np.float32)

    # Allocate memory on the GPU for E, B, E_new, and B_new
    E_gpu = gpuarray.to_gpu(E)
    B_gpu = gpuarray.to_gpu(B)
    E_new_gpu = gpuarray.empty_like(E_gpu)
    B_new_gpu = gpuarray.empty_like(B_gpu)

    # Compile the CUDA kernel
    mod = SourceModule(FDTD_UPDATE_KERNEL)
    update_fields = mod.get_function("update_fields")

    # Specify the block and grid sizes for the CUDA kernel
    block_size = (8, 8, 8)
    grid_size = (int(np.ceil(nx / block_size[0])),
                 int(np.ceil(ny / block_size[1])),
                 int(np.ceil(nz / block_size[2])))

    # Execute the FDTD update kernel
    update_fields(E_gpu, B_gpu, E_new_gpu, B_new_gpu,
                  np.int32(nx), np.int32(ny), np.int32(nz),
                  ↪   np.float32(dt),
                  block=block_size, grid=grid_size)

    # Fetch the results from GPU to CPU
    E_updated = E_new_gpu.get()
    B_updated = B_new_gpu.get()

    # Output the results
    print("Updated Electric Field:", E_updated)
    print("Updated Magnetic Field:", B_updated)

if __name__ == "__main__":
    main()
```

This code defines a CUDA kernel and utilizes PyCUDA for

344

compiling and executing it:

- The CUDA kernel, `update_fields`, performs the FDTD update on the electric and magnetic fields using representations derived from Maxwell's equations.

- `main` function initializes the 3D field arrays **E** and **B**, transfers them to the GPU, and then invokes the CUDA kernel to update these fields.

- The code retrieves the updated fields back to the CPU and prints them, demonstrating the GPU computation results.

In practice, the CUDA parallel framework yields computationally efficient simulations for applications such as communications technology, where Maxwell's equations play a pivotal role in modeling wave phenomena.

# Chapter 60

# Augmenting Database Queries

## Overview of Database Query Optimization

Database query optimization plays a crucial role in ensuring efficient data retrieval and processing. The execution time of a query often determines the feasibility of real-time analytics in large-scale data environments. CUDA (Compute Unified Device Architecture) provides a parallel computation framework that can substantially enhance performance by accelerating the computation of complex queries across large datasets. Traditional CPU-based query execution models can be supplanted by parallelized strategies that exploit CUDA's architecture, thus allowing for rapid query evaluation and data manipulation.

## Parallel Query Execution Model

The parallel query execution model leverages CUDA's ability to perform concurrent operations across multiple data points. Let $Q(T, P, F)$ denote a query comprising tables $T$, predicates $P$, and functions $F$. The transformation $\Phi$ from a sequential to a parallel execution plan can be expressed as:

$$\Phi(Q) = \{\texttt{execute\_parallel}(T, P, F) \mid \forall (t \in T, p \in P, f \in F)\}$$

The function `execute_parallel` distributes query components across CUDA threads, where each thread handles a subset of data, thus reducing the time complexity associated with sequential processing.

# GPU-Accelerated Join Operations

One of the most computationally intensive operations in database systems is the join. The join operation combines tables based on a set of specified conditions, often on the same columns. In a CUDA environment, the join operation benefits from parallel execution as follows:

## 1 Equi-join on GPU

The equi-join, where equality predicates are used, can be distributed across multiple GPU cores. Let $R \bowtie S$ represent the equi-join of relations $R$ and $S$ on attribute $A$. The CUDA-accelerated join exploits hashing techniques to distribute tuples into buckets, processed concurrently by CUDA threads.

$$R \bowtie S = \bigcup_i \left( R[h(r_i)] \times S[h(s_j)] \right) \quad \text{if } r_i.A = s_j.A$$

where $h$ is the hash function. The hashing partitions can be executed in parallel using the CUDA block grid strategy, each block handling a specific partition.

# CUDA-based Aggregation Functions

Aggregation operations, such as SUM, COUNT, AVG, MAX, and MIN, require efficient data traversal and accumulation. CUDA facilitates these operations by concurrently aggregating data from different partitions.

Consider an aggregation query $A(T)$ computing the sum of a column $c$. In parallel form, the calculation becomes:

$$A(T) = \sum_{i=1}^{|T|} t_i.c = \sum_{b=1}^{N_b} \left( \sum_{i \in B_b} t_i.c \right)$$

347

where $N_b$ represents the number of blocks and $B_b$ the $b$-th block of threads. Each block computes a partial sum, and a subsequent reduction step consolidates these into the final result.

# Algorithm for Parallel Query Execution

---

**Data:** Database tables T, query predicates P, and
   functions F
**Result:** Optimized query execution result
**Function** OptimizeQuery(*T, P, F*):
   Initialize CUDA context;
   **for** *each table* $t \in T$ **do**
     Transfer relevant table partitions to GPU memory;

   **for** *each predicate* $p \in P$ *in parallel* **do**
     Evaluate $p$ using GPU threads on table partitions;

   **for** *each function* $f \in F$ *in parallel* **do**
     Apply $f$ on GPU using parallel reduction
       techniques;

   Aggregate results from GPU memory;
   **return** aggregated results as final query output;

---

This algorithm achieves substantial performance gains by utilizing CUDA's threading model to process database operations concurrently, minimizing latency commonly associated with traditional CPU-bound execution models.

# Performance Evaluation and Benchmarks

The efficacy of CUDA in augmenting database query performance can be assessed through throughput and execution time benchmarks. Consider an experimental setup where a query workload is evaluated across CPU and CUDA-accelerated implementations. Metrics such as query response time $T_{cuda}$ vs $T_{cpu}$ highlight the operational gains:

$$T_{gain} = \frac{T_{cpu} - T_{cuda}}{T_{cpu}}$$

where a higher $T_{gain}$ indicates a favorable CUDA-enhanced query strategy, clearly indicating the practical advantages of employing GPU technology in modern database systems.

# Python Code Snippet

Below is a Python code snippet using PyCUDA to enhance the processing of database queries through parallel execution on GPUs. The code demonstrates the execution of a parallel query model with PyCUDA, focusing on join and aggregation operations.

```python
import numpy as np
import pycuda.autoinit
import pycuda.driver as drv
from pycuda.compiler import SourceModule

# CUDA Kernel for equi-join operation
kernel_code = """
__global__ void equi_join(int* R, int* S, int* result, int num_R,
↪   int num_S) {
    int tid = blockDim.x * blockIdx.x + threadIdx.x;
    if (tid < num_R * num_S) {
        int i = tid / num_S;
        int j = tid % num_S;
        if (R[i] == S[j]) {
            result[tid] = 1;
        } else {
            result[tid] = 0;
        }
    }
}
"""

# Compile the kernel code
mod = SourceModule(kernel_code)
equi_join = mod.get_function("equi_join")

# Initialize data
R = np.array([1, 2, 3, 4, 5]).astype(np.int32)
S = np.array([3, 4, 5, 6, 7]).astype(np.int32)

# Allocate memory on the device
result = np.zeros((len(R) * len(S)), dtype=np.int32)

# Execute the equi-join kernel
equi_join(
    drv.In(R), drv.In(S), drv.Out(result),
    np.int32(len(R)), np.int32(len(S)),
    block=(256,1,1), grid=(int(len(R)*len(S)/256)+1,1)
)
```

```python
# Extract and process results
matches = []
for i in range(len(R)):
    for j in range(len(S)):
        if result[i * len(S) + j] == 1:
            matches.append((R[i], S[j]))

print("Matched pairs:", matches)

# Aggregation example using CUDA parallel reduction
agg_kernel_code = """
#include <stdio.h>

__global__ void sum_reduction(int* input, int* output, int n) {
    extern __shared__ int sdata[];
    unsigned int tid = threadIdx.x;
    unsigned int i = blockIdx.x * blockDim.x + threadIdx.x;

    if (i < n) {
        sdata[tid] = input[i];
    } else {
        sdata[tid] = 0;
    }
    __syncthreads();

    for (unsigned int s=blockDim.x/2; s>0; s>>=1) {
        if (tid < s) {
            sdata[tid] += sdata[tid + s];
        }
        __syncthreads();
    }

    if (tid == 0) {
        output[blockIdx.x] = sdata[0];
    }
}
"""

mod_sum = SourceModule(agg_kernel_code)
sum_reduction = mod_sum.get_function("sum_reduction")

# Example data for aggregation
data = np.array([1, 2, 3, 4, 5, 6, 7, 8, 9, 10], dtype=np.int32)
result_sum = np.zeros((1,), dtype=np.int32)

# Temporary block-level sums
temp_blocks = np.zeros((len(data) // 256 + 1,), dtype=np.int32)

# Execute reduction in parallel on the GPU
sum_reduction(
    drv.In(data), drv.Out(temp_blocks),
    np.int32(len(data)),
```

```
    block=(256, 1, 1),
    grid=(int(len(data) / 256) + 1, 1),
    shared=256 * np.dtype(np.int32).itemsize
)

# Sum the results from each block on the CPU
final_sum = np.sum(temp_blocks)
print("Sum:", final_sum)
```

This Python code utilizing PyCUDA outlines key computational operations for enhancing database query performance:

- The 'kernel_code' defines the CUDA kernel for performing an equi-join operation, parallelizing the comparison of entries in two arrays.

- The 'equi_join' function facilitates the parallelized execution of the join operation on a GPU.

- The 'agg_kernel_code' provides another CUDA kernel that executes a parallel reduction to compute the sum of elements in an array, showcasing a method for efficient aggregation.

- The 'sum_reduction' function implements the summation of input data, allowing concurrent accumulation of data using shared memory within blocks.

Through these segments, the code exemplifies the practical implementation of core operations required to leverage CUDA for optimized processing in database systems.

# Chapter 61

# Exploration of Content-Based Image Retrieval

## Mathematical Foundations of Content-Based Image Retrieval

Content-Based Image Retrieval (CBIR) systems rely heavily on mathematical models to efficiently and accurately retrieve images based on visual content rather than metadata. At the core of CBIR systems, we define an image as a function $I : \Omega \to \mathbb{R}^n$, where $\Omega \subset \mathbb{R}^2$ represents the spatial domain and $n$ the number of color channels. Feature extraction transforms $I$ into a feature space $\mathcal{F}$, typically through a function $\phi : \mathcal{I} \to \mathcal{F}$. The similarity between two images $I_1$ and $I_2$ can be calculated through a distance metric $d(\phi(I_1), \phi(I_2))$, often the Euclidean distance or cosine similarity.

$$d(\phi(I_1), \phi(I_2)) = \sqrt{\sum_{i=1}^{m} (\phi_i(I_1) - \phi_i(I_2))^2}$$

where $m$ represents the dimensionality of the feature vector. This mathematical representation underpins further optimization in CBIR using CUDA for accelerated processing.

# GPU Acceleration of Feature Extraction and Matching

The implementation of CBIR systems in a GPU environment exploits CUDA's parallel architecture to optimize the computationally intensive feature extraction and matching processes. Feature extraction can be parallelized by distributing the operations across image blocks. Let $\Phi(I)$ be the parallel execution plan for extracting features, where each CUDA thread computes a portion of the image's features:

$$\Phi(I) = \{\texttt{compute\_features}(b_i) \mid \forall b_i \in \mathcal{B}\}$$

Here, $b_i$ denotes an image block defined as $\mathcal{B} \subset \Omega$ where the CUDA kernel computes local descriptors.

Subsequently, the retrieval stage involves comparing query image features against a large database:

---

**Data:** Query image features q, image database features db
**Result:** Ranked list of similar images
**Function** FeatureMatching(`q`, `db`):
  Initialize CUDA context;
  **for** *each feature vector $q_i$ in parallel* **do**
    **for** *each feature vector $f_i \in$ db in parallel* **do**
      $\lfloor$ Compute distance $d(q_i, f_i)$;
    $\lfloor$ Rank and select top $k$ matches;
  **return** ranked set of image matches;

---

# Optimization Techniques for CBIR on GPUs

To enhance CBIR performance, various optimization strategies are employed. These include:

## 1 Indexing with KD-trees and Hashing

Utilizing KD-trees and locality-sensitive hashing aids in reducing search space, improving retrieval times. KD-trees partition the feature space into hyperrectangles, enabling logarithmic search complexity in expectation:

$$\text{Search Complexity} \propto \log(N)$$

where $N$ is the number of database images. Hash functions $h : \mathcal{F} \to \mathcal{H}$ condense features to preserve similarity relationships, further optimizing retrievals.

## 2 Batch Parallelization Techniques

Batch processing of query images minimizes overhead associated with kernel launches. Utilizing shared memory within CUDA blocks allows efficient inter-thread communication, pivotal in feature normalization and vector quantization processes.

## 3 Memory Coalescing for Efficient Data Movement

Memory access patterns significantly impact performance. Coalesced memory access aligns thread memory requests into contiguous blocks, reducing access latency:

$$t_{\text{memory}} = \frac{t_{\text{coalesced}}}{k} + t_{\text{uncoalesced}}$$

where $k$ is the coalescence factor that denotes the degree of achieved coalescence. Proper indexing and alignment ensure optimal device utilization.

# Computational Complexity and Performance Analysis

The computational complexity of a CBIR system is typically $O(Nd + N\log(N))$ for $N$ images, incorporating both feature extraction $O(Nd)$ and retrieval phases $O(N\log(N))$. GPU acceleration redefines this through parallelized computation, manifesting as:

$$O\left(\frac{Nd}{g} + \log\left(\frac{N}{g}\right)\right)$$

where $g$ denotes the number of GPU threads. Empirical benchmarks illustrate a performance gain $G$, given by:

$$G = \frac{T_{\text{cpu}}}{T_{\text{gpu}}}$$

where $T_{\text{cpu}}$ and $T_{\text{gpu}}$ are the total execution times on CPU and GPU, respectively. This metric adequately portrays the effectiveness of adopting CUDA-based optimizations in CBIR systems.

# Python Code Snippet

Below is a Python code snippet that encompasses the core computational elements of image feature extraction, distance calculation, and feature matching within a CBIR system, powered by GPU acceleration using PyCUDA.

```python
import numpy as np
import pycuda.autoinit
import pycuda.driver as cuda
from pycuda.compiler import SourceModule

# Function to extract features from the image using CUDA
mod = SourceModule("""
__global__ void compute_features(float *image, float *features, int
    width, int height, int feature_dim){
    int idx = threadIdx.x + blockIdx.x * blockDim.x;
    if (idx < width * height * feature_dim) {
        int pixel_idx = idx / feature_dim;
        int feature_idx = idx % feature_dim;

        // Example feature calculation: normalized intensity
        features[idx] = image[pixel_idx] / 255.0;
    }
}
""")

compute_features = mod.get_function("compute_features")

def extract_features(image, width, height, feature_dim):
    '''
    Extract features from the image using CUDA.
    :param image: The input image as a flat float array.
    :param width: Width of the image.
    :param height: Height of the image.
    :param feature_dim: Dimension of the feature vector.
    :return: The computed features.
    '''
    image_gpu = cuda.mem_alloc(image.nbytes)
    features_gpu = cuda.mem_alloc(image.nbytes)

    cuda.memcpy_htod(image_gpu, image)
    block_size = 256
    grid_size = (width * height * feature_dim + block_size - 1) //
        block_size
```

```
        compute_features(image_gpu, features_gpu, np.int32(width),
        ↪   np.int32(height), np.int32(feature_dim), block=(block_size,
        ↪   1, 1), grid=(grid_size, 1))

        features = np.empty_like(image)
        cuda.memcpy_dtoh(features, features_gpu)

        return features.reshape((height, width, feature_dim))

    # Function to compute the Euclidean distance using CUDA
    mod_dist = SourceModule("""
    __global__ void compute_distance(float *features1, float *features2,
    ↪   float *dist, int feature_dim){
        int idx = threadIdx.x + blockIdx.x * blockDim.x;
        if (idx < feature_dim) {
            float diff = features1[idx] - features2[idx];
            dist[idx] = diff * diff;
        }
    }
    """)

    compute_distance = mod_dist.get_function("compute_distance")

    def euclidean_distance(features1, features2):
        '''
        Calculate the Euclidean distance between two feature vectors
        ↪   using CUDA.
        :param features1: Feature vector 1.
        :param features2: Feature vector 2.
        :return: Calculated distance.
        '''
        feature_dim = len(features1)
        features1_gpu = cuda.mem_alloc(features1.nbytes)
        features2_gpu = cuda.mem_alloc(features2.nbytes)
        dist_gpu = cuda.mem_alloc(features1.nbytes)

        cuda.memcpy_htod(features1_gpu, features1)
        cuda.memcpy_htod(features2_gpu, features2)

        block_size = 256
        grid_size = (feature_dim + block_size - 1) // block_size

        compute_distance(features1_gpu, features2_gpu, dist_gpu,
        ↪   np.int32(feature_dim), block=(block_size, 1, 1),
        ↪   grid=(grid_size, 1))

        dist = np.empty_like(features1)
        cuda.memcpy_dtoh(dist, dist_gpu)

        return np.sqrt(np.sum(dist))

    # Example usage
```

```
image1 = np.random.rand(1024 * 1024).astype(np.float32) * 255
image2 = np.random.rand(1024 * 1024).astype(np.float32) * 255
width, height, feature_dim = 1024, 1024, 1

features1 = extract_features(image1, width, height, feature_dim)
features2 = extract_features(image2, width, height, feature_dim)

distance = euclidean_distance(features1.flatten(),
↪    features2.flatten())
print("Distance between features:", distance)
```

This code defines several key functions necessary for the implementation and operation of a CBIR system:

- `compute_features` CUDA kernel performs parallel computation of image features, such as normalized intensity.

- `extract_features` function sets up CUDA memory management and kernel execution to retrieve feature vectors from images.

- `compute_distance` CUDA kernel calculates the squared differences across feature dimensions in parallel.

- `euclidean_distance` effectively calculates the root sum of squares, yielding the Euclidean distance between feature vectors.

The code snippet demonstrates efficient feature extraction and distance computation using GPU acceleration to optimize CBIR system performance.

# Chapter 62

# Using CUDA for Autonomous Vehicles

## Mathematical Modeling and Data Processing

In the realm of autonomous vehicles, rapid data processing is central to real-time decision-making. Consider a vector of sensory inputs $\mathbf{s}(t)$, where each component $s_i(t)$ corresponds to a sensory measurement at time $t$. The decision-making process is then formalized as:

$$\mathbf{d}(t) = f(\mathbf{s}(t), \mathbf{w}, \theta)$$

where $f$ denotes a possibly complex decision function, $\mathbf{w}$ represents learned weights of a model such as a neural network, and $\theta$ are parameters governing the system dynamics.

Efficient processing of $\mathbf{s}(t)$ can be optimized using CUDA. Specifically, the transformation of input data into actionable decisions leverages parallel computation, leveraging CUDA cores for operations such as matrix multiplications and convolutions intrinsic to deep learning models.

## Parallel Processing in Decision-Making

The decision function $f$ can be decomposed into several stages, each requiring parallel computation. For instance, a convolutional layer in a neural network processes an input $\mathbf{x}$ through a weight tensor $\mathbf{K}$ using:

$$(\mathbf{x} * \mathbf{K})(i, j) = \sum_{m,n} \mathbf{x}(i + m, j + n) \cdot \mathbf{K}(m, n)$$

The computational task above can be parallelized by assigning each convolution operation to a separate CUDA thread.

---

**Data:** Input feature map x, kernel weights K
**Result:** Output feature map y
**Function** Convolution($x$, $K$):
  Initialize CUDA context;
  **for** *each pixel* $(i, j)$ *in* $x$ *in parallel* **do**
    **for** *each kernel* $(m, n)$ *in K in parallel* **do**
      Accumulate convolution product;

  Synchronize threads;
  **return** y;

---

The convolution operations are parallelized by dispatching computations to CUDA kernels, thus reducing the latency associated with forward passes in neural networks deployed in autonomous decision systems.

# Sensory Data Analysis and Integration

The integration of sensory data from multiple sources—such as LIDAR, RADAR, and cameras—requires computing-intensive fusion techniques. Let $\mathbf{z}_i(t)$ represent sensory readings from source $i$ at time $t$. The fused state estimation of the environment $\mathbf{e}(t)$ is computed as:

$$\mathbf{e}(t) = g(\{\mathbf{z}_i(t)\}, \beta)$$

where $g$ is a fusion function and $\beta$ are the parameters for sensor tuning. Parallel processing with CUDA facilitates handling large volumes of data efficiently.

A Kalman filter may be reformulated to operate in parallel on a GPU by paralleling the key matrix operations:

$$\mathbf{K}(t) = \mathbf{P}(t|t-1)\mathbf{H}^T(t) \left[\mathbf{H}(t)\mathbf{P}(t|t-1)\mathbf{H}^T(t) + \mathbf{R}(t)\right]^{-1}$$

and this is executed in a manner amenable to thread-based decomposition across matrix elements.

# Optimization Techniques in CUDA for Real-Time Performance

Several strategies optimize CUDA usage for signal processing in autonomous vehicles:

## 1 Minimizing Memory Bandwidth Usage

Efficient memory usage is crucial. Techniques like memory coalescing are applied to organize data for concurrent access by CUDA threads:

$$t_{\text{effective}} = \frac{t_{\text{non-coalesced}}}{c}$$

where $c$ is the coalescence factor. Aligning arrays in memory provides essential bandwidth reduction.

## 2 Latency Reduction through Overlapping

Streaming enables overlapping data transfer and computation, leveraging async memory operations via CUDA streams, optimizing the execution pipeline as follows:

$$\text{Streamed\_Op} = \left( \sum_{\text{Ops}} \text{Async(Op)} \right)$$

## 3 Kernel Fusion for Reduced Launch Overhead

By fusing multiple computations into a single kernel, kernel launch overheads diminish, leading to more streamlined execution paths. Implementations may fuse separate matrix operations under one kernel framework to minimize inter-kernel synchs.

# Algorithmic Complexity Analysis

The complexities inherent in these processes are defined by the operations executed in parallel:

$$O\left(\frac{n^2}{p}\right) + O(\log p)$$

where $n$ denotes data dimensionality and $p$ the number of parallel CUDA processors. The overall computational gains are measured by:

$$\text{Gain} = \frac{T_{\text{serial}}}{T_{\text{parallel}}}$$

where $T$ is time. Benchmarks for these models delineate CUDA's efficacy in reducing processing times, providing the rapid response required for autonomous vehicle operations.

# Python Code Snippet

Below is a Python code snippet demonstrating the core aspects of using CUDA for autonomous vehicles, primarily focusing on neural network operations, including convolutions, data processing, and sensor fusion.

```python
import pycuda.driver as cuda
import pycuda.autoinit
from pycuda.compiler import SourceModule
import numpy as np

mod = SourceModule("""
__global__ void convolve(float *x, float *k, float *y, int width,
↪   int height, int k_width, int k_height) {
    int tx = threadIdx.x;
    int ty = threadIdx.y;
    int bx = blockIdx.x;
    int by = blockIdx.y;

    int row = by * blockDim.y + ty;
    int col = bx * blockDim.x + tx;

    if (row < height && col < width) {
        float value = 0.0;
        int half_k_width = k_width / 2;
        int half_k_height = k_height / 2;

        for (int m = -half_k_height; m <= half_k_height; ++m) {
            for (int n = -half_k_width; n <= half_k_width; ++n) {
                int currentRow = row + m;
                int currentCol = col + n;
                float imageValue = 0.0;
```

```
                if (currentRow >= 0 && currentRow < height &&
                ↪   currentCol >= 0 && currentCol < width) {
                    imageValue = x[currentRow * width + currentCol];
                }

                value += imageValue * k[(m + half_k_height) *
                ↪   k_width + (n + half_k_width)];
            }
        }
        y[row * width + col] = value;
    }
}
""")

def convolve_image(image, kernel):
    (image_height, image_width) = image.shape
    (k_height, k_width) = kernel.shape

    # Flatten the matrices for CUDA
    x = np.float32(image.flatten())
    k = np.float32(kernel.flatten())
    y = np.zeros_like(x)

    # Allocate device memory
    x_gpu = cuda.mem_alloc(x.nbytes)
    k_gpu = cuda.mem_alloc(k.nbytes)
    y_gpu = cuda.mem_alloc(y.nbytes)

    # Transfer data to the GPU
    cuda.memcpy_htod(x_gpu, x)
    cuda.memcpy_htod(k_gpu, k)

    # Define the grid and block dimensions
    block = (16, 16, 1)
    grid = ((image_width + block[0] - 1) // block[0], (image_height
    ↪   + block[1] - 1) // block[1])

    # Launch the kernel
    func = mod.get_function("convolve")
    func(x_gpu, k_gpu, y_gpu, np.int32(image_width),
    ↪   np.int32(image_height), np.int32(k_width),
    ↪   np.int32(k_height), block=block, grid=grid)

    # Transfer the result back to the CPU
    cuda.memcpy_dtoh(y, y_gpu)

    # Reshape to the proper dimensions
    result = y.reshape((image_height, image_width))
    return result

# Example Usage
image = np.random.rand(512, 512).astype(np.float32)
```

```
kernel = np.array([[1, 0, -1], [1, 0, -1], [1, 0, -1]],
↪   dtype=np.float32)
filtered_image = convolve_image(image, kernel)

print("Filtered Image:", filtered_image)
```

This code demonstrates the following:

- A CUDA kernel named `convolve` executes parallel convolution operations on image data.

- The `convolve_image` function prepares data for GPU processing, sets up CUDA memory allocation, and executes the convolution.

- The image is processed by dispatching parallel threads for convolution over input image blocks, leveraging the computational efficiency of CUDA.

- This snippet exemplifies how convolutions, a fundamental aspect of neural networks, can be parallelized in the realm of autonomous vehicle sensory data processing.

# Chapter 63

# Synthetic Aperture Radar (SAR) Imaging

## Mathematical Modeling of SAR

Synthetic Aperture Radar (SAR) imaging involves the collection of radar data while a platform moves. The data collected is then used to construct high-resolution images. The mathematical representation of SAR data can be modeled through the use of the complex-valued signal:

$$s(t, \tau) = \int \int \sigma(x, y) \, e^{j 2 \pi f_c \left( \frac{2 R(x,y,t)}{c} \right)} \, \text{rect} \left( \frac{t - 2R(x, y, t)/c}{\tau} \right) dx \, dy$$

where $\sigma(x, y)$ is the reflectivity function representing the scene, $f_c$ is the carrier frequency, $c$ is the speed of light, and $R(x, y, t)$ is the range function. The rect function is a time-domain rectangular window.

Efficient processing of SAR images requires significant computational power, optimized through parallel processing platforms such as CUDA, which can accelerate various parallel computations present in SAR image reconstruction.

# Signal Processing and CUDA Parallelization

The core process for SAR image reconstruction, often implemented using backprojection or frequency-domain techniques, can be framed as a series of linear transformations. The raw radar data $\mathbf{S}(f, t)$ undergoes transformations characterized by:

$$\mathbf{I}(x, y) = \mathtt{IFFT} \left\{ \mathtt{FFT} \left[ \mathbf{S}(f, t) \right] \odot \mathtt{W}(f) \right\}$$

where $\mathtt{FFT}$ and $\mathtt{IFFT}$ denote the Fast Fourier Transform and its inverse, and $\mathtt{W}(f)$ is a windowing function to manage bandwidth.

The following algorithm details the parallel implementation considerations for such transformations using CUDA:

---

**Data:** Radar data S, windowing function W
**Result:** SAR image I
**Function** Transform(*S, W*):
> Initialize CUDA context;
> S_d = Transfer S to device;
> W_d = Transfer W to device;
> S_fft_d = CudaFFT(S_d);
> S_fw_d = Multiply(S_fft_d, W_d);
> S_ifft_d = CudaIFFT(S_fw_d);
> I = Transfer S_ifft_d back to host;
> **return** I;

---

The computational workload is distributed across multiple CUDA threads, enabling substantial speeds in SAR data processing by reducing processing times during FFT and IFFT operations.

# Image Rendering and Data Structure Optimization

In SAR imaging, overlapping is used to maximize throughput. For vectorized operations, data is aligned such that operations leverage shared memory and cache efficiently, defined by the relationship:

$$t_{\text{overlap}} = t_{\text{compute}} + t_{\text{transfer}} - \min(t_{\text{compute}}, t_{\text{transfer}})$$

An advancement in SAR processing involves restructuring data to efficiently use CUDA's memory hierarchy:

$$\texttt{coalesced\_access} = \sum_i a[i] \cdot \texttt{stride}$$

Memory access patterns such as coalesced access ensure maximum throughput by aligning data accesses across threads to the hardware capabilities.

# Complexity Analysis and Computational Performance

The inherent complexity of SAR imaging algorithms is mitigated by parallel execution. Computational complexity factors can be expressed with respect to available resources:

$$O\left(\frac{n^3}{p}\right) + O(\log p)$$

where $n$ refers to the SAR image resolution parameter and $p$ to the number of processing elements. CUDA's capabilities lead to a computational efficiency, defined by:

$$\text{Speed-up} = \frac{T_{\text{serial}}}{T_{\text{parallel}}}$$

Technical benchmarks of CUDA-enhanced SAR processing demonstrate reduced latency and increased image fidelity, vital for real-time radar interpretations.

# Python Code Snippet

Below is a Python code snippet that encompasses the core computational elements for SAR imaging, including the formulation of SAR signals, FFT and IFFT processing, and optimization via CUDA using PyCUDA for efficient parallel computation.

```python
import numpy as np
import pycuda.autoinit
import pycuda.driver as cuda
from pycuda.compiler import SourceModule
import skcuda.fft as cu_fft
```

```
import pycuda.gpuarray as gpuarray

# SAR signal simulation parameters
n_points = 1024
carrier_freq = 1e9  # 1 GHz
speed_of_light = 3e8  # Speed of light in vacuum

# Create an example reflectivity function
reflectivity = np.random.rand(n_points,
↪  n_points).astype(np.complex64)

# Allocate space on the GPU
reflectivity_gpu = gpuarray.to_gpu(reflectivity)

# FFT and IFFT context setup
fft_plan = cu_fft.Plan(reflectivity_gpu.shape, np.complex64,
↪  np.complex64)

def sar_data_processing(reflectivity_gpu, fft_plan):
    # Perform FFT
    S_fft_gpu = gpuarray.empty_like(reflectivity_gpu)
    cu_fft.fft(reflectivity_gpu, S_fft_gpu, fft_plan)

    # Define a windowing function (example: Hanning)
    window_gpu =
↪  gpuarray.to_gpu(np.hanning(n_points).astype(np.complex64))

    # Multiply FFT output with window
    S_windowed_gpu = S_fft_gpu * window_gpu

    # Perform IFFT
    S_ifft_gpu = gpuarray.empty_like(S_windowed_gpu)
    cu_fft.ifft(S_windowed_gpu, S_ifft_gpu, fft_plan, scale=True)
    return S_ifft_gpu

# Process data using SAR defined transformations
image_data = sar_data_processing(reflectivity_gpu, fft_plan)

# Transfer result back to host
image_result = image_data.get()

print("Computed SAR Image Data:", image_result)
```

---

This code defines several key functions necessary for the implementation of SAR imaging using CUDA parallelization:

- `sar_data_processing` function encapsulates the core steps of SAR processing, including the Fast Fourier Transform (FFT), window application, and Inverse FFT (IFFT), leveraging GPU parallelization via PyCUDA.

- `cu_fft.Plan` is used to establish an FFT plan suitable for SAR data shapes on the GPU.

- The utilization of `gpuarray` ensures that data transfers between host and device are efficiently handled for fast computation.

The final block of code represents the application of these components by simulating SAR data, processing it in parallel on the GPU, and transferring the computed image data back to the host environment for further analysis or visualization.

# Chapter 64

# Quantum Chemistry Simulations

## Foundations of Quantum Chemistry

Quantum chemistry simulation involves the application of quantum mechanics to solve for the electronic structure of molecules. The fundamental principle guiding these simulations is the Schrödinger equation, encapsulated as:

$$\hat{H}\Psi = E\Psi \tag{64.1}$$

where $\hat{H}$ is the Hamiltonian operator, $\Psi$ represents the wave function of the system, and $E$ is the energy eigenvalue associated with $\Psi$. This partial differential equation forms the basis for many computational methods in quantum chemistry, such as Hartree-Fock and density functional theory (DFT).

## Hartree-Fock Method

The Hartree-Fock (HF) method reformulates the Schrödinger equation as a set of single-electron equations. Applying the Hartree-Fock approximation, one simplifies the many-electron interactions using a mean-field approach. The energy minimization leads to:

$$F[\phi_i] = \left(-\frac{1}{2}\nabla^2 + V_{\text{eff}}\right)\phi_i = \epsilon_i\phi_i \tag{64.2}$$

where $F[\phi_i]$ is the Fock operator, $\phi_i$ are the molecular orbitals, $V_{\text{eff}}$ is the effective potential, and $\epsilon_i$ the orbital energies. The computational demand scales as $O(N^4)$, where $N$ is the number of basis functions, proving suitable for parallelization on CUDA platforms.

# Density Functional Theory (DFT)

An alternative to HF is DFT which uses electron density ($\rho(\mathbf{r})$) as the primary quantity:

$$E[\rho] = T[\rho] + V_{\text{ne}}[\rho] + J[\rho] + E_{\text{xc}}[\rho] \qquad (64.3)$$

where $T[\rho]$ is the kinetic energy, $V_{\text{ne}}[\rho]$ is the nuclear-electron interaction, $J[\rho]$ is the classical electron-electron repulsion, and $E_{\text{xc}}[\rho]$ is the exchange-correlation energy. The complex nature of $E_{\text{xc}}[\rho]$ prompts advanced numerical solutions requiring extreme computational power, making DFT a candidate for CUDA optimization.

## 1 Parallelization Strategy for Quantum Simulations

Parallel computation in quantum chemistry involves distributing electron density calculations across GPU cores, accelerating matrix operations inherent in algorithms such as HF and DFT. This approach leverages the CUDA architecture:

---

**Data:** Initial electron density $\rho^{(0)}$
**Result:** Converged electron density $\rho^{(\infty)}$
**Function** DFTIteration($\rho^{(k)}$):
    | Construct Hamiltonian;
    | Diagonalize using CUDA;
    | $\rho^{(k+1)}$ from molecular orbitals;
    | **return** $\rho^{(k+1)}$;
Initialize $\rho^{(0)}$;
**repeat**
    | $\rho^{(k+1)} = $ DFTIteration($\rho^{(k)}$);
    | $k = k + 1$;
**until** *convergence*;

---

CUDA's parallel execution model reduces the time for matrix diagonalization and other linear algebra tasks, imperative for iterative methods inherent in quantum computations.

## Real-Time Molecular Dynamics

For molecular dynamics (MD), the integration of forces derived from electronic structure calculations results in:

$$F_i = -\nabla_i V(\mathbf{R}) \tag{64.4}$$

where $F_i$ are the forces on nuclei and $V(\mathbf{R})$ is the potential energy surface. Propagating the system dynamics requires solving Newtonian equations of motion, a process enhanced by CUDA's capability to manage computation across multiple threads:

$$\mathbf{R}(t + \Delta t) = \mathbf{R}(t) + \mathbf{v}(t)\Delta t + \frac{1}{2}\mathbf{F}(t)\frac{\Delta t^2}{m} \tag{64.5}$$

## Efficient Computational Techniques

In both HF and DFT frameworks, leveraging CUDA enables the application of sparse matrix techniques and iterative solvers which substantially reduce the computational overhead. The overall complexity of performing these simulations can be approximated by:

$$O\left(\frac{b^3}{g}\right) \tag{64.6}$$

where $b$ represents the size of the basis set and $g$ is the number of GPU cores. Speed-up metrics for quantum chemical calculations confirm enhanced computation time:

$$\text{Speed-up} = \frac{T_{\text{CPU}}}{T_{\text{GPU}}} \tag{64.7}$$

The CUDA framework offers remarkable capabilities in facilitating the exploration of molecular dynamics through parallel quantum chemical simulation, opening new avenues in both theoretical and practical chemistry domains.

# Python Code Snippet

Below is a Python code snippet that encompasses the core computational elements involved in quantum chemistry simulations, focusing on implementing the Hartree-Fock and Density Functional Theory methods, molecular dynamics, and efficient computational strategies using PyCUDA.

```python
import pycuda.autoinit
import pycuda.driver as cuda
import numpy as np
from pycuda.compiler import SourceModule
from scipy.linalg import eigh

# CUDA Kernel for basic matrix operations
mod = SourceModule("""
__global__ void matrix_mult(double *a, double *b, double *c, int N)
↪  {
    int idx = blockIdx.x * blockDim.x + threadIdx.x;
    if (idx < N * N) {
        int row = idx / N;
        int col = idx % N;
        double sum = 0;

        for (int k = 0; k < N; ++k) {
            sum += a[row * N + k] * b[k * N + col];
        }
        c[idx] = sum;
    }
}
""")

matrix_mult = mod.get_function("matrix_mult")

def hartree_fock_energy(basis_set, v_eff, cuda_block_size):
    """
    Function to compute the Hartree-Fock energy.
    :param basis_set: Matrix of basis functions.
    :param v_eff: Effective potential matrix.
    :param cuda_block_size: CUDA block size for parallelization.
    :return: Electron energy.
    """
    N = basis_set.shape[0]
    h_dev = cuda.mem_alloc(basis_set.nbytes)
    cuda.memcpy_htod(h_dev, basis_set)

    v_dev = cuda.mem_alloc(v_eff.nbytes)
    cuda.memcpy_htod(v_dev, v_eff)

    fock_matrix = np.empty_like(basis_set)
    fock_dev = cuda.mem_alloc(fock_matrix.nbytes)
```

```
        matrix_mult(h_dev, v_dev, fock_dev, np.int32(N),
        ↪  block=(cuda_block_size, 1, 1), grid=(N, 1))
        cuda.memcpy_dtoh(fock_matrix, fock_dev)

        # Diagonalize using CPU-based SciPy function for simplicity
        energies, orbitals = eigh(fock_matrix)
        electron_energy = np.sum(energies[:N // 2])   # Sum lowest
        ↪  occupied orbitals

        return electron_energy

def dft_energy(density, kinetic_energy, v_ne, j, e_xc):
    """
    Compute the DFT energy.
    :param density: Electron density.
    :param kinetic_energy: Kinetic energy term.
    :param v_ne: Nuclei-electron interaction term.
    :param j: Classical electron repulsion.
    :param e_xc: Exchange-correlation energy.
    :return: Total DFT energy.
    """
    return kinetic_energy + v_ne + j + e_xc

# Initialize matrices and parameters
N = 128  # Number of basis functions
basis_set = np.random.rand(N, N)
v_eff = np.random.rand(N, N)

cuda_block_size = 16

hf_energy = hartree_fock_energy(basis_set, v_eff, cuda_block_size)

# Initialize DFT variables
density = np.random.rand(N, N)
kinetic_energy = np.sum(np.random.rand(N))
v_ne = np.sum(np.random.rand(N))
j = np.sum(np.random.rand(N))
e_xc = np.sum(np.random.rand(N))

dft_total_energy = dft_energy(density, kinetic_energy, v_ne, j,
↪  e_xc)

print(f"Hartree-Fock Electron Energy: {hf_energy:.4f}")
print(f"Total DFT Energy: {dft_total_energy:.4f}")
```

This code defines several key functions necessary for executing quantum chemistry simulations on a GPU:

- The `matrix_mult` CUDA kernel performs matrix multiplication, a critical operation in computational chemistry.

- The `hartree_fock_energy` function computes the Hartree-Fock energy by diagonalizing the Fock matrix.

- The `dft_energy` function calculates the Density Functional Theory energy using key energy components.

The final block of the code demonstrates how to compute these energies using dummy data matrices, leveraging the power of GPU-based computation with `PyCUDA`. The integration of CUDA helps automate and parallelize computationally intense tasks, optimizing performance significantly.

# Chapter 65

# Financial Risk Analysis

## Mathematical Foundations of Risk Measurement

In financial risk analysis, the accurate quantification and modeling of risk are critical. One of the cornerstones of this quantitative process is the Value at Risk (VaR) metric, defined as:

$$\text{VaR}_\alpha = \inf\{x \in \mathbb{R} : P(L > x) \leq \alpha\} \tag{65.1}$$

where $\alpha$ denotes the confidence level, and $L$ represents the loss. This measure is widely used due to its simplicity in capturing potential losses over a fixed horizon.

Another robust risk metric is the Conditional Value at Risk (CVaR), which offers an expectation over the tail of the loss distribution:

$$\text{CVaR}_\alpha = E[L \mid L > \text{VaR}_\alpha] \tag{65.2}$$

Such metrics demand sophisticated computation, especially in scenarios involving large datasets.

## Leveraging CUDA for Parallel Risk Computation

The computational intensity of financial risk analysis can be significantly mitigated using CUDA. Implementing Monte Carlo simulation, a prevalent technique for risk assessment, benefits from parallel processing:

$$L = f(X_1, X_2, \ldots, X_n) \tag{65.3}$$

Here, $X_i$ are stochastic inputs, and $f$ represents the loss function. The parallelism in Monte Carlo simulations emerges from the independence of $L$'s evaluations.

## 1  Monte Carlo Simulation on CUDA

Monte Carlo methods entail generating a large volume of scenarios, which involve complex mathematical computations. The use of CUDA allows simultaneous generation and evaluation of these scenarios across GPU cores:

---

**Data:** Random scenarios $X_i$
**Result:** Estimated risk measures VaR and CVaR
**Function** MonteCarloSim(*num_scenarios*):
| Parallel **Generate**$X_i$;
| Evaluate $L = f(X_1, X_2, \ldots, X_n)$ on CUDA;
| Sort $L$, Compute VaR$_\alpha$;
| CVaR$_\alpha$ using sorted $L$;

Initialize scenarios;
MonteCarloSim($10^6$)

---

With this setup, the algorithm leverages CUDA's ability to perform parallel number generation and scenario evaluation, thus accelerating the convergent computation of risk measures.

# Covariance and Correlation Analysis in Portfolios

Covariance and correlation are vital in understanding the risk dynamics between different financial assets. Given $n$ assets with return vectors $\mathbf{R} = (R_1, R_2, \ldots, R_n)$, the covariance matrix $\Sigma$ is:

$$\Sigma_{ij} = E\left[(R_i - \mu_i)(R_j - \mu_j)\right] \tag{65.4}$$

Depicting the linear dependence structure, facilitating enhanced risk predictions and management protocols.

# Principal Component Analysis (PCA) for Dimension Reduction

For high-dimensional risk profiles, PCA reduces dimensionality by transforming to a set of uncorrelated variables, the principal components:

$$\mathbf{Z} = \mathbf{X}\mathbf{W} \tag{65.5}$$

Here, $\mathbf{W}$ represents the orthogonal matrix of eigenvectors derived from the covariance matrix of $\mathbf{X}$. CUDA expedites the eigen-decomposition required for this transformation, enhancing computational efficiency.

# Risk Mitigation Strategies via Efficient Computation

Employing advanced computational techniques and CUDA, risk mitigation strategies are formulated by optimizing asset allocation:

$$\min_{\mathbf{w}} \ \mathbf{w}^T \Sigma \mathbf{w} - \lambda \mathbf{w}^T \mu \tag{65.6}$$

subject to budget constraints $\mathbf{w}^T \mathbf{1} = 1$, where $\mathbf{w}$ is the weight vector of allocations, $\Sigma$ the covariance matrix, and $\mu$ the expected returns. This optimization takes advantage of CUDA's parallel capabilities to handle large-scale portfolios and complex constraints efficiently.

# Python Code Snippet

Below is a Python code snippet that encompasses the core computational elements of financial risk analysis, including the calculation of risk metrics, Monte Carlo simulation using PyCUDA, and portfolio optimization.

```python
import pycuda.autoinit
import pycuda.driver as cuda
import numpy as np
from pycuda.compiler import SourceModule

# Initialize CUDA kernel for Monte Carlo Simulation
```

377

```python
mod = SourceModule("""
__global__ void monte_carlo_simulation(float *results, float
↪ *d_randoms, int n, float strike) {
    int idx = blockIdx.x * blockDim.x + threadIdx.x;
    if (idx < n) {
        float loss = 0;
        for(int i = 0; i < n; i++) {
            loss += d_randoms[idx * n + i]; // Simulated scenario
            ↪ computation
        }
        results[idx] = loss > strike ? loss - strike : 0; // Payoff
        ↪ calculation
    }
}
""")

def compute_var_cvar(results, alpha):
    """
    Compute VaR and CVaR from simulation results.

    :param results: Array of simulated losses.
    :param alpha: Confidence level.
    :return: VaR and CVaR.
    """
    results_sorted = np.sort(results)
    var_index = int((1-alpha) * len(results_sorted))
    var = results_sorted[var_index]
    cvar = np.mean(results_sorted[var_index:])
    return var, cvar

def main():
    num_scenarios = 1000000
    strike_price = 100.0
    alpha = 0.95

    # Random scenarios (using normal distribution as an example)
    randoms = np.random.normal(0, 1,
    ↪ num_scenarios).astype(np.float32)

    # Allocate memory on GPU
    d_randoms = cuda.mem_alloc(randoms.nbytes)
    cuda.memcpy_htod(d_randoms, randoms)

    # Prepare output array for results
    results = np.zeros_like(randoms)
    d_results = cuda.mem_alloc(results.nbytes)

    # Setup CUDA parameters
    block_size = 256
    grid_size = (num_scenarios + block_size - 1) // block_size

    # Run simulation
    kernel = mod.get_function("monte_carlo_simulation")
```

378

```
    kernel(d_results, d_randoms, np.int32(num_scenarios),
    ↪  np.float32(strike_price),
            block=(block_size, 1, 1), grid=(grid_size, 1))

    # Retrieve results
    cuda.memcpy_dtoh(results, d_results)

    # Compute VaR and CVaR
    var, cvar = compute_var_cvar(results, alpha)

    print("Value at Risk (VaR):", var)
    print("Conditional Value at Risk (CVaR):", cvar)

if __name__ == "__main__":
    main()
```

This code defines several key functions necessary for the implementation and analysis of financial risk using Monte Carlo simulation:

- The CUDA kernel, `monte_carlo_simulation`, is responsible for performing Monte Carlo simulations on the GPU, calculating payoffs for each scenario.

- `compute_var_cvar` function computes the Value at Risk (VaR) and Conditional Value at Risk (CVaR) from the simulated losses, providing crucial risk metrics.

- The main function initializes data, copies it to the GPU, invokes the kernel for parallel computation, and retrieves the results to calculate and print the risk measures.

The implementation leverages the parallel processing capabilities of GPUs using PyCUDA, significantly accelerating the computation of risk metrics over large datasets.

95140019R10213